Fantasyland

Fantasyland

A Season on Baseball's Lunatic Fringe

Sam Walker

VIKING

VIKING

Published by the Penguin Group

Penguin Group (USA) Inc., 375 Hudson Street, New York, New York 10014, U.S.A. • Penguin Group (Canada), 90 Eglinton Avenue East, Suite 700, Toronto, Ontario, Canada M4P 2Y3 (a division of Pearson Penguin Canada Inc.) • Penguin Books Ltd, 80 Strand, London WC2R 0RL, England • Penguin Ireland, 25 St Stephen's Green, Dublin 2, Ireland (a division of Penguin Books Ltd) • Penguin Books Australia Ltd, 250 Camberwell Road, Camberwell, Victoria 3124, Australia (a division of Pearson Australia Group Pty Ltd) • Penguin Books India Pvt Ltd, 11 Community Centre, Panchsheel Park, New Delhi – 110 017, India • Penguin Group (NZ), Cnr Airborne and Rosedale Roads, Albany, Auckland 1310, New Zealand (a division of Pearson New Zealand Ltd) • Penguin Books (South Africa) (Pty) Ltd, 24 Sturdee Avenue, Rosebank, Johannesburg 2196, South Africa

Penguin Books Ltd, Registered Offices: 80 Strand, London WC2R 0RL, England

First published in 2006 by Viking Penguin, a member of Penguin Group (USA) Inc.

10   9   8   7   6   5   4   3   2   1

LIBRARY OF CONGRESS CATALOGING -IN-PUBLICATION DATA

Walker, Sam.

   Fantasyland : a season on baseball's lunatic fringe / Sam Walker.

   p. cm.

   Includes index.

   ISBN 0-670-03428-2

   1. Rotisserie League Baseball (Game)   2. Fantasy baseball (Game).   I. Title.

   GV1202.F33W35 2006

   793.93—dc22   2005044532

Printed in the United States of America

Designed by Carla Bolte • Set in Dante

For Gus

Acknowledgments

Books like this only get written when a fairly large number of people agree to do things they never considered doing before and, by all rights, shouldn't have.

Rick Kot at Viking performed editorial miracles while keeping me grounded. He did this by responding to every Rotisserie crisis I had with several minutes of immobilizing laughter. Ever since she yanked the proposal from my hesitant fingers, Emma Parry, my agent, has been, as they like to say, a "gamer." Paul Steiger, Joanne Lipman, Amy Stevens, and Jonathan Dahl at *The Wall Street Journal* gave me space to do this without once asking why on earth I wanted to. Sandy Alderson and Phyllis Merhige of Major League Baseball offered early guidance and Rick Cerrone of the New York Yankees took a leap of faith. Baseball media specialists Benny Agosto, Brian Britten, Debbie Gallas, Glen Geffner, Sean Harlin, Nancy Mazmanian, Tim Mead, Scott Reifert, Chris Stathos, Jay Stenhouse, Bill Stetka, Bart Swain, and Jim Young knew my purpose but still saw fit to issue me credentials. Inside Edge, STATS LLC, and Baseball Info Solutions gave me glimpses into three of the world's greatest troves of baseball data. Greg Ambrosius of the FSTA and John Hunt of *USA Today Sports Weekly* were generous with their expertise and Bill Meyer of USA Stats let me bother hundreds of his subscribers.

Researchers Jon Steinberg, Andre Archimbaud, and Fred Meyer provided early pinch hitting. I would have made an even worse mess of things without my "mock auction" leaguemates: Hal Cohen, Anthony Di Fino, Michael Fishman, Steve Lawrence, Larry Repanes, Jim Sias, David Wadler, and Teddy Werner. Christine Price turned in a performance worthy of an Oscar nomination and Laura Howson, Dave Jacobs, and HalfShaq helped with team aesthetics. I owe a great debt to Matt Davis, Erin Friar, Chad Millman, Jim Tobin, and Joe Veltre for un-mixing my metaphors and filling the gaps in my baseball knowledge.

Though they also appear in these pages, the members of the Base-ball Seminar, the founding fathers of Rotisserie, and the members of Tout Wars performed many selfless acts they may live to regret. I'd also like to thank the dozens of ballplayers who gave me time, and in particular, Miguel Batista, Jacque Jones, Doug Mientkiewicz, Bill Mueller, and David Ortiz. I hope to see you all in Cooperstown.

Some contributors are unaware of their munificence: the makers of F&F vitamin C tablets, the pilots of Continental Airlines, the cooks at Chez Brigitte, various purveyors of espresso, the guy who coined the word "shebazzle," the insurance experts at GEICO who covered the rental car I totaled in Puerto Rico (still not my fault), and the woman who found my cellphone in a taxi and dropped it off without leaving her name.

To Janet Stein, the world's greatest obstetrician, we will think of you on every birthday. To everyone whose wedding I missed (Neal and Diane, Matt and Lauren, Molly and Jeff), all I can say is there was considerably more beer for you. As for Sig and Nando, I still vacillate between wondering how I could have been so lucky to find you and, in other moments, thinking I should have fastened you to trees with duct tape.

My mother, Linda, not only provided brilliant edits, but showed that her baseball education continued beyond the 1984 Detroit Tigers. Max, Helene, Vincent, and Tony offered strength and encour-agement in the too-infrequent moments when I remembered to call.

Most of all I want to thank my wife, Christy, whose patience, grace, brilliance, competence, and generosity of spirit are beyond my powers to describe. For the record, she thought I traded Curt Schilling a month too early.

Contents

Fantasyland

Something about Jones

Jacque Jones sits on a padded folding chair in a quiet corner of the Minnesota Twins clubhouse, thumbing through a dog-eared paperback. It's the last day of February 2004, and practice has been over for an hour. The rest of the Twins have cut loose in shorts and flip-flops to savor the last Sunday afternoon in Florida before the real slog of spring training begins. There are putts to sink and fishing poles to bend with Spanish mackerel. The coaches have gone bowling.

Before he opened the book, Jones, the team's $4.35 million right fielder, had showered, moisturized, slipped on track pants, and collected his car keys from the top shelf of his locker. He was all set to head home to his wife of three months when he noticed its title, asked me if he could take a look at it, and then, before I could refuse, pried it loose from the crook of my arm. From the moment he turned to page 55, I've felt like eating a rosin bag.

The book's title is the *Baseball Forecaster*, and its author is a guy named Ron Shandler, whom I'd met only two weeks earlier. Bearded, studious, and somewhat reclusive, Shandler lives on the outskirts of Roanoke, Virginia, in the foothills of the Blue Ridge Mountains. He did not play professional baseball, and he's never worked as a scout, set foot in a clubhouse, or stuffed his gums with chewing tobacco. Growing up in Queens, the son of a Borscht Belt bandleader, he spent most of his childhood at the piano.

But every October Shandler retreats to his basement for six weeks to download all the raw statistical data from the previous baseball season and run it through a phalanx of proprietary mathematical formulas and algorithms. When he's finished, he has a complete projection for every ballplayer who might wear a major-league uniform the following year, from the number of home runs Barry Bonds will hit to the precise number of batters Tim Spooneybarger is liable to strike out. The results are printed in the *Baseball Forecaster*, which he publishes himself and sells for $23.95.

His primary audience is the throng of Americans who play a parlor game called Rotisserie baseball or, more specifically, the subset of these people who are obsessively committed to winning. His predictions are often so uncannily accurate and so boldly counterintuitive that his followers consider him a soothsayer, a bearded prophet, and an undiscovered genius. He also happens to be the world's most decorated Rotisserie champion.

For the last eight days, I've lugged the *Forecaster* across Florida following the old sportswriter circuit of sleepy ballparks, sticky motels, and improvised breakfasts at Amoco. Along the way I've met with general managers and coaches, interviewed superstars and minor-league nobodies, and watched more "pitchers' fielding practice" than I care to remember. In a typical year, I'd have come to spring training to dredge up material for my sports column in *The Wall Street Journal*, but the purpose of this trip is far less rational: I'm here to scout talent for my first Rotisserie team.

Four months ago, after years of principled resistance, I decided to play fantasy baseball and, rather than testing the waters in a beer league for novices, to aim for the top. After some lobbying, I was invited to compete in an expert league called Tout Wars, which is typically reserved for the nation's most accomplished Rotisserie players. By way of comparison, this is kind of like trying to learn the cello by joining the London Philharmonic.

I'm not carrying Ron Shandler's book just to imbibe his wisdom. I'm also using it to study his predilections and find the rare instances where he's clearly wrong. Not only is Shandler a competitor in Tout Wars, he invented it.

On page 55 of this year's *Forecaster*, the Bearded One renders his judgment on Jacque Jones, the ballplayer now seated in front of me. According to Shandler's statistical gauges, Jones is a lousy bet to hit another 25 home runs in a single year, and his batting average last season was "grossly inflated." Shandler doesn't specifically mention that Jones is an impatient hitter who strikes out five times more often than he draws a walk, but the numbers are printed in the accompanying row of stats. To anyone who follows his teachings, there's only one proper conclusion to draw.

This guy is horseshit.

The moment Jones read Shandler's blurb for the first time, an improbable smile spread across his face. As he read it again, his shoulders started to bounce as if he were laughing, but there was no sound. Soon he began flipping through the projections for other outfielders and the smile evaporated. Creases have formed on his forehead now, and he's chewing a fingernail.

"Can you believe that?" I say, trying to snap him back from wherever he's headed. Jones lifts his chin for a second, staring past me to a distant row of lockers. The clubhouse is completely empty now, save for a pair of laundry kids tossing damp socks and undershirts into rolling canvas hampers. He returns to the book.

Most professional athletes are made of emotional granite. They are not sensitive to the evaluations of strangers or burdened by the ability to imagine failure. Jacque Jones is made of something else, something more like a ripe avocado. From his Little League days in San Diego all the way through to the major leagues, his emotions have always been painfully apparent. Something about the topography of his face—the chestnut eyes, the thin black mustache, the pearly teeth, and the prominent cheekbones—gives it an expressiveness that can veer quickly from joyous to fierce to despondent. His mother, Linda Faulk, claims she can tell what kind of a game he's going to have just by looking at him.

Here in this dimly lit room, as he flips through the pages of the *Forecaster,* his eyes have taken on a mournful glaze. It seems entirely possible that Jacque Jones is about to cry.

———

Rotisserie League Baseball was invented in 1980 when a group of Manhattan publishing swells, led by a book editor named Daniel Okrent, sat down in a Park Avenue apartment one morning to settle a tired old argument: who among them would make the best general manager. Since none of them was likely to ever own a major-league team, much less to be hired to run one, they decided to create an elaborate simulation. The concept has since morphed into countless variations and subspecies, but the original rules, the purest form of the game, are still widely used.

The central event of a Rotisserie season is a draft that takes place once a year in March or April, near the beginning of the real baseball season. At this meeting the members of a Rotisserie league (usually about twelve people) gather around some commodious table to pick "teams" composed of real major leaguers—a process that is nearly impossible to complete in less than six hours. While it's called a draft, it's really an English auction. Each team "owner" pays $260 in real money to the pot in exchange for the right to spend that exact sum on ballplayers. When the auction starts, contestants take turns calling out names for bidding. Superstars tend to sell first for as much as $50, while bench players and pitching scrubs rarely cost more than a buck. The auction continues until every owner has filled out a roster of twenty-three players in the following combination:

   9 pitchers
   5 outfielders
   2 catchers
   1 first baseman
   1 second baseman
   1 shortstop
   1 third baseman
   1 middle infielder (second or short)

1 corner infielder (first or third)
1 utility player

Since Rotisserie teams are composed of a mishmash of players from different ballclubs, there's obviously no way for them to properly play one another. The goal therefore isn't to win games but rather to accumulate points in eight statistical categories: home runs, stolen bases, runs batted in, batting average, saves, wins, earned-run average, and WHIP.* In a Rotisserie league with twelve teams, whichever one fares best in a given category (collecting the most saves, for instance) will earn twelve points, while the second-place team earns eleven, and so on, all the way down to one. The owner with the highest overall score in all eight categories at the end of the regular baseball season wins the lion's share of the pot.

While its goal is to give ordinary shlubs a taste of what it's like to run a major-league ballclub, the Rotisserie game is, in some ways, *more* complicated than the real one. For one thing, there are no contracts. Most classic "Roto" leagues require all players to be released at the end of the season and to therefore be eligible at the next auction. That being the case, a dedicated owner has to come to the draft ready to pass judgment on every ballplayer who might step between the chalk stripes in the forthcoming season. To make solid predictions, one must account for hundreds of variables, from something as tangible as a hitter's likely spot in the batting order to murkier topics like the sturdiness of his hamstrings or the relative nastiness of his divorce proceedings. At a reasonable pace of assessing ten players a day, this process would take five months.

Then there's the challenge of watching one's Rotisserie team play baseball. While real GMs can keep tabs on their players from the comfort of a luxury box, their fantasy counterparts have to stay abreast of simultaneous action happening in every corner of America, which forces them to flip channels like restless insomniacs. When

---

*WHIP, also known as composite ratio, measures a pitcher's ability to keep hitters from reaching base. The formula is walks allowed plus hits allowed divided by innings pitched.

they're not juggling the roster, making trades, signing free agents, reading injury reports, and evaluating minor-league call-ups like any other baseball executive, they're pasted to their workstations watching a schizophrenic online scoreboard where a single stolen base in Cleveland can cause a seismic tremor in the standings.

Although polls say somewhere between three and five million Americans play "fantasy" baseball, the hobby is about as regulated as a neighborhood game of kickball. There's no National Rotisserie Association to sanction events or set standards. There's nothing to buy and no licensing fees to pay. But the concept behind it, the notion of playing an imaginary game based on the outcome of a real one, has crossed more borders than the bubonic plague.

From the original Rotisserie seed in 1980, thousands of derivations have sprouted: football, golf, bass fishing, curling, jai alai, bowling, and beach volleyball each have their own fantasy equivalent. There's a fantasy sumo league with contestants in twenty-four countries from Portugal to Mongolia, and the *Daily Telegraph* hosts a fantasy cricket league where participants construct teams composed of Bangladeshi batsmen, Sri Lankan bowlers, and West Indian wicket keepers. One survey found that fifteen million Americans, or about 7 percent of the population, play some form of fantasy game, which, if true, makes this pastime more popular than recreational tennis and ice-skating combined.

For the longest time I was determined to ignore the movement. Whenever somebody invited me to join a Rotisserie league, my typical response was to laugh politely and say something generous and enlightened like "Fuck that." It's not that I thought this game was too geeky, though it clearly leans in that direction. What turned me off was that I could tell it was powerfully addictive. I didn't want to become one of *those* guys, the ones you'd happen upon at a party locked in an impenetrable exchange that went something like this:

"Who's your closer?"

"Alfonseca."

"How much?"

"Twenty-three."

"Whoa, no way!"

"For thirty saves?"

"Try half that."

Every spring, without fail, one of these same people will sidle up to me on the subway and ask to borrow my *USA Today* sports section. The moment I hand it over, this otherwise unremarkable commuter will flip to the baseball "notes" section where every banal lineup change, injury update, and nightclub misadventure is chronicled in compressed type. By the time I get to my stop, they're already so engrossed that all I can say is, "No, you keep it."

There was nothing outwardly peculiar about these Rotisserie addicts. They didn't wear purple shrouds and matching Nikes. They managed to hold down respectable jobs and even stable marriages. As best I could tell, the game appealed to people who would still be playing Dungeons & Dragons if it wasn't such a powerful antidote to getting laid in high school.

But on a summer afternoon in 2002, something happened that caused me to reexamine my view. After a New York Mets game at Shea Stadium, down in the clubhouse, I stopped to talk with Mo Vaughn, the team's burly cleanup hitter. It had been a humbling year for Vaughn, who'd come to New York with World Series ambitions, only to become a sports-page punch line. He was fatter than a porpoise, colder than a snowdrift at the plate, and by any standard, a $12 million disaster. Up in the stands that day, the hecklers had been merciless: "I didn't know Mo Vaughn was pregnant!"

At the moment, however, the strain of this very public humiliation was second in his mind to another, more private form of ridicule. Some of his buddies back home had drafted him on their Rotisserie teams, he told me, and like fantasy players the world over had come to regret it. The only difference was that these people had a tool more powerful than shouted insults at the ballpark. They had his cellphone number. "Crazy fools," Vaughn sniffed, casting his eyes to the floor. "They've been killing me all year."

From then on, in the normal course of my reporting, I started asking ballplayers how often, if ever, they heard from the Rotisserie crowd. The answer was, quite emphatically, *all the time.* "They tell me to steal bases," said Andruw Jones of the Atlanta Braves. "For some reason, they want me to hit more doubles," said Mike Lowell of the Florida Marlins. "People are always telling me I'm doing well for them on their fantasy team," Pittsburgh closer Mike Williams observed. "I get that a lot more than 'You're doing a great job out there.' "

Such encounters were not limited to players. In 2001 Frank Thomas of the Chicago White Sox suffered a triceps injury that knocked him out for the season. But for mundane clerical reasons, the ballclub waited a couple weeks before placing him on the sixty-day disabled list, which, unbeknownst to them, prevented scores of Thomas owners in Rotisserie leagues from replacing him on their imaginary rosters.

To these people, this move was an outrage akin to the sinking of the *Lusitania.* They were so mad, in fact, that they started calling. And calling. First they just vented at the ballpark receptionists, but after a while they began demanding to speak directly to the general manager. "Bizarre," a team spokesman called it.

By the end of the 2002 season, I'd collected enough of these anecdotes to write a column for the *Journal* about the not-so-subtle influence that Rotisserie zealots exert on the major leagues. When it appeared, it wasn't the volume of correspondence that surprised me but the fact that nobody had much of anything to say about the column itself. All they wanted to do was recap their own fantasy seasons. One message, typical of the lot, said, "I can't believe I traded Kevin Millwood!"

Slowly, my aversion to Rotisserie baseball began to soften. Part of it was a case of professional burnout. Over the last few years, baseball had generated an abundance of news, none of it especially good. Rather than researching stories at the ballpark, most of my baseball "coverage" consisted of hunching over my desk like a garment worker, talking in conspiratorial whispers to labor lawyers, agents, investment bankers, doping experts, orthopedic surgeons, insurance brokers, disgruntled umpires, and vituperative taxpayers. The high point was the day I broke the news that retired superstar Jose Canseco had finally admitted pumping his body with anabolic steroids during his playing career.

I was so caked with baseball muck that I couldn't watch a ballgame without working myself into a lather about some tangential issue. Name a team, and I could tell you more than you'd ever want to know about the liquidity of its ownership group and a lot less than you'd expect about its pitching rotation.

It was then that I actually started to envy those Rotisserie nutjobs. If anything, they had the *opposite* problem. While I was consumed by steroids and ballpark financing, whatever punch they were drinking had intoxicated them to the point where they could dismiss, if not fully ignore, the game's systemic problems. While I'd forgotten what it was like to watch a ballgame when you have an emotional investment in the outcome, these people had an emotional investment in the outcome of *every pitch*.

The following November I arranged to cut back on my column schedule at the *Journal* to spend the entire next season exploring the parallel galaxy of Rotisserie baseball. The question was no longer whether to play. It was which league to join.

————

Jacque Jones is bent forward now, elbows on knees, still poring over the *Baseball Forecaster*. Six minutes have turned to ten, and he's barely finished with the Ms. If he wasn't anchoring the book with a thumb in the center crease, I'd be tempted to grab it and make a dash for the parking lot.

It's not that Jones is overreacting. At this particular moment in baseball history the timeless game of white-ash bats and emerald lawns is being upended by the notion that the inherent value of a ballplayer is, at bottom, far more quantifiable than most people realize. There's a growing school of belief, inside and outside the game, that the old scouts, the traditional surveyors of baseball talent, might someday be replaced by laptops.

Two events had tilted the balance. The first came in November 2002 when the Boston Red Sox announced that Bill James, the standard bearer of baseball's analytical revolution, would join the team as an adviser. The following spring, Michael Lewis published the best-seller *Moneyball*, which revealed the quantitative magic that helped the Oakland A's win so many games on a shoestring budget.

Suddenly, numbers were *hip*.

For elite Rotisserie players like Ron Shandler, this cultural shift was a welcome development, though long overdue. Shandler and others like him had embraced the statistical revolution years ago, in large part because they had no choice. For outsiders who weren't privy to the intelligence collected by scouts, coaches, and trainers, the numbers were the only means of making informed, unemotional decisions in Rotisserie drafts. And after years of tweaking their formulas, these experts had become better at reading the numbers than all but a handful of major-league general managers.

For Jacque Jones, this sea change couldn't have come at a worse time. Back before the statheads rose to prominence, baseball would have embraced a guy like him. He played good defense, he could run a bit, he hit for average and power and wasn't afraid to play hurt. The fact that he hit .300 on a team that won its division two years in a row would have been proof enough of his value.

Better still, Jones was the kind of player people could relate to. He wasn't exceedingly tall or freakishly proportioned or preposterously muscled. Coming up, scouts told him he was too small to hit home runs and too slow to steal bases. What they didn't know was that Jones was a firm believer in the great American tradition of working your ass off. He made it despite them.

But in the new baseball calculus, Jones was suddenly suspect. To mathematicians like Shandler, his defects weren't physical limitations that could be overcome at the gym; they were psychological. Jones swung at too many first pitches, he walked too infrequently and struck out too often. His on-base percentage was too low; his home-run totals were dubious, given his growing tendency to hit ground balls; and his batting average had been bloated by an unusually high rate of hits per balls in play. The clear implication is that Jones isn't as good as he is lucky.

Because of these prejudices, and concerns about his size and speed, Jones has not been able to secure his baseball future beyond the end of this season when his contract with the Twins expires, assuming he lasts that long. A few days from now, Terry Ryan, Minnesota's general manager, will make a rare appearance at batting practice to tell Jones there's no truth to a rumor, printed that day, that he's about to be traded to Los Angeles. It will be the first Jones has heard of this. Soon afterward, there will be so much speculation about his future that Twins manager Ron Gardenhire, noticing the strain on his right fielder, will attempt to lighten the mood by greeting him in the clubhouse with a question.

"Jacque, you still here?"

Jones is now finished with the *Forecaster*. He closes it firmly and flips it over to have a look at the author photo. Shandler is wearing a black shirt and tossing a baseball in the air, his head cocked. When I first saw the picture, it seemed sort of jaunty, but now, in the hands of Jones, I observe that Shandler's lips are pursed and his graying beard is slightly unkempt. The whites of his eyes are magnified by his glasses, and one side of his face is cast in shadow. Upon further review, he looks like an ax murderer.

"It's sad that people write books like this," Jones says with deliberate softness. "I hit .300 in the major leagues and still people are writing this stuff."

Jones hands the *Forecaster* back to me, visibly deflated but still determined to defend himself. He offers a list of reasons why Ron Shandler is wrong: Some hitters take more time to mature, luck is a big part of baseball, and it's good to hit ground balls because they force errors. If he'd listened to the opinions of so-called experts, he'd have quit this game years ago.

"All this stuff can be rebutted," he insists.

In the ensuing silence, Jones notices a sheet of paper stuck in the back of my notebook that's covered with numbers. It's my personal evaluation of Jones, one of hundreds I'd drawn up back home in New York, never imagining that a ballplayer would want to read it.

"What's this?" he asks.

———

I'd prefer to claim that it came to me in a dream and I woke up bathed in celestial light or that I heard about it from a disembodied voice on a subway platform. But the truth is that I stumbled upon it in the way so many of us find our destinies these days: I followed a few links on the Internet, and *boom,* there it was.

Tout Wars: Battle of the Experts.

Founded by Ron Shandler in 1998, Tout Wars is, by any reasonable standard, the national championship of Rotisserie baseball. To be invited, you have to have one foot in the fantasy-baseball information business, whether it's running a Roto advice site, publishing a book of projections, working for a baseball-statistics company, or writing a column for some prominent Rotisserie organ. In other words, you need to be engaged in the business of "touting" ballplayers.

The Tout Wars auction is held at the end of March in a hotel conference room near some major airport, like O'Hare or LaGuardia. There are two separate competitions, one where the player pool is limited to the American League and the other to the National League. The auctions are broadcast on the Internet and dissected by fans in a chatroom. There's no prize money, no trophy, and no celebratory banquet for the winner. To the men who compete in this contest (and they're all men) the only payoff is the right to brag. And judging from the blurbs on their books and Web sites, brag they do.

Last year's roster of contestants includes three lawyers, only one of whom is practicing. There's an MBA, a Hollywood screenwriter, a pair of computer engineers, and a guy with a master's in Victorian literature. Most of them appear to be in their thirties, while a handful are over fifty. They hail from Los Angeles and Chicago to the Washington suburbs and dozens of points between. In addition to Ron Shandler, whose three Tout Wars titles are the most of anyone, there are a few names I've seen before: Mat Olkin, the 1999 American League champion, writes an occasional baseball statistics column for *USA Today* 's *Sports Weekly,* and Jason Grey, the defending AL champion, is a regular fantasy-baseball advice columnist on *Sports Illustrated* 's Web site.

As I click through the photos from the 2003 draft, there's only one common thread: Nobody is smiling. Some of the Tout warriors look mildly scared, others unmistakably hostile. Nobody seems to have shaved, and a few have random tufts of hair sticking up at odd angles, as if they'd forsaken showers. These people have taken a goofy parlor game and turned it into a winner-take-all death match. They don't just want to beat you, they want to chew your organs.

Nonetheless, the notion of joining this league stuck to me like a dollop of ballpark mustard. Some of the lure, I'll admit, was my own intellectual vanity. If I was going to devote all my brainpower to playing this game, what was the sense in aiming low? Just as intriguing was the fact that the more I looked into the matter, the more I could tell that these guys were *going places.*

One Tout Wars alumnus was already working in the front office of the Toronto Blue Jays and another had caught on as a scout for the Milwaukee Brewers. One current player had a contract to do confidential research for the Boston Red Sox, another had recently been contacted by the New York Mets, and every year a handful of major-league teams ordered copies of Ron Shandler's *Baseball Forecaster.* Tout Wars wasn't just a bunch of hobbyists gone haywire, it was a laboratory for new baseball ideas.

But the most compelling reason to play was also the most straight-forward one: I was convinced that I could compete at a high level. While some of these touts clearly had contacts inside the game, there's no way any of them had a baseball Rolodex deeper than mine. While they evaluated players by the numbers from their various cubicles, I could pick up the phone and talk to a scout or a general manager and get the *real* story. I had to believe that my years of experience as a reporter were worth at least as much, if not a hair more, than the sum total of their number crunching.

Moreover, I was in a position to do something these guys could never dream of. With ready access to press credentials, I could spend a year systematically *managing* my own team. I'm not talking about juggling my lineup once in a while but actually showing up at the ballpark and working with the players I drafted: learning their idiosyncrasies, passing along tips from scouts, lobbying managers on their behalf, or just taking them out in the middle of a slump for a frosty one. In other words, treating them like people.

Playing in Tout Wars would be a noble experiment. A chance to determine, once and for all, which device was better at predicting a ballplayer's performance: the laptop or the human eye, cold, hard data or gut hunches and intuition. If I could interpret human intelligence the way these guys decode the numbers, I was sure I could do more than just tread water in this league. I could win.

On a cold, gray day in December 2003, I sat down at my desk, cleared my throat, and picked up the phone.

"Shandler Enterprises," said the voice on the line.

"Uh, yes. Is Ron Shandler in?"

"Speaking."

After introducing myself, I launched into my pitch, which I'd carefully laid out on a series of index cards and rehearsed in the shower. The problem, of course, was that I didn't meet any of the criteria for membership in Tout Wars: My Rotisserie credentials weren't just lacking, they were nonexistent. And while I did cover baseball, I also wrote about hockey, basketball, boxing, and the Tour de France. My only hope was that back in 1998, a pair of sportswriters from *Newsday* and the *New York Post* played in Tout Wars and finished in the middle of the pack. As far as I could tell, they hadn't disgraced themselves.

Though I stammered a bit, my argument was lucid, persuasive, and altogether brilliant, or at least I thought so. "That's interesting," Shandler said once I'd finished. His voice was flat and faint, as if he were talking to me from Alaska, and he sounded sort of exasperated. Shandler said he'd have to check with the other guys in the league, so I asked him how long he thought this would take.

"Not long," he said.

Two weeks later, after my application had been batted around via e-mail by the broader Tout Wars membership, the phone rang. It was Jason Grey, the current league administrator.

"I have news," he said.

I held my breath.

"Welcome to Tout Wars."

———

After two months of shaking the trees for confidential baseball data, I'd collected two unusual bits of information about Jacque Jones, which were laid out in detail on the evaluation sheet he's just pinched from my notebook.

One says that 38 percent of the pitches Jones swings at are outside the strike zone, making him, as my data sheet says, "one of the least selective batters in the major leagues." Another stat shows that the season before, Jones had turned twenty more weakly hit balls into base hits than the average ballplayer, a curious feat for a hitter who's not especially fast. These figures only back up the unspoken point Shandler made in his book: that when you break his performance down to its component parts, Jones appears to be playing at a level he cannot sustain.

Jones lets the paper hang limply from his fingers. "Look, I'm never satisfied," he says, staring at the carpet. "Last year was a difficult year. I was very disappointed with the results. It burned in the off-season. I've let everything go now, but it hurt for a while." Jones claps a hand over his eyes and squeezes it. He runs his palm over his forehead and down to the base of his neck. His eyelids are heavy. "Sometimes when you're winning, people don't realize how hard it was," he says in a near whisper. "It's tough to survive in baseball. People have family issues, problems you don't even know about. It's tough enough to play the game when you're healthy."

Jones hands the sheet of paper back to me without hurry or malice. He's still crouching forward, his car keys wrapped around one finger, betraying no desire to get up and leave. The only sound in the locker room is the buzz of a dying fluorescent bulb.

When I came here to visit the Twins, Jones was one of the players I wanted to meet most. Not because the mathematicians love him, but precisely because they do not. If I was going to compete at the highest levels of Rotisserie, I knew I would have to find cases where the numbers failed to tell the whole story. I'd come here to see if there was something about Jones, some incalculable trait that explained how he'd been able to defy the percentages. As he sits here, torturing himself on a sun-splashed afternoon, I have my answer. No matter how much the scouts or the statheads trash him, Jacque Jones will always find a way to succeed. Not because he's the most gifted ballplayer, but because he can't bear to imagine the alternative.

Standing up to go, collecting all my incendiary materials, I feel a concussive wave of guilt. As a sort of peace offering, I tell Jones that despite all this stuff, the data, the numbers, I'm still thinking about picking him for my Rotisserie team.

"What do you think?" I ask.

There's no smile this time, only a faraway glance. Then a shrug.

"It's up to you," he says.

Jacque Jones just made the cut.

THE PRESEASON

The Winter Meetings

December 2003

Austin Metzger of Rochester, New York, decided to join an online fantasy baseball league and compete against eleven people he had never met. Through a solid draft and a few decent trades, "Austin's Team" shot up in the standings and eventually finished second. Only then did Austin Metzger reveal his secret: He's eight.

· · ·

Under a hanging moon on the second Friday night in December, the streets of New Orleans are thick with the usual crowd of tap dancers, pickpockets, transvestites, police horses, and huggy drunks from Nova Scotia. It's barely past supper time, and the gutters are already choked with daiquiri cups.

Or so I'm told.

For the last ten hours I've been circling the lobby of the Marriott on Canal Street like a mallwalker on amphetamines, stopping only so often to slouch against a wall and stretch my knotted calf muscles. The occasion is Major League Baseball's winter meetings, an annual convention where everybody who's anybody in the horsehide bureaucracy gathers under one roof to mix, mingle, and talk shop.

There's Tommy Lasorda over by the revolving doors, his potbelly protruding from a cream sport coat. Superagent Scott Boras, looking tan and smug in jeans and a sweater-vest, holds court with reporters ten paces from the lobby Christmas tree. Jack McKeon of the Florida

Marlins—last seen winning the World Series—stands to my left, chewing an unlit cigar. Over by the bar obscured by a wall of plastic ferns, a pair of general managers, John Schuerholz of the Atlanta Braves and Walt Jocketty of the St. Louis Cardinals, are politely negotiating a five-player trade.

For the dozens of reporters on hand, this weekend is an exercise in competitive stalking. Interviews aren't so much scheduled here as they are accidents of timing. If you spot Chicago Cubs general manager Jim Hendry locked in conversation near the elevators, the trick is to check his pivot foot to see which way he's likely to break. Guess correctly, and your prize is three minutes of his time.

But even with an ESPN satellite truck idling outside, the winter meetings don't generate a lot of news anymore, unless you consider "Blue Jays Pick Up Justin Speier" one for the history books. "A dry hump" is how one baseball official describes them. Over by the escalators, Anthony McCarron of the New York *Daily News* is bracing himself against the back of a chair. "This," he says, "is the worst assignment in sports."

Years ago, the winter meetings were an intimate affair, a baseball salon where a crackling fire and a steady flow of Scotch loosened the lips of baseball executives. Bawdy stories were told, blockbuster trades executed, and dynasties artfully shaped. These days it's more like a swap meet.

Just about everybody in the building has something to sell, whether it's an agent peddling an unsigned client, an unemployed pitching coach looking for a fresh start in the minors, or a salesman hawking foam fingers that glow in the dark. As a rule, the more time you loiter, the less important you are and the more likely you'll be to earn the weekend's lowest designation, *First Team, All-Lobby*.

At the bottom of the food chain is the mob of eager collegians that flocks here every year, all hopped up on Bill James and hell-bent on landing a job with a big-league club in "baseball ops." They sleep five to a motel room, charge their cellphones in the lobby outlets, and pass out résumés on Kinkos card stock. Some wear blue blazers and introduce themselves as "Brian from Harvard," while others describe the valuable experience they gained Xeroxing game notes for the Montgomery Biscuits. The moment anyone over the age of thirty tries to take a breather for a few seconds, as I've just done, they'll descend like a swarm of tsetse flies.

The one standing before me now is named Scott. A few hours ago, I'd seen him wandering the lobby dressed like one of Al Capone's hitmen: black pants, black shirt, yellow tie, and a bulky canvas duffel bag that, when slung over his shoulder, bends him forward like a bridge troll. He's a bit plump and sweating from the exertion.

"You here looking for a job?" I ask.

Scott nods, drops the duffel, and begins telling his story. This is his third pilgrimage to the winter meetings. Last year, he landed a job in the marketing department of a minor-league team, passing out bobbleheads and the like. What he really wants, of course, is a job in a big-league front office, and to that end, he's been keeping an eye out for Montreal Expos general manager Omar Minaya. "I chased him all over Opryland last year," he says, proudly.

On a whim, I ask him if he plays Rotisserie. He nods again.

"How'd your team do?"

"You mean my *teams*."

Scott the minor-league intern plays in eight Roto leagues. The competition is so intense, he says, that he used to stay up until three o'clock every morning, waiting for Yahoo! to update the standings. For the next ten minutes, he walks me through his shrewdest trades last season, his favorite being Albert Pujols for Mark Prior. Finally, after checking the hands of a watch I'm not actually wearing, I simply turn and start walking. "Wait," he says. "I haven't even told you about my pitching staff!"

The Tout Wars draft has been tentatively scheduled for Saturday, March 27, somewhere in New York, which gives me fifteen weeks to prepare. These proceedings, then, represent the first leg of my Rotisserie odyssey. I haven't come here to gather news, exactly, but to chase after baseball intimates, copy down their cellphone numbers, and pump them for classified information about ballplayers.

I'm still not entirely sure why the members of Tout Wars agreed to extend me an invitation, but there was apparently no dissent. I'd like to think that these guys devour my weekly columns and think I'm positively brilliant, but I have a hunch the reason they allowed me to join is so they can thoroughly beat my ass. The last "insider" who tried his hand at Tout Wars was a guy named David Rawnsley, a former assistant scouting director for the Houston Astros, who wound up finishing *ninth*.

Even so, standing here at the Marriott with a blank notebook, surrounded by the guardians of baseball's most classified intelligence, I'm feeling a lot more cocky than intimidated. No matter what my Tout Wars opponents might be doing to prepare for the season, they're not doing it *here*.

Extracting useful information from real baseball executives in the name of winning your Rotisserie league is, at the moment, sort of hard. Spring training is still two months away, and, I'm told, it's a little premature to be making judgments about players. "Call me at home in a couple weeks," says Omar Minaya. "That's a question for spring training," says new Boston manager Terry Francona. At this point I'm not even sure which set of players to focus on—the Tout Wars elders haven't decided whether to put me in the American League or National League side of the contest. Then there's the thorny issue of why anybody who makes a living trying to win baseball games would disclose secrets to a Rotisserie geek. "I can't help you with that," barks Bill Stoneman, the flinty GM of the Anaheim Angels. "Scouting information is confidential."

On those occasions when the insiders do talk, they don't always agree. Over by the bar, I collar San Diego Padres GM Kevin Towers, who has nothing but praise for one of his young pitchers, Jake Peavy. "He's smart, he studies the game and watches a lot of video," Towers says, sipping a Bud Light. "I sat down with him when he was eighteen, and he was talking about how hitters don't make adjustments. I could have been talking with Greg Maddux." Minutes later, I bump into Scott Boras, who happens to be the agent who represents Greg Maddux. When I tell him what Towers has just said, he nearly spits out a mouthful of Poland Spring.

PEAVY?

After completing yet another lap, I take a post between a marble column and a ceramic pot to stalk my next victim. But in five seconds I can feel somebody's gaze. My pursuer is a tall guy with a backpack and a practical haircut who's wearing a white dress shirt with no coat and the kind of explosively colorful tie you wear when you don't wear ties very often. He has the tan, lanky, and slightly stooped look of someone who spends a fair amount of time hiking. Technically he's one of the kids, but from the creases at the corners of his eyes I can tell he's pushing forty. Our eyes meet. I'm a dead man.

"My name's Sig," he says.

The man who calls himself Sig tells me he's flown to New Orleans from his home in Silicon Valley to try to fulfill a dream he's had since the first time he flipped over a baseball card and saw numbers on the back: getting a job mining data for a major-league ballclub. He reaches into his backpack and hands me a color brochure he's been distributing. The theme: why your baseball team should hire Sig. "I can't provide you with traditional scouting," it says. "I wouldn't know a player tipping his pitches from one tipping his cap. But I can provide you with advanced and thorough quantitative analysis."

Sig works for NASA as a biomathematician in the Fatigue Countermeasures Group, where he helps determine, among other things, the optimal sleep schedules for astronauts. Before that, he had a job with the Air Force, where he was engaged in the business of launching spy satellites from the space shuttle. He has a B.S. in aeronautical and mechanical engineering and two master's degrees—one in mathematical modeling and another in human-factors engineering. In his spare time, he's finishing a Ph.D. in applied mathematics and statistics. He didn't tell his NASA colleagues why he was coming to New Orleans, he says, because they would have thought he was insane.

Inside the brochure, there's a picture of Sig looking earnest in front of a giant NASA placard as well as an inexplicable photo of Don Mattingly standing in the outfield grass beneath a giant billboard of a hot dog. In a text box, Sig promises innovative insights into how players age, how to make sense of minor-league data, and the wisdom of signing veterans to fat contracts. He lists a range of statistical tools he's familiar with: logistic regression, stochastic processes, and Markov chains. On the back is a smattering of quotes, including one from Leonardo da Vinci ("No human investigation can be called true science without passing through mathematical tests") and one from Billy Beane, the unabashedly quantitative GM of the Oakland A's ("If he's that good a hitter, why doesn't he hit better?").

When I ask Sig what he thinks he can bring to a major-league team, he explains he's got a spreadsheet on his laptop containing the complete statistics of every ballplayer who's worn a uniform since the Korean War, which he can use to divine heretofore unknown truths. He says he's a member of the Society for American Baseball Research (SABR), which recently published a paper he wrote on the surprisingly large influence pitchers have in throwing out basestealers. Sig seems to have no doubt that given the right opportunity, he'll find a way to break the game of baseball down into a series of equations, all of which end with a tidy figure on the right side of an equals sign.

Sig offers me a business card, which I take politely and stuff into a front pocket of my pants. I wish him good luck and then step off, notebook in hand, to resume my perambulations. I can't imagine what might happen if a guy this hypereducated got ahold of a major-league baseball team. Algorithms in the dugout? Baserunners with jetpacks? I'll say this for baseball's winter meetings: You meet the damnedest people.

———

Observe the crowd at the Marriott long enough, and every so often you'll see a skinny guy, no more than forty, lurking around the edges of the room. He'll be wearing hair gel or a goatee or maybe some fashionable trousers. He's usually carrying something: a laptop, a thick binder, or a cappuccino. Chances are he's one of the new front-office appliances—the latest wave of prestigiously schooled assistant GMs and in-house statisticians, people who like to slip terms like "sample size" and "equivalent adjusted ERA" into casual conversation. Few, if any of them, ever played the game, but they're not the least bit humbled by the fact. They consider themselves to be just as genetically blessed as the ballplayers, only in the brainpower department. For the most part, they don't socialize. To them, baseball is a business, and backslapping is just another market inefficiency.

On the other side of the room are the old scouts, the ex-players, the traditional baseball men. They stand in clots of five or six, identifiable by their lumpy sweaters, encroaching baldness, and the thick gold championship rings jammed above their knuckles. Every ninety seconds or so, there's an eruption of coarse laughter from their ranks. You could set your watch by it.

When I arrived in New Orleans, I knew baseball was in the middle of an ideological cold war and that these two groups, with their very different philosophies about baseball, were increasingly at odds. For years, these rivals had had few occasions to draw their revolvers. Other than learning how to turn on a laptop, the life of a scout hadn't changed much in half a century. The grunt work of baseball, the process of evaluating talent, was still carried out in dusty ballyards from Honduras to Terre Haute, the sorts of places MBAs and computer scientists rarely tread. No matter what silliness was taking root in the front office, their marching orders remained clear: Have a seat, apply sunscreen, watch a few kids play baseball.

But over the last few years, people who subscribed to the teachings of baseball newthink, a discipline known as "Sabermetrics," had begun to assume positions of influence. While the scouts described the game in the old vernacular of a player's physical "tools," the new breed spoke strictly in scientific terms, making analogies to subatomic particles and discussing paradigm shifts, false dichotomies, and the teachings of Karl von Clausewitz. To this quantitative counterculture, baseball's Old Testament was full of dubious doctrine. There was no such thing as a clutch hitter, no sense in designating one pitcher as the "closer," and no reason why a guy who hits forty bombs a year can't be platooned. As far as they were concerned, anybody who made a habit of swinging at the first pitch ought to be selling bathroom fixtures at The Home Depot.

These were not necessarily bad ideas. Most of them were backed by sturdy math, if not plain old common sense. The problem was the terms the scientists used to describe anyone who didn't agree with them. These ranged in severity from "boobs" and "halfwits" to "gorillas" and "recalcitrant dopes." As the baseball establishment returned fire, what should have been a logical step in the sport's evolution became a food fight at lunch period: jocks on one side, honor students on the other. What I failed to understand was how thoroughly the jocks were being routed.

That same evening, up in a banquet room at the Marriott, I'd attended an awards banquet called Scout of the Year. A couple dozen baseball big shots wandered in to show their faces and pick at the buffet, but only a handful stayed for the presentation, where a few elderly scouts were honored for lifetime achievement.

At the end of the program, with the room nearly empty, Dave Yoakum of the Chicago White Sox came to the podium. Yoakum had helped set up a charitable foundation to deal with a specific problem: the growing number of old scouts who'd been fired by major-league teams and had fallen on hard times.

"We have to do a better job of explaining what our scouts do," Yoakum said toward the end of his remarks, his voice turning impassioned, even grave. "Many new owners are not aware much of the history of the game. They made their money in buildings or highways or the stock market, I don't know what. They haven't dealt much with the human being."

The room turned silent then, like a funeral mass. "This new technology and these modern philosophies are all well and great," Yoakum continued, "but it still comes down to having good scouts. People who are loyal. People who are great students of the game."

———

By cocktail hour on Friday night, I've come to terms with the fact that this is not the time or place to bombard general managers with questions about fantasy baseball. Some of them are so besieged they haven't shown their faces.

But there's one group of experts that likes nothing better than to spend an evening talking about ballplayers between pops at the lobby bar: the old scouts. These guys are characters, for sure. Al Goldis of the Mets makes the scene in a tweed fedora. Pat Dobson, a former pitcher now working for the Giants, sports a pair of alligator loafers. Outside the revolving door, I bump into Tampa Bay scout Stan "Big Daddy" Williams, a former teammate of Sandy Koufax, who's puffing a Marlboro and observing the scenery on Canal Street. "I'm looking at all these young girls," he says with a wink. "But I can't remember *why*."

After three hours at the lobby bar and more than a few vodka martinis, the scouts have filled my notebook with the names of "sleepers" to watch for my Rotisserie team. I've listened to stories about fleabag motels, pimply kids with nasty curveballs, and the quirks of the first radar guns. I've marveled at their ability to lace almost every sentence with an F bomb and winced at some truly appalling jokes. I've stood rapt as they explained the mysteries of the physical game—wrapping their hands around imaginary bat handles and crooking their fingers around phantom baseballs. I've inhaled four gallons of Aqua Velva.

Maybe it's the vodka talking. Maybe it's the fact that I didn't exactly ace the math portion of the SAT. But I'm starting to think that baseball's infatuation with advanced statistics is something less than a panacea. In every other walk of life, quantitative types have already made their presence felt, and in most cases the results have been dubious. On Wall Street, the number crunchers brought us derivatives, an investment vehicle so advanced that some people who invested in them still can't tell you what happened to all the money they put in their retirement accounts. Consumers already up to their necks in debt get fifty credit-card solicitations a day courtesy of some thoughtful database. And it's no longer possible to buy a curtain rod without disclosing your zip code.

The problem with running a business strictly by the data is that it creates a tedious sameness. If baseball goes this route, it won't be long before the Indians, Yankees, and Diamondbacks are as indistinguishable as the Hilton, the Sheraton, and the Hyatt. As far as I'm concerned, baseball without variety would be soccer.

Bob Schaefer is the bench coach for the Kansas City Royals. He's a taciturn guy with piercing eyes who talks in a low rumble without moving his jaw much. He's the former director of player development for the Red Sox and a former scout whom I'd met a few years ago at a ballgame in Kansas City. Last season the Royals had been one of baseball's bright surprises, making an improbable run at the postseason with a team that played a lot better than the statisticians expected. While they faded in September, the season was hailed as a tour de force of positive coaching.

Schaefer is an old baseball guy out of central casting, and I'm curious to hear his take on the gathering feud. It takes about ten seconds to see where he stands. "Guys who only go with stats do it because they don't know what the fuck they're doing," he says. "The further you get from third base, the smarter you get."

If there was a perfect science to projecting ballplayers, Schaefer continues, there wouldn't be so many famous anomalies: Wade Boggs, one of the greatest hitters of his generation, spent five long years in the minor leagues. Raúl Ibañez was all but discarded from baseball three times before he finally earned a job though sheer determination. Boston outfielder Trot Nixon turned out to be a better player in the majors than he'd ever been in the farm system. "Stats don't win games," he says, his jaw muscles bulging now. "It's makeup, toughness, character."

Schaefer points to a crowd near the escalators. "Some of these people have never been in a dugout, they don't know shit about how to handle players. On the Royals, we played for each other." At this, his voice drops an octave, and his cheeks return to their normal pallor. "We're talking about ballplayers here, not robots."

Walking back to my hotel that night, kicking those discarded daiquiri cups, I'm starting to think playing by the numbers is the wrong way to win a contest in which human beings are the chess pieces. After all, isn't the point of Rotisserie baseball to identify players whose performances will *defy* prediction? Maybe I should try to win Tout Wars by ignoring the technocrats and listening exclusively to the advice of the old scouts. Maybe all you need to dominate Rotisserie is a splash of Aqua Velva.

———

"You have a package," says the desk clerk on the other end of the line. Last night's cocktails have taken a bit of a toll, and when I roll over to look at the clock it's a quarter past nine. I throw on some clothes, run a washcloth over my face, and put on two pairs of socks to insulate my aching feet. Over a plate of crawfish and eggs in the lobby restaurant, I open the envelope, which my wife has forwarded from home. Inside, hot off the presses, is a copy of *Ron Shandler's 2004 Baseball Forecaster*.

After my invitation to Tout Wars, I'd logged on to Shandler's Web site and ordered a copy, but I'm astonished that it's already here. Before I'd even heard of Tout Wars, Shandler was already holed up in his basement, tinkering with last year's data like a bathtub bomb maker. While I've spent exactly one day researching players, he's done.

"You are about to embark on a strange journey," Shandler writes in his introduction, "How to Use This Book." "This is a land where a career .250 hitter could be projected to contend for a batting title. It's a place where today's frontline closers become tomorrow's mop-up men. Within these pages, you'll find performance breakouts and regressions that occur at odd times to unusual players. At face value, lots of what you read will look completely counter-intuitive. It's almost like we're making the whole thing up."

Exactly, I agree, slurping coffee.

Skipping forward, I decide to give Shandler a pop quiz based on some of the information I gathered from the scouts. Out on Canal Street, Big Daddy Williams had raved about Ron Villone, a lefthander recently acquired by Seattle who had been, he said, "beating the shit out of left-handed hitters."

Flipping to page 127 of the *Forecaster*, I find Shandler's assessment of Villone. In the familiar measures of wins, strikeouts, ERA, and innings pitched, Villone had shown steady improvement. But scattered around these traditional statistics was a bouillabaisse of bizarre acronyms: S%, R$, Dom, and BPV. I'm sure there's a glossary in the back, but there's not enough coffee in Louisiana to get me there. Instead, I turn to the summary blurb. It says: "Got everyone all excited by posting early PQS scores of 5,4,4,4,3,5, but only had three more DOM starts in his next 13. BPIs were as mediocre as ever, so keep your excitement in check."

I have no idea what any of this means, but I've caught Shandler's general drift. Ron Villone was the sort of pitcher who will fool a lot of observers, but not him. Scanning the small type, I see a statistic called "opponent batting average," which measures how Villone fared against right-handed and left-handed hitters. There, it shows that lefties hit .267 against Villone over the full season, which was—despite Big Daddy's glowing account—his worst showing in five years.

Hmmm.

My next subject is Pedro Feliz, an emerging San Francisco first baseman who'd been swinging some heavy lumber. Pat Dobson, the scout in the alligator mocs, had raved about Feliz and told me he will "definitely" see more playing time, which was *exactly* the type of inside tip I'd come to New Orleans to get. While the other Touts might play it safe with Feliz, I could bid aggressively knowing the organization believes in him.

On page 45 of the *Forecaster*, Shandler writes: "Happy Pedro hacked his way to a career high 16 HR in just 235 AB." Not only did Feliz suffer a steep decline in the second half, Shandler notes, but he struck out 43 times more often than he walked. His prediction for the 2004 season: just eleven home runs.

Ten minutes later my coffee is cold, and the pop quiz is not turning out the way I'd hoped. Reading them again, I realized most of the treasured tips I'd collected from the scouts were really just vague bromides like "not ruling out injuries," "burnout candidate," and "pretty good young pitcher." On the other hand, Shandler's predictions couldn't be more exact. His numbers were authoritative, his conclusions firm and supported by precedent. The Bearded One, who lives five hours from the nearest major-league ballpark and attends one or two games a year, seems to know just as much, if not more, than the people who get paid to sit behind home plate.

As I trudge back to the Marriott to put another six miles on my cushioned insoles, I realize I have just learned two important lessons.

First, anybody who would choose to ignore the numbers in an expert Rotisserie league has, in all likelihood, been drinking vodka. Second, it might take me four months to figure out what all of Ron Shandler's acronyms mean, let alone how to apply them. If I'm going to mount a serious campaign in Tout Wars, I need more than just a crash course in statistics, I need a Ph.D.

Fumbling through my pockets, I fish out my collection of business cards and shuffle through them. I remember the résumé, but the name escapes me.

Oh yes, *Sig.*

The Front Office

January 2004

For once, Rick Sangerman had everything nailed down. He'd read every forecasting book. Studied all the stats. Bought all the magazines. So when pitcher Jim Gott came up for auction, Sangerman confidently bid $32 and won. As he penciled Gott's name onto his roster, he was handed a copy of the one source he hadn't bothered to check: the morning paper. Gott was out for the season with an elbow injury.

• • •

It's a frigid afternoon in December, and ice crystals have formed on the windows facing my desk. In the week since I returned from the winter meetings in New Orleans, I've been hunkered down in my apartment in Greenwich Village, studying the finer points of the game I'm about to play and trying not to hyperventilate.

The phone rings. It's Jason Grey.

The purpose of his call is to announce that the Tout Wars elders have decided to put me in the American League side of the draw, which is both good news and bad. On the plus side, I've been an American League fan from the cradle. While I was growing up in Ann Arbor, Michigan, the walls of my bedroom were flecked with tape marks from a continuous parade of posters of various Detroit Tigers: Alan Trammell, Kirk Gibson, and Ron LeFlore, among others. When the Tigers won the 1984 World Series, the only thing that prevented me from drinking a twelve-pack of Stroh's and rioting in the streets was the fact that I was an eighth-grader. My allegiance to the Tigers has waned through the subsequent lean years, but my connection to the American League hasn't. Living in New York, I've learned that anybody who covers sports for a living had better keep up with all the minutiae of the Yankees or else suffer the wrath of friends, colleagues, and, worst of all, the Slovenian guy at the corner deli. "You call yourself a *sportswriter?*"

Beyond that, the American League is altogether more interesting right now. The GMs tend to be younger and more unorthodox, and the owners a lot less provident. Lately they've been treating the National League like a glorified farm system—paying princely sums to lure away superstars with names like Schilling, Sheffield, and Guerrero. The competition is so daunting that even Theo Epstein, the unflappable thirty-year-old Yale-educated general manager of the Boston Red Sox, is getting chill bumps. "I'd give a grand to be in the NL this year," he says.

Not coincidentally, Tout Wars has shifted in the same direction. Already the roster of contestants in the American League includes three former champions: Jason Grey, Lawr Michaels (the guy with the master's in Victorian literature), and Mat Olkin of *USA Today*. In a couple of weeks, for reasons that won't be immediately clear, Ron Shandler will switch over from his preferred slot in the National League. The rest of the field includes last year's runner-up, Rick Fogel of USA Stats, and three more contestants who've finished in the top four. The only other rookie will be Joe Sheehan, a columnist for Baseball Prospectus, the brash Sabermetric Web site that's becoming the *Paris Review* of the baseball intelligentsia. When I ask Grey to rate the quality of the field, he calls it the tightest he's ever seen. "There are no guppies in the pond."

Great.

As we're hanging up, Grey, feeling suddenly benevolent, leaves me with one final word of caution. "Don't overload yourself with information," he tells me, "or you will go nuts on draft day."

Since I committed to playing in Tout Wars, I've collected every bit of Rotisserie wisdom I've heard and dutifully typed it into a file called "Advice." But this time there's really no point. If there's any postulate I'm likely to violate in the most flamboyant fashion, it's this one.

What Jason Grey doesn't understand, and what I would never tell him, is that ever since I cracked the cover of the *Baseball Forecaster*, I've been waking up with my stomach in knots, wondering how I'm going to close the prohibitive knowledge gap that separates me from people like him. To play this game the way my opponents do, I will have to develop a working knowledge of about five hundred ballplayers and, when the draft rolls around, be prepared to make instantaneous judgments on each of them.

Swallowing hard, I decide to punch up Jason Grey's Web site, the humbly titled Masters of Fantasy Baseball. I've known that several of my Tout Wars opponents have some writing gig or statistical job that gives them access to one or more major-league locker rooms and that they do, on occasion, talk to ballplayers. But when Grey's home page pops up, my worst fears are confirmed. One link takes you to a photo showing a pile of *Sports Illustrated* press credentials he's been issued by various ballclubs. Another link summons a sample of *audio files* from clubhouse interviews, including a recording of Kansas City's Carlos Beltran explaining why he hasn't been stealing so many bases.

Most of Grey's columns have one unifying trait: some phrase designed to convey the idea that Grey is a baseball insider; something like, "my pals in the Tigers press box confirm it," or, "I've heard from multiple sources in the Dodgers organization," or, "I can personally vouch for the fact the infield grass is grown a little extra thick on the third-base line." At other points he speculates about players with gambling problems, bad attitudes, or a propensity to party too much. To Grey, clubhouse visits aren't just occasional romps, they're the centerpiece of his sales pitch.

This sort of access, of course, was supposed to be *my* secret weapon. By hanging around the players more than anyone, I figured I would break new ground. Turns out I'm not a Rotisserie pioneer after all.

As the winter sun vanishes across the Hudson River, I decide to stop postponing the inevitable. I close all my study guides, shut off my computer, and sit down at the kitchen table with nothing but a blank sheet of paper. Now that I know which side of the draw I'm playing in, I begin to write down, purely from memory, the likely starting lineups and pitching rotations for every team in the American League. As a sports generalist at the *Journal*, I didn't expect to nail the identities of all two hundred of these ballplayers, or even most of them. But after an hour of intense concentration, I count up all the names on my list and write the tally at the top.

Sixty-two.

The following morning I wake up from a vivid dream. It's nighttime, and I'm being chased by the police through an endless, empty parking lot. At one point I'm carrying a stadium hot-dog steamer, and New York Yankees catcher Jorge Posada is jogging next to me, shouting encouragement: "Run, dude, run!" When I wake up, my jaw is tender from grinding my teeth.

Just as I'd learned at the winter meetings that I was outgunned statistically, I've now realized that my knowledge of players is even lousier than I thought and that one of my opponents may already be my equal in gathering secret intelligence. Staring at the bathroom mirror, waiting for my abdominal muscles to unclench, I realize I won't be able to master the player pool by myself.

It's time to hire a scout.

———

Take out an online classified that contains the term "fantasy baseball research assistant" and this is what you'll get: one hundred and seventy-two résumés.

Sifting through my in-box, I find responses from a cigar salesman, an oncology nurse, a radio news anchor from Poughkeepsie, and a guy who says he'll be available as soon as he wraps up a research project on the Republic of Turkmenistan. There's a high-school junior in the pack, as well as a former technology executive who graduated from college the year I was born. One résumé, tacked immediately to the bulletin board, comes from a guy in his thirties who lists his employer for the last ten years as Vito's Pizza. His "responsibilities" at his place of employment include "resolving customer complaints."

Yo, this pizza *sucks!*

If there's one clear theme to all these responses, it's that the word "Rotisserie" sends some primal code to the brain indicating that it's okay to make yourself sound like a compulsive nutcake. One applicant says he scores parts of *five* baseball games a night on television, on his own, for no apparent purpose. Another brags that he used to play entire 162-game baseball seasons on his Nintendo, keeping track of the "stats" of all the players. "755, 56 and 0," one letter opens. "These numbers represent, of course, Hank Aaron's home run record, Joe DiMaggio's hitting streak and the times I played in a fantasy baseball league without capturing the championship."

After reading one query, I nearly knocked over my coffee grabbing for the phone. It was from a pitcher who played in the minor-league system of the Cleveland Indians. As I was dialing his number, though, I noticed he'd only be available until May, when he'd be due back on the mound to audition for the Kansas City T-Bones of the independent Northern League.

When I'm through whittling down the list, the finalists for my scouting position include a woman who's finishing an internship with the Boston Red Sox, a former writer for the Oakland A's team magazine, and an aspiring player agent with some formal training as a scout. In the end, I contacted four people and scheduled interviews at a café around the corner from my apartment.

At 8:00 A.M. sharp, the first of the batch, Ferdinando Di Fino, twenty-five years old, wanders in from the cold. He's wearing a gray suit with no tie, and there's a pencil jammed behind his ear. He's a big, square guy with wide-set eyes, a meaty chin, and the stiff comportment of a football coach. But between his bashful smile and the way he stands until offered a chair, it's clear that he's not the bullying type. "Call me Nando," he says.

Nando (rhymes with *condo*) is a lifelong Yankees fan of Italian extraction who grew up in Syracuse. His father is a doctor, his mother a nurse. His own baseball career ended in the seventh grade, when he was cut from the junior varsity. He's a graduate of Boston College who recently earned a master's in history from Fordham. He wrote his thesis on the topic of the American horror movie.

While none of this immediately suggests that Nando might be a front-runner for the job, there is one detail that separates him from the pack: He'd paid his way through graduate school by working at SportsTicker, a company that supplies instant baseball data to newspapers and Web sites. His job was to come in at about noon, sit down between a TV and a computer terminal in a room filled with rabid sports freaks, and score three baseball games in a row. Over the full season, he'd seen every player in the majors at least four times. "My baseball knowledge is at a level that is way too high because of this job," he wrote in his cover letter, "and my own fantasy teams (I had three last year) all finished in the top two."

But what I liked about Nando was the sheepish way he relayed this information. In fact, he seemed to think of himself as a recovering Rotisserie addict, a guy who'd been on a summerlong bender. Every night, despite his better judgment, he would belly up to the bar to squint at the ESPN "crawl" for updates on his fantasy players. "Hypnotic and girl-repelling," he called it.

After finishing school and quitting SportsTicker, things got a little murky. Turns out there are precious few job openings for a guy with a master's in history who, by some accident of brain chemistry, can remember obscure biographical details about every ballplayer in the major leagues. So Nando moved home to Syracuse and took a job in a produce warehouse, where he's been reporting to work at sunrise to unpack grapefruits and bananas and perform all the menial jobs reserved for the warehouse low man. "They won't let me near the forklift," he says.

While he clearly knows ballplayers, I'm worried Nando is just a kitchen-table fantasy player who may not be prepared for the rigors of Tout Wars. In the winter of 1980, when Dan Okrent unveiled the rules of this game, he determined there should be eight scoring categories in all, four in hitting and four in pitching. For years, this "4x4" format was the unchallenged standard. But lately, some of the more progressive leagues, including Tout Wars, have added two more categories, runs and strikeouts. "Does a 5x5 league seem intimidating to you?" I ask.

Nando sets his water glass down with a thud and presses the back of his hand to his mouth, raising a finger as if to say "hold on a second." His face turns red as he tries not to cough a mouthful of water all over the table. "Dude," he says, clearing his throat, "I played in a 7x7 last year. This is nothing."

The other candidates are impressive enough, but it's pretty clear that I'm only going through the motions. I already have my man.

———

It's commonly believed that most Rotisserie leagues are won during the preseason. To hold my own in Tout Wars, therefore, I've drawn up a blueprint that's comparable in scope and ambition to von Schlieffen's plan to conquer France by way of Belgium.

The first two phases are already complete. Phase one was my December trip to the winter meetings in New Orleans, which was followed closely by phase two, a trip to Puerto Rico over the holidays, where I dropped my wife at the beach in the mornings and spent eight days traveling the island to scout major-league prospects who'd gone there to play in the annual winter league. Next month, I'll pack my bags and spend three weeks at spring training, dividing my time between Florida and Arizona, where I plan to visit every American League campsite and, if I can manage it, interview two hundred ballplayers. When I'm done, I won't just be able to name 100 percent of the likely starters in the American League, I'll be able to tell you how many of them have goatees.

In the first week of January, however, the task at hand is to set up my own front office, a communications bunker where I can monitor the pulse of Major League Baseball, wheedle confidential information from insiders, make deals, talk deals, and just generally behave like a sociopath without frightening my neighbors.

I've settled on a desk in the basement of my wife's office building near Union Square: an old carriage house on a leafy block of brownstones that's close to a bookstore, a Starbucks, the subway to Yankee

Stadium, and, most importantly, Pete's Tavern. In a week's time, I have shuffled all the dusty boxes stored there to a far corner and armed myself with phone, fax, and DSL. After a trip to Barnes & Noble and a flurry of shopping on Amazon, I've built a baseball library nearly eleven feet long, which includes two baseball encyclopedias, the *Bill James Handbook*, John Benson's *Future Stars*, two books on scouting, two of Ron Shandler's *Forecasters*, player handbooks from *Baseball America* and *The Sporting News*, and a dozen team media guides. I spend another three hundred dollars signing up for the sites run by my Tout Wars opponents: Ron Shandler's Baseball HQ, Jeff Erickson's RotoWire, and Joe Sheehan's Baseball Prospectus. A subscription to Jason Grey's Mastersball, with its orgy of scouting detail, sets me back forty bucks.

In his first week on the job at a salary of $1,500 a month, my chief scout, Ferdinando Di Fino, rumbles into the front office in a navy peacoat and plops into a chair, wearing a knit cap. He will continue to wear this cap all day, I discover, because his hair is unevenly buzzed. When I met him, he'd been pomading his hair forward to give it a trendy slope, but he was getting sick of the trouble of maintaining it, so he made a pit stop to the hardware store. "I got some clippers," he explains, "and did the job myself."

After accepting my job offer, Nando quit his brief career in fresh produce and fled Syracuse with all his possessions in the back of a Pontiac. He's since installed himself in an apartment in Hoboken where, other than a busted heater, his only complication is the arrival of Bosco, an unemployed college buddy with designs on his sofa. Nando says he can stay, but only if he pays the electric bill.

Our first priority is a project I call "The Board." In almost every general manager's office in the major leagues, there's one common decorative element: a giant magnetic board where the name of every active ballplayer is posted. Some GMs use color coding to denote injuries, unsigned free agents, scouting reviews, and players who can't be sent down to the minors without clearing waivers. Staring at one of these things can induce drowsiness, but in a business where trades are often made on the fly, they're indispensable. During the two days it takes for his magnetic board to be unbolted from his office in Kansas City and shipped to spring training, Royals general manager Allard Baird says, "I feel naked."

One trip to Staples and $142 later, we have a three-foot metal board, a thousand magnets, and Sharpies in five different colors. The process of making a magnet for every player will take Nando four days and come to be referred to as "arts and crafts time."

Overall, Nando's chief responsibility is to collect biographical information on every player in the American League—basically anything that is *not* quantifiable. If a player just signed a new contract, went through salary arbitration, had a religious conversion, got married, learned jujitsu, visited New Zealand, failed a Breathalyzer test, or had a bad palm reading, I want to know about it.

One Tuesday, well past midnight, Nando calls me at home. He's been cooped up in the front office for fifteen hours, but you wouldn't know it from the tone of his voice. "You wouldn't believe some of the crazy shit you can find on the Internet," he says. His discoveries include an Ohio electronics technician who keeps updated evaluations on thousands of players in the minor leagues, a blogger called the "transaction guy" who does nothing but comment exhaustively on every major-league roster move, and a University of Illinois physics professor who took a break from studying nucleons to discover that curveballs, not fastballs, are the easiest pitches to hit for home runs. There's a chatroom on a sports gambling site where wiseguys gossip openly about which players are using steroids. There's another site where dozens of major leaguers describe the moment they found God. There's a forum where gay fans talk about everything from the Yankees' baffling lack of plate discipline against a lightly rested Josh Beckett in the World Series to whether Javy Lopez has pushed Baltimore out of the basement in "total team hotness."

More surprising is how much of this analysis is available for free. Without spending a dime, you can see all the player statistics since 1871, download box scores from ten thousand games, and find out how many extra-base hits there were in the National League in 1935. Some of these sites have caught the attention of real baseball executives. When I ask Yankees general manager Brian Cashman if he reads any of this stuff, he rattles off a list of obscure sites he's browsed, including something called Baseballgraphs.com, which maps the history of the game using advanced quantitative methods like defense efficiency ratio and fielding independent pitching. "Some of it is useful, and some is useless," Cashman says. "But it's incumbent on every one of us to keep up." If you're not careful, he observes, "the game will pass you by."

In a matter of days Nando has absorbed so much information about ballplayers that he can no longer keep it down. "A. J. Hinch says he wants to be a general manager someday," he announces over take-out chicken salad. In an e-mail message sent well past midnight, he writes, "Carlos Lee has a brother in the Chicago farm system who is also named Carlos." Over gyros at a Greek place around the corner, he tells me how White Sox pitcher Kelly Wunsch, back in his minor-league days, surprised his future wife by proposing to her while dressed as the team mascot.

After two weeks of this, Nando stomps into the front office with a disgusted look. He tells me he's been listening to baseball columnist Rob Neyer, a protégé of Bill James and one of the chief proselytizers of baseball newthink. "That guy is a cocky prick," he fumes. "He was just on TV saying that Derek Jeter is a terrible shortstop and spouting off his holier-than-thou Sabermetric jargon. I really hate these guys." This is, of course, music to my ears. Forced to examine nothing but personal details about players, Nando is starting to sound like one of the old scouts from New Orleans. He's becoming a baseball humanist. By the time he's finished with his rant, I've settled on his new front-office nickname.

"Bonecrusher."

———

Sig from New Orleans, my new chief of statistics, is taking his sweet time answering his cellphone. He's in Orlando at a NASA conference, helping chart the future course of intergalactic travel, but he swore he would take a few minutes off today to talk baseball. "Sorry," he says, finally picking up. "I just got off some space simulator."

I haven't so much decided to hire Sig to help me with the numbers as Sig has decided to adopt me as an experiment, a sort of quantitative Eliza Doolittle. As I'm about to find out, Sig is more than a little confident in his analytical abilities and enjoys nothing more than using them to flatten people—especially a bunch of guys who call themselves "experts." Once he got a load of the Tout Wars Web site, he was ready to start immediately. While keeping his regular hours at NASA, he's agreed to join my team, at least through the draft, at a part-time salary of $1,200 a month. The purpose of this call is to make final arrangements for his trip to New York in the last week of January, where he plans to unveil our statistical battle plan. Already he's sent me a series of elaborate graphs based on Tout Wars results from previous years. I have no idea what they mean, but in a side note he said something about our opponents that popped off the screen: "I don't think they're all that smart."

Sigurd Mejdal (it's pronounced "MY-dell") is thirty-eight. He grew up in San Jose, the son of a career army officer who was born in Denmark and his wife, a nurse from Colombia. He played Little League baseball for six years, where he was assigned sporadically to center field, took a lot of walks, and once went three full seasons without hitting anything but a single. He hasn't played Rotisserie in almost a decade, so he's constantly mangling player names. In Sigspeak, "Brad Fullmer" becomes "Bill Fumer" and "Frank Catalan-otto" is renamed "Fran Cataloni." First baseman Doug Mient-kiewicz gives him such fits that he's shortened his name to "Mint."

Sig isn't the least bit defensive about this. To him, players aren't so much individual people as distinct data troves. A few weeks ago, I would have scoffed at this view, but not now. The less Sig knows about a player's reputation, the more ruthlessly he can evaluate his statistical prospects. My time with Ron Shandler's book taught me that the numbers have their own compelling narrative, and when their story collides with the conventional wisdom about a ballplayer, it's not a failure but an opportunity.

My goal in hiring both Sig and Nando was to create the world's most outlandishly bipolar advisory team. At the auction table, I'll have Nando in one ear telling me that he likes Seattle outfielder Raúl Ibañez because he's been taking karate lessons to improve his balance. In the other ear, Sig will ask, "How do you spell 'Ibañez'?" Then he'll type his name, run a forward stepwise multiple-sigmoidal regression with linear weights, and tell me there's a 76.3 percent chance that Ibañez will have a career season. If all goes well, they'll agree on twenty-three players, just enough to fill out a Tout Wars roster. If I can combine the best of the numbers with the best of traditional scouting, there's no way I can lose.

On January 27, the day Sig arrives in New York, the streets have been hushed by the first hours of a heavy blizzard. The native Californian tromps down the stairs to the front office, kicking the snow off his feet and brushing it from his sleeves as if it were toxic ash. Under the dim fluorescent lights, he plunks down on a cardboard box and cracks open his Sony Vaio.

During working hours, Sig uses this machine's linear algebra–based optimizing software to simulate the performance of cosmonauts on the International Space Station. But when the whistle blows, it's all baseball. Loaded on its hard drive is an Excel file with the final box scores for about 38,000 games dating back over the past seventeen years. On another, he's got the complete career numbers for every player in the major leagues since 1950. Whenever he has a question, he types in a series of commands, hits "enter," and in seconds some segment of baseball's DNA is revealed to him: from the precise value of a double (.49 runs) to the negative impact of a player who is caught stealing (−.33 runs).

"Computer magic," he calls it.

Sig's baseball philosophy is that human perceptions are, for the most part, garbage. When humans watch a baseball game, they give too much weight to first impressions, recent events, and unusual occurrences. They make causal connections when they don't exist, rely too heavily on existing theories, and give too much weight to evidence that confirms them. All human observers, the scouts included, are sort of like drunks in a bar brawl: their abilities are severely limited, but the more they indulge, the more confident they become. As he sees it, thousands of humans have played professional baseball. They have appeared on the scene, struggled, succeeded to different degrees, struggled some more, failed, and ultimately retired. But their stories live on in the numbers. While he can't know exactly what any particular player will do in the future, he can find out what all yesterday's players did with their tomorrows. So rather than sitting behind home plate with a stopwatch and a radar gun, he only has to look at a player's career numbers, find a few hundred similar players from the past, and then use their "futures" to determine what the modern player is liable to do.

Hanging in Sig's office at NASA is a close-up photograph of a snowflake that reveals its intricate pattern and wondrous complexity. Under the picture there's a caption: "Remember, you are very unique and very special, just like everyone else."

The job I've given Sig is to devise a software program that will take all the data available about this year's players and spit out projections for next year or, as Sig puts it, "write tomorrow's sports pages today." Crazy as it sounds, this exact process has become something of an obsession among baseball statisticians, not unlike a ballplayer's quest to hit .400. Deep inside the most progressive front offices and baseball think tanks, such systems are already up on the lift. The Yankees use a mathematical formula, pioneered by former GM Gene Michael, that allows them to measure the caliber of each new Yankees team against championship squads of the past. The Orioles have a tool that weighs a team's offense, defense, and pitching and spits out a baseline value, while the Oakland A's developed a Markov model—an actuarial table of everything that happened in the major leagues over five years—to develop an entirely new set of statistics to evaluate players. Theo Epstein of the Red Sox uses a secret predictive "metric" developed by team statistician Voros McCracken.

Although they're scarcely advertised, and only a tiny fraction of fantasy-baseball players know they exist, several advanced projection engines have become available to the public. One was created by Tom Tippett, the founder and president of Diamond Mind Baseball, an Oregon company that sells software for computer simulation games. He sells his predictions, based on his own proprietary formula, on a CD that costs twenty-five dollars. Another version is PECOTA, a system engineered by another Tout Wars participant, Nate Silver of Baseball Prospectus, who makes the results available to BP subscribers. Ron Shandler's computer projections, which appear in the *Forecaster*, are the most widely known. The numbers these programs generate are just as reliable, if not more so, than what the majority of major-league teams use internally.

Sig tells me that all of these systems produce roughly the same results: a correlation coefficient of .700 for hitters and .490 for pitchers, or a total of about .600 for everyone.

This means that after taking into account dozens of factors, from a player's previous statistics to his age, the dimensions of his home ballpark, and the number of games he's likely to play, they can account for about 60 percent of the statistical deviation. In other words, computers can predict the baseball future with about 60 percent accuracy, while the remaining 40 percent remains a mystery. (By comparison, the correlation between a typical student's high school and freshman college grade-point averages is about 48 percent.)

What's remarkable about Sig's attempt to build his own predictive system is that he's only got sixty days to do so. He's already looking for software that will allow him to run six hundred locally weighted regressions with little effort and for reliable minor-league data— which turns out to be prohibitively expensive. In a single day of work a week earlier, late at night after all the other engineers had gone home, Sig put together a rough draft of a model that topped out at .611 for hitters—just 13 percent behind the best software in the business. "That was a bit disappointing," he says.

Once this task is finished, Sig will develop another system to convert every player's projected performance into a dollar value based on the parameters of Tout Wars, where each owner has exactly $260 to spend.* Next Sig plans to write a software program that will keep track of all the bids during the draft in March and reveal any hidden market trends we might be able to exploit. To refine his formulas, he's already made appointments to talk to an economist at the Federal Reserve and to sit down with Dr. Ben Polak, a Yale statistics professor who specializes in game theory.

When it's all done, he's proposed calling the system Zoladex, after a drug that chemically sterilizes those who take it. When the other Touts get a taste of it, he figures, "we will not only separate them from their egos but also from their manhood."

Zoladex it is.

As Sig's tutorial winds down, I could really use a drink. Nando is so confused that his eyebrows seem to be stuck in the arched position. Ever since Sig walked through the door, my chief scout has been eyeing him suspiciously, like a department-store detective. I have no idea if these two will be able to work together.

While we're packing up for the bar, I hand Sig a printout of the chart he sent me shortly after taking a first look at the Tout Wars site. Sig had gone back to the previous season and looked up what Ron Shandler and a few other contestants had predicted players were worth before the 2003 Tout Wars auction, then plotted these projections against the actual amounts paid at the draft. "I fit a linear regression through the line and also a polynomial to see how well the line describes the data," he explains.

I nod as if this is obvious.

After a few minutes of digression during which phrases such as "prediction mean," "positional volatility," and "marginal revenue difference" spill out, I'm starting to get the general point. Sig wanted to see if the Touts were holding any aces up their sleeves—whether they were making one set of projections for their books and Web sites and then deviating wildly from them at the auction. The fact that his

---

*To properly value any one player's projected statistics, you must first put them in context. If you expect Alex Rodriguez to hit 45 home runs, for instance, you can't place a value on them until you've determined how many home runs will be hit by every other American League player who is likely to be drafted.

chart was linear, that there was a 90 percent correlation between the x- and the y-axis, means that the answer is, as he puts it, "a big fat *no.*"

Over the last six weeks, I'd made peace with the notion that no matter what, I'd always be a step behind the experts at the auction table. Trying to catch up to the laptop huggers with two months of preparation was patently foolish. But something in Sig's tone, his extreme confidence in the data—even the way he clacks and spins his wireless mouse with a mischievous expression—has started to change my view. "So this," I say, waggling the graph under his nose, "means exactly what?"

Sig rises from his cardboard box and stretches his back. He snaps the monitor of his laptop closed and shoves it in his backpack. He snatches the paper from my hands and waggles it back at me with a loud crinkling noise.

"It means we can win."

Fanalytics

February 14

On his wedding day while seated at the head table with his bride, Beth,
Tim O'Day couldn't erase one idea from his mind: trading Willie Hernan-
dez for Luis Leal. Knowing the possible consequences of excusing himself
to make a Rotisserie trade, he waved leaguemate David Lewis over and
told him to make the offer on his behalf. Ten minutes later, Lewis returned
from a pay phone flashing a furtive thumbs-up.

"It was one of the worst trades in history," O'Day says.

· · ·

Every February for the last seven years, Ron Shandler, the Bearded
One, has emerged from his basement in Roanoke, said good-bye to
his wife, Sue, grabbed a box of *Forecasters,* and trundled off to the
bustling metropolis of York, Pennsylvania, to appear at a free public
forum called Talkin' Baseball.

This year's event takes place on Valentine's Day at the old Martin
library downtown in a Victorian room with parquet floors, red velvet
curtains, and a grandfather clock. Ten minutes before the scheduled
start, more than seventy people have turned up from six neighboring
states, overwhelming the supply of folding chairs. Library marketing
director Frances Keller has pulled out all the stops, laying out a spread
of turkey sandwiches and peanut-butter pie, all carefully swathed in
Saran Wrap. "This is one of our biggest days of the year," she says.

I've driven here today to meet Ron Shandler for the first time, although I already feel as if I know him. It's been two months since I opened my copy of the *Baseball Forecaster*, and ever since it has served as my Rotisserie baseball security blanket. Already its pages are smudged, its spine cracked, its cover shredded like a flag in high winds. It's been stuffed in bags, dropped in snowbanks, and thoroughly marked over with ballpoint ink. But there is one thing that distinguishes me from the other baseball hobbyists in this room: I'm here to perform reconnaissance.

One of the awkward aspects of being a famous Rotisserie pundit who also competes in Tout Wars is that whenever you speak in public, as Ron Shandler is about to do, you are accountable to your readers and, as such, obligated to tell the truth, even in the presence of an opponent. By the time he's finished Talkin' Baseball, I'm betting Shandler will have tipped his hand on a hundred ballplayers.

The best demographic study of serious Rotisserie players was conducted by Don Levy, a University of Connecticut sociologist, who found them to be 94 percent white, 98 percent male, 63 percent married, and overwhelmingly college educated. As the meeting comes to order, a quick scan of faces and ring fingers in this room suggests that he's exactly right. Blue jeans, ballcaps, and sensible jackets are *de rigueur,* but there's still a whiff of affluence. I'd bet the number of dentists exceeds the number of bricklayers by a factor of four to one. The average age is about forty, but the far ends of the range are wider than I expected. Sitting in the front row, there's an elderly guy in a cardigan who seems constantly on the verge of nodding off. Three seats to his left, there's a pair of twentysomethings demonstrating all the classic symptoms of being painfully hung over.

Shandler sits at the head table between the moderator, a library official named Frank Baker, and another panelist, Paul White, a columnist for *USA Today* who writes about general baseball topics. Shandler is forty-six, average in height and build, with a slight paunch. His beard, which could use a trim, is streaked gray in spots. His eyes are framed by a large pair of glasses with a purplish tint. There's a cellphone clipped to his belt on a battered leather holster, and he's wearing jeans, lumpy brown shoes, and a heavy green button-down. He looks like he's dressed for a hayride.

In the ten years since Shandler asked to be included on this panel, his stock in the Rotisserie business has grown considerably. In addition to his Web site, which has more than 7,000 subscribers, he will sell roughly 17,000 copies of the *Forecaster* this year at $24 apiece. His audience has grown to the point that he's started hosting forums each year in a handful of major cities from Boston to Phoenix, where his acolytes pay forty bucks at the door to engage in a Socratic dialogue with the world's greatest Roto player. It's not unusual for people to show up early to get a choice seat.

But here in York, to my surprise, Shandler is something of an afterthought. Paul White, the columnist, is clearly the headliner for the afternoon, and he dominates the early hours with digressions about his experiences covering the *real* game. The moderator seems to have a very loose idea of who Shandler is, asking him at one point, "Didn't you play in one of those expert leagues?" From the tenor of the questions, I can tell that some of the people in the audience aren't familiar with Shandler's work. Before it's over, he will repeat the basic tenets of his bedrock theory, Component Skills Analysis, five or six times. As the hours wear on, he sinks farther into his chair with an expression that falls somewhere between tedium and grim resignation.

For all his prominence in the elite circles of Rotisserie, Shandler has grown accustomed to being invisible just about everywhere else. Most mainstream baseball fans, no matter how rabid, have never heard of him. The same goes for hundreds of thousands of casual fantasy players, many of whom would be reluctant to buy a book that doesn't have pictures.

Watching him talk, you get the feeling that Shandler isn't terribly upset by this. The frumpy clothes, the clinical tone, the general air of reluctance all suggest that he's perfectly comfortable being known as a bearded stat geek who wears sandals most of the time and drives a Hyundai. The public side of his job may be crucial to his livelihood, but "celebrity" isn't something he greatly enjoys.

Still, there is one professional slight that absolutely burns him up.

After twenty years of baseball research, some of it original and much of it groundbreaking, Shandler continues to be shunned by the most unlikely group: the larger establishment of serious baseball mathematicians and researchers. The chief culprit, he told me before the forum, is the Society for American Baseball Research, the loose federation of amateur baseball wonks for which Sabermetrics is named. The group has never invited Shandler to speak at its annual convention or published his work in its journal.

To the potentates at SABR, Shandler is to baseball analysis what supermarket tabloids are to serious journalism. Rather than toiling humbly for the betterment of the game, Shandler uses the latest tools and techniques to pander to the masses in the name of earning a few bucks. To these critics, Rotisserie baseball isn't just a frivolous game, it's a handbrake on progress. While esteemed Sabermetricians like Bill James devote themselves to finding better ways to measure the skills of ballplayers, Rotisserie encourages people to fixate on precisely the kind of statistics—RBI, batting average, wins, and saves—that the Sabermetricians have labored for years to discredit. If it wasn't for the opiate of Rotisserie baseball, they say, some of this dreck might have been excised from the box scores by now. No matter what sort of knowledge Shandler digs up in his basement, he's still guilty of aiding and abetting the quackery.

For a time, Shandler tried to fight this perception. In 1991, he rented a table at the SABR convention in New York to introduce the *Forecaster* to the members of the academy. And as he manned his table at the exhibit hall, a browser stopped in front of him and slipped a copy off the stack.

It was Bill James.

Shandler could barely contain himself. It had been James's 1984 *Baseball Abstract* that kindled his passion for baseball numbers and set him off on his current course. The book had, quite literally, changed his life. Even then, the tall and bearded James was considered the nation's top serious baseball analyst and the gatekeeper to the analytical tree house. It was a career moment.

James choked out a gruff "hello" and began thumbing through the

Forecaster. It had been several years since James had quit writing the *Abstract*, and all sorts of imitators had tried to fill the void. While Rotisserie players were Shandler's intended audience, he'd incorporated some of James's innovations into his own player evaluations, always giving him full credit. He'd also done some cool things on his own, which he was hoping James would notice and approve of. If these SABR guys would actually read his work, Shandler believed, they would understand that Rotisserie baseball doesn't have to be a mindless exercise.

Three agonizing minutes ticked by. James kept his head down, eyes on the pages, with an impenetrable poker face. Finally, he splayed the book open and turned it around so Shandler could see it. He pressed his finger to a single number in the book's vast ocean of data: the batting average of Atlanta Braves prospect Andy Tomberlin.

"This is wrong," he boomed.

Without speaking another word, James snapped the book shut, placed it neatly on the pile where he'd found it, and moved on. As soon as he was out of view, Shandler looked at the number. In those days of data entry by hand, he'd mistyped Tomberlin's total at-bats— his batting average *was* wrong. He hasn't seen Bill James since.

While he has stopped making overtures to the SABR crowd, Shandler hasn't given up his quest to "legitimize" Rotisserie baseball. In an impassioned essay in the 2003 *Forecaster*, he launched a campaign to encourage his audience to drop the term *fantasy* entirely and replace it with a word he invented, "fanalytics." "All of the work we do is serious analysis," he told me before the York program began. "In a different venue, it would be looked at no differently than the work that Bill James does." Later, I flipped over my *Forecaster* and asked him why he wasn't smiling in the author photo. "It's a serious book," he said, curtly. "There's nothing funny about it."

What the Sabermetric establishment never bothered to notice is that Shandler is, to the core, one of *them*. He, too, believes standard Rotisserie stats paint an incomplete picture and that there are better ways to measure the skills of ballplayers. Shandler's method of player evaluation centers around one basic idea: Players do not control the stats but are responsible only for their skills. If a player's performance changes drastically, Shandler wants to know if there's evidence that suggests his skills have improved or if it just appears to be a statistical anomaly. If a player's batting average spiked the season before, Shandler checks to see if the individual components that contribute to batting average explain the change: Did he take more walks? Did he make contact with the ball more frequently? Or did his batted balls just become hits at a greater rate? Likewise, if a player suddenly hits more home runs, Shandler looks to see if he was also hitting a higher percentage of fly balls, as opposed to grounders.

Some of his innovations are, to those who deign to read them, clear advancements in baseball thinking. One of his discoveries involves a pitcher's "strand rate," or the percentage of baserunners he allows who fail to score. Shandler determined that 72 percent of baserunners, on average, never cross the plate, and that if a pitcher's personal average is significantly higher or lower than that, there's an 80 percent chance that it will affect his ERA in a concomitant direction. In other words, a pitcher who strands an unusual number of baserunners is probably lucky and, therefore, likely to fare a lot worse the next season. Shandler wasn't just using the tools invented by the Sabermetricians, he was inventing *new ones.* "If a general manager isn't aware of what Ron has done," Mat Olkin likes to say, "he's probably throwing away millions of dollars."

While the baseball intelligentsia continued to thumb its nose, Shandler bided his time by using his knowledge to throttle the world's best Rotisserie players. At the first Tout Wars auction, held in 1998 at Manhattan's All-Star Café, Shandler fielded a team in each league. For some years now, he'd been using his proprietary formulas and gauges to pick out a few unheralded pitchers at the draft. But that year, he decided to give his numbers their stiffest test.

In the American League draft, Shandler chose the middling Charles Nagy as his staff anchor and supplemented him with a grab bag of nobodies including Eric Milton, Tim Worrell, and Eddie Guardado, who together cost about as much as one superstar. Some of his opponents laughed when he paid $1 in the National League auction for a journeyman named José Lima, who'd posted a lousy 5.28 ERA the season before. Just about everyone assumed that Shandler, always hunched over his spreadsheets, had finally snapped. "Hey, Ron," one of his subscribers wrote afterward, "how come you drafted such a crappy pitching staff?"

Under Shandler's microscope, however, these pitchers were anything but crappy. José Lima might have had a high ERA the season before, but he'd also posted career highs in strikeout-to-walk ratio (3.9), strikeouts per nine innings (7.6), and rate of home runs allowed. He'd also been the victim of a dismal 59 percent strand rate.

As the season wore on, Shandler didn't just stay afloat, he manhandled Tout Wars, winning *both* titles by a combined margin of nearly twelve points. In the NL, his pitching staff led the way, anchored by José Lima, who won sixteen games with a 3.70 ERA.

Shandler decided it was time to give his "crappy pitching strategy" a proper name, so he asked his subscribers to suggest some ideas. The winner was "Low Investment Mound Aces," or simply LIMA. For the next five years, the LIMA Plan would grow in stature to become the most influential and widely copied Rotisserie auction strategy of all time. Shandler would use it to win four expert-league titles and, more important, thousands of customers for life.

Back at the York symposium, it's hour four. Paul White has exhausted his repertoire of war stories, and now the assembled Shandlerites have taken the floor. To the casual fans here in York, their questions sound baffling. They want to know what to expect from pitchers in their second season after undergoing Tommy John surgery, whether PQS is applicable to pitchers in the minor leagues, and how long it will take for Craig Wilson to play five games as a catcher. Leaning back in his chair, legs splayed out in front of him, Shandler is finally in his element, pointing out hands coolly and delivering concise responses at a metronomic pace: "Be risk averse. . . . Look at peripheral gauges. . . . Positional scarcity is paramount." After a few minutes of this, the lone woman in the crowd, a youngish brunette with a softball build, rises to ask Shandler whether there's a couple of arms worth considering on the Detroit Tigers staff. "I can think of two," he says. "Jeremy Bonderman and Jeremy Bonderman." There's a ripple of laughter.

When the show's over, a line forms in front of Shandler's table. One guy has a follow-up question about the Texas outfield, another about the Baltimore bullpen. But the last straggler isn't here for Rotisserie enlightenment. He shakes Shandler's hand, looks him in the eye, and says, "Congratulations. It's about time."

For years now, Shandler's *Forecaster* has been quietly making inroads in baseball's front offices. Tal Smith, longtime president of the Astros, was a regular reader. Doug Melvin of the Brewers, Allard Baird of the Royals, and former Dodgers GM Dan Evans have owned copies. In 2003, *Money* ran a feature about the Red Sox that revealed that Theo Epstein kept a copy of the *Forecaster* in a prominent spot on his bookshelf. But even if Shandler's projections were doing more than just propping up the short leg of a desk, no major-league executive had ever acknowledged his work.

So when a message arrived in Shandler's mailbox on an otherwise unremarkable day in October, he had to Google the name of its sender, Jeff Luhnow, to make sure it wasn't a hoax. Late in the 2003 season, Bill DeWitt Jr., the owner of the St. Louis Cardinals, had hired Luhnow, a Northwestern MBA with no prior baseball experience, to fill a new position in the front office—vice president of baseball development. Luhnow's "charter," as he described it in press reports, was "to ensure that the Cardinals have the skills and capabilities necessary to compete most effectively in today's rapidly changing environment." In other words, the owner wanted to get more quantitative. What the articles didn't mention is that Luhnow was a serious Rotisserie player and a devoted reader of the *Baseball Forecaster*.

The proposition in the e-mail was this: Luhnow was forming an outside board of advisers to help the team make personnel decisions, and he wanted to know if Shandler might be interested in contributing. After several weeks of talking it over, Shandler accepted the job—on the condition that he could use the affiliation to promote his Rotisserie empire and continue to compete in Tout Wars.

When the paperwork was filed, Shandler decided to switch to the

American League side of Tout Wars to protect himself from the temptation to use privileged information. He wrote a column announcing his new role and posted it on his Web site on Friday, February 13.

In other words, *yesterday.*

There would be a handful of blurbs and blog items about Shandler's new gig, but no satellite trucks showed up at his house. The only national press was a brief mention in, of all places, *The New Republic.* But in an online chat a week after the news broke, Jeff Luhnow wrote a sentence that, to Shandler, was both perfectly obvious and incalculably gratifying. "Those of you who have read Shandler's book, the *Baseball Forecaster,* know that he is more than a fantasy baseball analyst. He is a baseball analyst."

As the last members of the York audience head out to salvage what's left of Valentine's Day, Shandler packs his computer bag and checks the day's take. He's sold exactly thirteen *Forecasters* at a discounted price of twenty dollars, a quantity he calls "a little light." In a few minutes, the Bearded One grabs the box of unsold books and marches out the library door to catch a flight home.

Driving back to New York that evening along the Pennsylvania Turnpike, I can't shake the idea that there was something odd about Shandler's behavior. Never mind that he's just received the biggest professional honor of his career and broken down the invisible wall between the fantasy game and the real thing. Never mind that the pompous Sabermetricians who shun him are crying in their beers right now. Over a period of five hours, in a roomful of potential customers with a stack of books to sell, Shandler had not mentioned his new job with the Cardinals. Not even *once.*

After shaking hands with that subscriber who'd come to congratulate him on the achievement, the Bearded One had managed to project only one discernable reaction: skepticism.

"Thanks," he said. "We'll see."

The Right Sort of Braincase

For all the time Jim Regan and Gil Pappas have been playing fantasy base-ball together through the mail and over the Internet, they've had a curious knack for missing each other. One rendezvous was scratched by a funeral. Another was scuttled by an illness. And one time they showed up at differ-ent Howard Johnson hotels in Kissimmee, Florida. One of these days, they'll get it right. (It's only been twenty-seven years.)

• • •

In the beginning, there was vichyssoise, or at least that's the story that stuck. Most of the news clips, dissertations, and documentaries will tell you that Rotisserie League Baseball, if not the entire megaplex of fantasy sports, was the spontaneous undertaking of a group of men who met for lunch in 1980 at a Manhattan restaurant called La Rotis-serie Française. But in truth, this was only the live birth. The concep-tion took place two decades earlier in Cambridge, Massachusetts, about one mile west of Harvard Yard, on a homely brown sofa be-longing to a fellow named Bill Gamson.

It was April 1960. It could have been a weekday or a weekend—hell, it might have been March for all the principals can remember. At the time it was just three shlumpy guys, all about twenty-six, getting together to try some half-baked contest the host had thought up. If you'd told Bill Gamson he was about to become the Thomas Edison of a worldwide sports movement, he would have assumed you were making fun of him.

Gamson had just landed a job as a research associate in social psychology at Harvard's School of Public Health, and had taken up residence in a college-town tenement on Foster Street that was boxy, beige, and hard up to the street with no semblance of a yard. The floors in Gamson's unit were so badly warped that a baseball placed on the high end would roll to the opposite baseboard. The "sofa" was actually a twin mattress with bolster pillows and a brown slipcover his wife, Zelda, had made.

Under the rules of Gamson's game, each player anted up $10, which would translate into an imaginary budget of $100,000 to be used to bid on the services of real major leaguers. Armed with a copy of *The Sporting News*, Gamson and his friends, Dick Snyder and Marty Greenberg, ran through the rosters of each team until somebody threw a playing card on the coffee table, indicating they wanted to bid. This continued until everyone was out of money. The idea was that during the season, each of their "teams" would be measured by eight handpicked statistics, though Gamson can't remember them all. By the time they were finished, midnight had come and Zelda, pregnant with the couple's first child, was feeling sorry for the neighbors. "The whole thing was pretty raucous," she remembers.

Through a modern lens, this may look like a perfectly normal way for three baseball nerds to spend an evening in April. But in 1960, the whole exercise was thoroughly radical. Baseball was still a rigid institution. The old reserve clause bonded players to teams as if they were indentured servants. Fans still wore suits to the ballpark, and owners and managers ruled with baronial authority. It wouldn't have occurred to most people that baseball could be toyed with, the players could be put into the service of your own imagination, or, for that matter, there could be more to being a fan than just buying a ticket and clapping at appropriate junctures.

But Bill Gamson was not most people. As an undergraduate at Antioch, the small Ohio college whose first president was the social reformer Horace Mann, he'd been drilled in the school's fundamental mission: empowering students to question the accepted tenets of society. And in the spring of 1960, Gamson was already putting his training into practice: carrying homemade picket signs to civil rights protests all over Greater Boston. Joining others to play a game that subverted a set of established rules was, at least to him, an entirely reasonable thing to do.

Word of Gamson's game spread quickly on the Harvard campus, and the following year, he expanded the number of teams to ten. To simplify the scorekeeping, he winnowed the categories to four: batting average, runs batted in, earned-run average, and wins. And in a nod to domestic tranquillity, Gamson split the bidding into three rounds and asked the contestants to send their bids by mail. To throw off anybody at the post office who might suspect him of being a bookie, he decided to give his creation the tweediest name he could think of: the Baseball Seminar.

Gamson wasn't the first person to invent a parlor game powered by the statistics of real ballplayers. The first known version was a board game called National Pastime, which was patented in 1925 by a Wisconsin man named Clifford Van Beek. While it wasn't a big seller, one set fell into the hands of a Pennsylvania teenager named J. Richard Seitz, who, in 1951, began selling his own improved version called APBA. Eleven years later, Hal Richman introduced the market to a game called Strat-O-Matic Baseball, which would ultimately dominate the genre.

The basic goal of these games was, like the seminar, to build a team that could beat the teams constructed by one's idiot friends. To make them work, the creators took the past statistics of ballplayers and broke them down into probabilities, which were then printed on cards. A player who'd posted a .250 batting average, for instance, would get a base hit 25 percent of the time. To determine the outcome, you would roll dice or flick a plastic spinner and look up the result on a player's card.

To Gamson, these tabletop games lacked one crucial element: immediacy. As a high school student in Philadelphia, Gamson had played in a friendly pool where the object was to pick three major-league batters who would collect five hits in total the following day. The prizes never amounted to more than milk money, but Gamson didn't care. Suddenly, the simple act of reading the box scores had become a daily thrill ride. If Richie Ashburn was one of your picks, he wasn't just playing for the Phillies, he was playing for *you*. It was the memory of this game that inspired the Baseball Seminar.

In 1962 Gamson moved to the University of Michigan, and there the seminar blossomed. At the time, advanced quantitative methods, aided by early computers, were reshaping academic research in much the same way they've upended baseball more recently. Gamson's generation of social scientists was the first to be drilled in statistics, psychometrics, and econometrics, and Michigan was on the cutting edge. The seminar gave them an informal way to flex their new analytical muscles.

Soon the game had grown to twenty-five teams and the competition stiffened. Academic conventions became excuses to sneak in ballgames, office hours were canceled in the name of bid preparation, and before long the machinery of academic research was pressed into service. One seminar participant, a political scientist and sociologist named Pat Crecine, recruited a pair of graduate students from his 1967 computer-simulation course to run a regression analysis on baseball stats. Phil Converse, one of Michigan's most renowned social scientists, used inferential statistics to perform a study on seminar bidding patterns that Gamson called "the most incredible data analysis I've ever seen."

After several years, a former faculty member named Dave Goldberg moved to Detroit, where he founded a sister league. Through a mutual friend, he convinced Ernie Harwell, the venerable Detroit Tigers radio broadcaster, to field a team for two years. And in 1974, *New Yorker* baseball writer Roger Angell accepted an invitation to play. As a real "baseball guy" who talked to players and managers and visited clubhouses, Angell entered the game as the heavy favorite. But after two years of mediocre finishes, he had become so engrossed by his seminar team that he forced himself to quit. "I had to give up or lose my job," Angell says. "It was that bad."

In fifteen years, Bill Gamson's strange little contest had never rated a mention in the sports pages. But it had proven to be an intellectual weed that, once planted in the right sort of braincase, was nearly impossible to eradicate. Anyone who joined the seminar would inevitably ask himself the same question: Why didn't anybody think of this sooner?

———

After graduating from the University of Michigan, Dan Okrent moved to New York in 1969 to take a job as the assistant to the publisher at Alfred A. Knopf. For the next seven years, he rose quickly through the editorial ranks of book publishing until, to his own astonishment, he was named editor in chief of Harcourt Brace.

In the middle of the libertine 1970s, most young hotshot New York junior executives were content to ride out the decade groping through a haze of sex, barbiturates, and disco. But Okrent managed to escape the era with only one appreciable vice: baseball.

No morning could begin without box scores, and not a week passed without a trip to see the Yankees or Mets. He became so infatuated with Strat-O-Matic, the tabletop game, that he'd play for six hours at a time, even during weekends in the Hamptons. His addiction became so legendary in New York media circles that when *Newsweek* ran a story about "Strat" zealots, they sent over a photographer to take his picture.

As it turns out, the young Okrent was heroically unprepared to be the chief executive of a major publishing house. So after less than two years on the job at Harcourt, he resigned his post and fled New York, as he puts it, "with my tail between my legs." He moved to the tiny town of Worthington, Massachusetts, where he set up shop with his second wife, Becky, in a rambling old Dutch Colonial farmhouse. To pay the mortgage, he hung out a shingle as a publishing consultant, but his real ambition was to start writing books and magazine articles about baseball. By 1985, he had published two books, including the critically acclaimed *Nine Innings*.

But long before then, in the space of a single year, Okrent would make two significant contributions to baseball. The first came on the day in 1978 when he opened *The Sporting News* and noticed a tiny ad for a book that promised "18 Statistical Categories You Can't Find Anywhere Else." Curious, Okrent sent a money order for $2.50 and received a homemade pamphlet. The writer, it turned out, was an overnight security guard at the Stokely Van Camp bean-canning plant in Lawrence, Kansas. But Okrent was so dazzled by his provocative theories that he booked a flight to Kansas to profile him for *Sports Illustrated*. The security guard's name was Bill James. And when the article finally ran, Okrent effectively launched his career.

The second discovery came to him sometime in the winter of 1979 in the cabin of an American Airlines jet bound for Austin, where he'd been hired to help *Texas Monthly* organize a new books division. Somewhere along the way his thoughts turned, as they always did, to baseball or, more accurately, the depressing absence thereof. In the dead of winter, with no box scores to amuse him, he remembered an old friend.

In late August 1965, Okrent, then a mopheaded freshman, sat down for the first time in the office of Robert Sklar, an assistant professor of history at Michigan. When he wasn't teaching, Sklar served as an academic counselor to undergraduates, and Okrent, the son of an attorney and a schoolteacher from Detroit, was one of his latest crop of mentees. Within minutes, Sklar took a liking to the precocious kid, and over the next four years the two men would overcome their ten-years age difference to become close friends. Close enough, in fact, that after Okrent moved to New York, Sklar paid him a visit at his apartment in Brooklyn.

In all the time they'd known each other, Sklar had never mentioned the baseball simulation game he played with fellow faculty members at Michigan. Or if he had, Okrent had tuned him out. But during this visit, sometime around Opening Day, Sklar was in the middle of making his bids for the Baseball Seminar and Okrent, a newly minted baseball nut, was eager to help. Sitting at Okrent's kitchen table, Sklar explained the game.

Okrent couldn't remember many details about this "assistant professors' league" or whatever the hell it was called. All he'd retained was something about an auction and a few statistical categories. But there in that Pan Am cabin, feeling bereft of baseball, he suddenly realized this game's fundamental genius. By forcing themselves to form opinions on hundreds of ballplayers before the season began, Sklar and his friends had found a workable excuse to gorge on baseball nearly all winter long.

Back home in Worthington on a snowy afternoon in December, Okrent sat down at his rolltop desk with a calculator, a few sheets of graph paper, and his Macmillan *Baseball Encyclopedia* to sketch out the rules of his own variation. Like the seminar, there would be an auction, a salary cap, and an equal number of scoring categories for pitchers and hitters. But while seminar contestants could spend their money on as many (or as few) players as they wished, Okrent decided to add a new level of complexity.

One of Okrent's first baseball interview subjects had been Earl Weaver, the legendary manager of the Baltimore Orioles, who had told him that the toughest decision he made every year was choosing which twenty-five players to take north from spring training. Oftentimes, Weaver said, the difference between winning and losing was the presence of some bit player on the bench who could fill in at shortstop if needed or steal the occasional base. Okrent decided to make this the central challenge of his own game. Each contestant would have to think like Earl Weaver did, assembling a full roster with a balance of speed and power, starting pitching and relief, superstars and role players. In other words, to build a team that, in real life, would probably win a fair number of games.

The trick was to figure out how to keep score. To do this, Okrent realized he'd have to determine which statistics were most important to a winning ballclub, so he opened his Macmillan and jotted down the final standings for the last four seasons in the National League East. Then, for each team, he copied down their totals in every measurable category.

For two days, Okrent meticulously ranked every team by each

variable and compared these rankings to the final standings to see how they corresponded. Right away, he noticed that home runs, wins, and saves were almost always present in large quantities on a winning club, while fielding percentage had no bearing. Stolen bases, runs batted in, and earned-run average were strong correlates to success, while doubles and strikeouts were less so. He also tossed in a statistic for pitchers he'd thought up while playing Strat-O-Matic: walks allowed plus hits allowed divided by innings pitched. At the time, he called it "innings pitched ratio" or IPRAT, but it's now more commonly known as WHIP. In the end, Okrent took the eight best indicators and anointed them as the official categories.

On occasional trips to New York in 1979, Okrent would lunch with a pack of friends and acquaintances who belonged to a loose group called the Phillies Appreciation Society. Their regular venue was a Midtown restaurant called La Rotisserie Française, which, if not for this particular party of regulars, would have vanished forever into the mists of culinary mediocrity. (About four years later, to the surprise of no one, the Rotisserie would serve its last *croque monsieur.*) By January 1980, with the rules to his new game polished to a high sheen, Okrent was ready to perform his dance of seduction. If this group from *"La Rot"* wouldn't play his game, he figured, nobody would. His first mark was an easy one: *Esquire* editor in chief Lee Eisenberg, who bit the hook like a blackfin tuna. Corlies "Cork" Smith, a forty-nine-year-old editor at Viking, signed up immediately, too. Other members of the Phillies Appreciation Society—editor Walter Lippincott and painter Sheridan Lord—declined Okrent's invitations, assuming that he must have suffered a head injury.

For several days, Okrent, Eisenberg, and Smith worked the phones until each of them had rounded up three recruits. Okrent called a meeting at an East Side pub called P. J. Moriarty's, and it was there, over plates of corned beef and cabbage, that the game took root. With Okrent acting as chief parliamentarian, the categories were adopted as is, the roster size set at twenty-two, the auction scheduled for April, and the ante fixed at $250, which was somewhere between what the high rollers wanted and what the book editors could afford.* To make sure that contestants would have to know bench players, too, the game was limited to the National League. And though none of these people ever returned to the restaurant, "Rotisserie" was chosen as the official league handle.

The draft was held the following April on a Sunday over the dining-room table at Cork Smith's opulent Park Avenue apartment. As the league assembled, anybody who thought this would be a lighthearted way to spend an afternoon got a rude surprise. "The talk before the draft was dazzlingly erudite," says advertising writer Bruce McCall. When he discovered that some people had memorized the entire farm system of the Houston Astros, he recalls, "I realized I was doomed." Okrent, who arrived unshaven and unkempt, coped with the tension by smoking a dozen unfiltered Camels.

"I think I threw up," he says.

Nobody had a tougher adjustment than Bob Sklar, who had since moved to Manhattan to work as a film historian and television critic. That morning, Sklar had attempted to explain to his girlfriend, an artist, how he planned to spend the afternoon. She told him that if this was something he really intended to do, he should not trouble to call her *ever again*. Sklar arrived looking ashen and sat motionless for the first few minutes. But then he picked up Mike Schmidt for $26, and it was *c'est la vie*.

If Gamson's invention in 1960 was a product of a golden age of social dissent, the first Rotisserie draft was more like Woodstock for smart-asses. For team names, Okrent went with Okrent Fenokees, Smith with Smith Coronas, Bruce McCall with McCall Collects, and *Esquire* research chief Rob Fleder with the Fleder Mice. When book publisher Tom Guinzburg drafted Kim Seaman and John Urrea, he referred to them as his "urological bullpen." During the bidding on Aurelio Lopez, Okrent identified him as the only major leaguer to have five different vowels in his first name. "It was like a low-rent Algonquin roundtable," McCall says.

When the season began, the members of the Rotisserie League

---

*In 1981, the league extended the rosters to twenty-three and raised the ante to $260.

Baseball Association started to lose their composure. Glen Waggoner, an administrator at Columbia University, found himself writing ballclubs asking for glossy photos of his players to put in a team yearbook. Peter Gethers, an editor at Random House, discovered Sports Phone, a service that offered a recording of updated baseball scores for twenty-five cents a minute—and began running up monthly bills in excess of one hundred dollars. Attorney Michael Pollet of the Pollet Burros found himself standing in a sea of glowering Mets fans at Shea Stadium, shouting encouragement to Rick Sutcliffe, who happened to be pitching for the Dodgers.

The most immediate problem was calculating the score. In the days before spreadsheets and the Internet, the stats had to be tallied by hand, a process that could take seven hours a week. Naturally, the job fell to Okrent, the only member of the league who could possibly enjoy such an exercise. Soon he found himself driving to a distant newsstand to obtain *The Sporting News* two days before it would otherwise arrive in his mailbox, and while on vacation, rowing across the harbor from Cuttyhunk Island to a pay phone, where Bob Sklar would read him the late box scores.

By July word of the league had spread through the New York media grapevine, and Lee Eisenberg got a call from *New York Times* reporter Fred Ferretti. For the group interview, Eisenberg booked a stately *Esquire* conference room overlooking Park Avenue. He warned Okrent to behave and told Waggoner to wear a suit. As the current leader and likely first champion, Eisenberg was determined to project the idea that the Rotisserie League was something other than a collection of myopic weirdos.

When Ferretti arrived, the Rotisserie League was impeccably turned out (Okrent wore a bow tie) and politely gathered around an imposing conference table, discussing some minor procedural issues. The change was subtle at first, Ferretti remembers, with an "Oh, for Chrissake" and a "What the hell do you know?" But within minutes, the decorum unraveled like a cheap sweater. On July 8, 1980, New Yorkers woke to a story that began, "What George Steinbrenner is to the American League, Lee Eisenberg is to the Rotisserie League."

The response was swift and direct but, contrary to what the founders expected, overwhelmingly positive. *CBS Morning News* followed up with a segment on the league, and all of a sudden Okrent was the toast of every cocktail party.

"People were galvanized," he says.

By the end of September Eisenberg's pitching had failed him, and the winner of the first Rotisserie season was the Getherswag Goners, a team operated jointly by Peter Gethers and Glen Waggoner (neither one of whom could afford the entire entry fee by himself).

Okrent finished eighth.

At the awards banquet Gethers and Waggoner arrived in rented tuxedos accompanied by their girlfriends, who wore cheerleader costumes. In real clubhouse celebrations champagne is the preferred bath of champions. But in this case, the winners were marched into Cork Smith's bathroom and told to lean over the tub, where they were drenched in something more in keeping with the spirit of the league: chocolate Yoo-hoo. As the cold, syrupy goo slipped under his collar and trickled down the length of his back to puddle at his belt, Waggoner stared off in the distance, his face aglow. "I've never had more fun in my life," he says.

————

In March 1981 Dan Okrent wrote an essay about the Rotisserie League for *Inside Sports* called "The Year George Foster Wasn't Worth $36." The story was all well and good, but what really got people talking was something that appeared in a sidebar: the rules.

That spring, dozens of baseball writers cribbed them from the magazine and started their own press-box leagues. And when a baseball strike dragged into July, these same writers filled the news void by penning requiems for their own suspended Roto teams, lending the whole enterprise an air of trendiness.

Peter Gethers got a call from a *New York Times* reporter who wanted to know how the strike was affecting his life.

His girlfriend answered the question for him.

"We have sex during baseball season," she said.

Two years later Bantam approached the founders to collaborate on an official Rotisserie book, which was published in 1984 with a subtitle that proclaimed it to be "The greatest game for baseball fans since baseball." If there was any chance that Rotisserie might be viewed by major-league executives as an intellectually rigorous simulation, this lime-green paperback killed it. In the acknowledgments, Okrent thanked relatives Babe, Honus, Ty, Felipe, and Jesus Okrent. Gethers listed his hobbies as "volleyball and Nazi hunting," and the official "Constitution" instructed people to abstain from sex three weeks before drafting.

In the context of the times, however, the tone was pitch-perfect. In the same year that Rotisserie took hold, David Letterman began his career as a talk-show host. A young comedian named Jerry Seinfeld moved to Los Angeles to work in television, and ESPN was winning viewers with an irreverent brand of sports commentary. It was the dawn of the age of irony, and the Rotisserie League was, as Waggoner puts it, "smartalecky as can be."

Better yet, baseball was undergoing a popular renaissance. Nielsen ratings were near their historical peak, and the 1980 tilt between Philadelphia and Kansas City still shares the highest World Series rating ever recorded. Fans from the Me Generation were longing for a level of involvement deeper than just watching the game, and Rotisserie was the stiffest drink at the bar.

At the same time, free agency had switched off the gravity that once held teams together. As established stars changed uniforms with greater frequency, fans were increasingly attracted to a game that allowed them to buy and sell players like the commodities they'd become.

In 1982, when Ballantine published the first mass-market version of *The Bill James Baseball Abstract*, it was a runaway hit. And even though most of James's advanced statistical explorations were, as Okrent puts it, "the antithesis of what we did in Rotisserie," the two entities fed off each other. Frothing Jamesians took to Rotisserie as a way to let off steam, while Rotisserie leaguers started reading James as a way to get an edge. That they prospered together, Rob Fleder says, "wasn't an accident."

Over the next eight years, Rotisserie leagues sprang up organically in every corner of North America with names like the Farrah Fawcett Major League, the Irrational League, and the Raucous Baseball Caucus. ESPN did a two-part series on the phenomenon, and Waggoner and *Ms. Magazine* associate publisher Valerie Salembier, the original league's only female participant, appeared on a CBS show hosted by Charlie Rose. Bryant Gumbel, Ron Howard, and Bob Costas joined leagues. *Boston Globe* baseball writer Peter Gammons became the proprietor of the Gamonsters, and *Sports Illustrated* baseball writer Steve Wulf joined the founder's league in its second season. New York governor Mario Cuomo was so preoccupied with his team, the Queens Alliance, that even sensitive budget negotiations could be pushed aside. "If I heard about a Cuban guy who just landed on a raft and Castro said he was the best he ever saw, I'd want to get the son of a gun," he says. After Bill Giles, one of the *real* owners of the Phillies, formed a league in the team's front office, there was no looking back. "Go into our lunchroom," a spokesman said, "and that's all people are talking about." In 1988, *USA Today* estimated that five hundred thousand people were playing.

As the madness spread, the founders of the first Rotisserie League had only one collective goal: figuring out how to cash in. Accomplished as they were in their various wordy pursuits, the founders were not the most astute businessmen. As entrepreneurs go, they fell somewhere down at the far end of the spectrum between lazy and grossly incompetent. There was a membership drive that stalled, a statistical service that never took off, a clothing line that flopped, a nibble from a software developer that never panned out, and a quixotic bid to buy the Holyoke Millers, a *real* minor-league team. One of the more elaborate schemes was an annual convention during spring training, where the Rotisserie public could hobnob with the founders. "There would be 150 nerds walking the hallways of the hotel," Peter Gethers remembers, "and you'd hear things like 'I think that's Glen Waggoner!' " The net proceeds were just enough to cover their expenses, plus the odd round of golf.

Early on, the founders had copyrighted the rules and the term "Rotisserie" and fought off anyone who attempted to use them for profit.

But after a while, people who wanted to publish draft guides for Roto players realized they could just call the game "fantasy baseball" and everybody would know what they meant. To compete with these up-start magazines, the founders added player projections to the annual Rotisserie book, but most of them lacked one somewhat important element: research. "We know he can run," said one player evaluation, "but can he hit?"

From 1991 to 1994, as the founders looked on in horror, Rotisserie became the Monster That Ate Everything. The number of players jumped from one million to three. Aided by the boom in personal computers, the number of private "stats providers" jumped from nine to sixty. Fantasy annuals jammed the newsstands, a Roto radio show was launched, and ESPN aired a preseason pay-per-view special. "No way," Okrent said at the time, "did I have the idea that it would mushroom to the preposterous size it has reached."

Then came the Internet. While it might be foolish to suggest that Rotisserie leaguers played a leading role in establishing the viability of the World Wide Web, one thing is indisputable: Their eagerness to embrace the medium was surpassed only by those who wanted to look at pictures of naked women. Just when it seemed that the 1994 baseball strike had slowed Rotisserie's momentum, a company called Commissioner.com opened for business in 1996. For three hundred dollars, these guys would put your league stats on a home page where everybody could see them. It was such a hit that two years later, Sportsline bought the company for $31 million.

Today, millions of people play fantasy games online and pay hundreds of dollars to have their league statistics tabulated in real time. Nearly every major Web portal—Yahoo!, America Online, and ESPN, to name a few—has fantasy games and content.* The concept is even spreading beyond sports. There are fantasy games for people who would like to manage movie studios, record labels, or stock funds. This year roughly nine hundred legal buffs (I'm not kidding) will

---

*The hobby is so pervasive that some companies, including General Motors, have blocked access to fantasy sites on their internal networks.

play a game called Fantasy Supreme Court, in which the goal is to predict the outcome of every case on the High Court's docket before the term begins.

After years of guarded suspicion, even Major League Baseball is getting into the act, offering fantasy games and analysis on its official site. There are minor-league Roto leagues, historical games that use bygone players, and "ultraleagues" with nearly sixty scoring categories including complete games, holds, and passed balls. There's a national fantasy-baseball draft contest in which the winner pockets one hundred thousand dollars. Fantasy football, a simpler game inspired by the baseball version, now has something like ten million participants. In the future, there will be fantasy-sports bars and travel agencies. Fantasy owners will be able to see daily video highlights of "their" players, and there's a system in the works that would allow fantasy leaguers to make injury substitutions or even pull struggling players *before* their real managers do.

If you add up the annual revenues of the fantasy-sports service industry, the total would be about $150 million. But when you include all the ancillary spending on things like league dues, Internet upgrades, and premium sports packages (to say nothing of psychotherapy), there's little doubt that total fantasy expenditures are well north of one billion dollars. At this pace, the monster that used to be known as Rotisserie League Baseball seems to be lurching toward a once unthinkable milestone. Someday, these derivative games may be just as profitable as the real ones.

————

It took only two days for Dan Okrent to plot the rules of Rotisserie baseball, but he's spent the better part of three decades dealing with the consequences.

He's been followed into restaurant bathrooms, hounded at ballgames, and cornered in elevators by Roto nuts who want to know if they should pick up Ryne Sandberg or trade John Candelaria. A Maryland woman once wrote him a letter blaming "your stupid game" for destroying her marriage. And even though Okrent has never claimed the idea was his alone (Bill Gamson's name was included in the acknowledgments of the first Rotisserie book), every now and then somebody grumbles that the founders are *frauds*. The moment Roger Angell, the former seminar player, first heard about Rotisserie, he says, "I thought they were ripping us off."

By the mid-1990s, these nuisances had begun to pile up. Forget that he never got rich or that he scarcely had time to run an imaginary baseball club. The more Rotisserie grew, the more Okrent became convinced that no matter what else he accomplished, his obituary would say: "Okrent Dies, Invented Rotisserie Baseball."

In the spring of 1996, he let his son, John, manage the Fenokees and the following season contracted the franchise. His players were dispersed to the free-agent pool, his meticulous records stuffed in a desk drawer. For the first time in three decades, Okrent turned to the box scores in the morning paper and had no compelling reason to read them.

There were several attempts to lure him back. Waggoner called. Eisenberg called. Stories of his defection ran in *The New York Times* and *USA Today*, with the latter likening it to "the Earl of Sandwich becoming a vegetarian." But his mind was made up. Dan Okrent was determined to become Dan Okrent, the guy who did other stuff, too. In 1999, he entered the American Crossword Puzzle Tournament and finished thirtieth.

In April 2004, the five remaining members of the original Rotisserie League will meet in Glen Waggoner's dining room on the Upper West Side to draft National League ballplayers for the twenty-fifth time. Waggoner, sixty-three, better known as "Shooter," is now deputy editor of *ESPN: The Magazine* and has assumed the role of league den mother. As the draft begins, he'll squeeze his giant frame into a chair at the head of the table, where he will observe the proceedings while stroking his untamed beard and raising his bushy eyebrows, which poke out in all directions like overgrown privet. He'll address the table with the vocabulary of an English barrister, always using a word like "knave" or "varlet" when "dumbass" would probably suffice. And even though he will still be recovering from major heart surgery, he'll be sipping one of his trademark gin martinis, which have a reputation for tasting like a cross between Everclear and Quaker State.

Lee Eisenberg will arrive in a cranky mood and hunch down in his usual corner, eyebrows arched, brooding over various scouting books and grousing about his pitching staff. These days, he's a shadow of the character who, the first year he won the league, showed up at the banquet with two leggy dates dressed in fur coats. Rob Fleder, now an executive editor at *Sports Illustrated*, will arrive in a fashionable shirt, load up on West Coast players he'll never be tempted to stay up and watch, and depart in a Town Car. Peter Gethers, now a successful screenwriter and best-selling author, will sit at the far end of the table exhibiting all the enthusiasm of a captive polar bear.

Four hours in, one member of the league will have made a hash of his roster. He will have used the word "shit" about six dozen times, compared himself to Donald Rumsfeld, and relieved his frustration by sampling the contents of an abundant pastry tray.

His name is Dan Okrent.

To coax the beloved founder of Rotisserie back from his Blue Period, his leaguemates had to make some concessions to old age and decrepitude. They formed a new, simplified league called AARP, the official motto of which is, "so easy you might even forget you're playing." Okrent rejoined them in 2002 as the proprietor of a new franchise, the Dan Druffs.

In 2004, Okrent agreed to become the first public editor of *The New York Times*, a position that made him, overnight, the world's most influential media critic. At fifty-six, with a contemplative crease between his eyebrows and a mane of silver hair, he looks distinguished enough to be an ambassador. But to his colleagues in the Rotisserie League, he's got all the gravitas of a fry cook. To them he'll always be Danny, the poor slob who's never managed to win the game he made up. That's never, as in *not once*.

When the draft is over, the founders will have polished off a few bottles of Foster's, a platter of crudités, several tubs of pretzels, and something in the neighborhood of two thousand fudge cookies. They'll limp out the door in various stages of gastrointestinal discomfort, wondering why they continue to play a game that none of them is especially good at. Lee Eisenberg will say the same thing he always says. "Let's not play next year."

It's been more than a decade since the members of the Rotisserie League sold off the licensing rights to the name and the rules and agreed to split the modest fees. All told, over all these years, the founders have divided up about five hundred thousand dollars in various royalties. They have walked away from the business having earned nothing of consequence from what Rob Fleder calls "the one great idea we ever had." Someday, Waggoner says, "Harvard Business School will do a case study."

But while they would rather prance around in lingerie than admit it, this game has been pretty good to them. Nobody's marriage fell apart, there were never any punches thrown, and everybody prospered. If they hadn't done what they did, baseball, if not the larger world, might look a bit different. Rotisserie played a role in the popularization of everything from the Internet to *USA Today*. WHIP, that statistic Okrent made up, now appears on the scoreboard at Fenway Park. You can't watch a World Series game or an NFL broadcast without meeting the "fantasy player of the game." And in the eleventh edition of its *Collegiate Dictionary*, Merriam-Webster recognized Rotisserie Baseball as a term. They even sent over a plaque.

Mention any of this to the founders, and the best they can do is roll their eyes and make yawning motions. As far as they're concerned, the novelty is long gone. But there is one topic that's guaranteed to make any of them brighten: that first year. "It was more fun than we deserved to have," says Bruce McCall, now a humorist for *The New Yorker*. "You can't believe what innocent good fun it was," adds Rob Fleder. "There was something pure about it, something you would never imagine looking at the phenomenon now."

———

Bill Gamson is seventy, trim and balding with a snowy white beard and a wan smile. In 1982 he left Michigan to take a faculty job at

Boston College, where he still teaches once a week, commuting from Martha's Vineyard, where he and Zelda now live.

His academic career has been distinguished. Four years after founding the Baseball Seminar, he invented a game called Simulated Society, or SimSoc, where contestants take positions in social conflicts like strikes, natural disasters, and political protests. It's become a classic tool of leadership training and has sold more than 350,000 copies. In 2002, he was elected to the American Academy of Arts and Sciences alongside actress Angelica Huston and violinist Itzhak Perlman.

His other creation, the Baseball Seminar, is forty-four years old and thriving. It has players in eleven states from Florida to Oregon and has since been renamed the *National* Baseball Seminar. The rules have been tweaked a tiny bit, but the bids are still submitted by mail, and the initials WAG can still be found on the list of participants.

While he's always known the seminar was older than the Rotisserie League, Gamson just assumed it had sprung up independently from the mind of another baseball neurotic. It wasn't until 2001 that he finally made the connection: Gamson to Sklar to Okrent to worldwide pandemonium. "It came as a complete surprise to me," he says.

Talking to him on the phone, I decide to ask this eminent sociologist the obvious question, whether he has any regrets about this engrossing social movement he has unwittingly unleashed on the populace. There's silence on the line. Gamson is thinking through all the angles, calculating all the probabilities. Then he starts to laugh.

"If only I'd charged a nickel!"

The Grapefruit League

February

Randy Simmons, pastor of the Gulf Coast Church of Christ in Fort Myers, Florida, doesn't turn to the Holy Spirit to help him win his Rotisserie league. He's got a better source: the group of major-league umpires who are members of his congregation. One year, they turned him on to an unheralded pitcher named Mike Moore, who, they said, has ungodly movement on his fastball. "He won seventeen games that year," Simmons remembers, "and seventeen the next."

• • •

On February 22, just over a month before the Tout Wars draft, I touch down at Tampa International Airport where a smiling employee of the Hertz Corporation provides me with the keys to a phantom-gray Toyota Camry.

She suspects nothing.

In the next ten days, I will roll up seven hundred miles on the odometer visiting all eight American League spring training camps from here to Fort Lauderdale. Along the way I will leave the windows open during a downpour, tromp mud all over the floorboards, drive at speeds in excess of eighty-five miles per hour, and paste the cabin with a mixture of sunblock, powdered sugar, coffee drizzles, ballpoint ink, and fryer grease.

"Is everything out of the car?" they'll ask me when I return it.

"Basically, yes."

If I've abandoned any of my usual rules of the road, it's the notion that I ought to pack light. Inside my bags is a metric ton of scouting books, Rotisserie magazines, and media guides, plus something like nine hundred pages of printouts. For each Florida team, Nando has assembled a thick dossier with scouting reports, head shots, news clips, and capsule biographies for every player in camp. If the defending Tout Wars champion, Jason "Don't Get Overloaded" Grey, could get a look at this arsenal, he'd be *horrified*.

Every time I told a seasoned Rotisserie player about my plan to spend ten days and $2,400 scouting ballplayers in Florida and then, in short order, ten days and $3,000 in Arizona for the same purpose, the response was more or less consistent: *You are an idiot.*

No matter how idyllic it may seem to frostbitten Northerners, spring training is one of the sports world's great anachronisms, a relic of the days when ballplayers had to take real jobs in the off-season and needed a full six weeks just to firm up the love handles. With the exception of pitchers, who still need the time to build up arm strength, most veteran ballplayers think it's too long by half. They fight the tedium by fooling around with a heavier bat or a screwball or something else they'll never actually use during the season. And at this early stage of training, most managers can't tell you the location of the clubhouse coffee pot, much less who's liable to bat seventh in the order on Opening Day.

After booking my flights, I sat down with Cory Schwartz and Gregg Klayman, the statistics and fantasy coordinators for Major League Baseball's official Web site, to ask them for some spring-training scouting pointers. What they gave me was a synopsis of all the clichéd ballplayer quotes I was likely to hear.

"I'm in the best shape of my life."

"I got a personal chef."

"I had Lasik surgery."

"I'm on a macrobiotic diet."

By the middle of May, Schwartz continued, most of the players who say these things will go right back to sucking.

"Sucking," Klayman echoed.

Even so, I'm convinced I'm making the right move. No matter how many experts implore me to be ruthlessly objective about players, to think of them purely as data sets, I still think that's a half-witted approach. When it comes down to it, the twenty-three players I select next month will be, in some perverted sense, my employees. Would you hire two dozen people by looking at résumés alone?

In the two months since I wandered into the winter meetings with a blank notebook, I've been walking around New York with the rosters of every American League team stuffed in my pockets for quick review. On my last ballplayer quiz I was able to name 82 percent of the league's likely starters and, in most cases, some intriguing factoid about them. If Sig Mejdal is right when he says 60 percent of the baseball future is calculable, that means 40 percent lies somewhere outside the realm of logic and reason, and that's why I've come to Florida. While Sig irons out the math from his NASA cubicle, I'm going to hang my press pass around my neck and try to see things that can't be explained by the statistical record. If a shortstop has something weighing on his mind, I'll try to coax it out of him. If a pitcher has started throwing twice as many changeups, I'll see if there's an interesting story behind it. Put simply, I'm here to chase a hunch—that there's a lot of valuable information about ballplayers that nobody knows about because nobody's ever bothered to ask.

Day One: The Devil Rays

I'm standing on a sticky blue carpet inside Tampa Bay's spring clubhouse in St. Petersburg with an empty notebook and a Styrofoam cup of instant coffee. It's early. I've got a thicket of printouts under my arm. And I'm *terrified*.

In all the time I've spent preparing to conduct auditions for my Tout Wars team, I never could anticipate how the typical ballplayer would respond to a fusillade of questions from a Roto dweeb, especially if some of them weren't entirely nice.

As I'm working up my nerve, outfielder Rocco Baldelli saunters by, making a loud and slurpy mess of a green apple. Baldelli is one of those guys you hated in high school because he looked like a *Baywatch* lifeguard. As he sits down backward on a folding chair in front of his locker, all he needs to complete the picture is a whistle and a flotation device. *Baldelli, Baldelli.* Shuffling through my notes, I'm reminded that the knock on Baldelli, who was a rookie last season, is that he tends to swing at anything that comes within a kilometer of home plate. The obvious question is whether he's content with this approach or determined to be a little more selective.

I stride up, introduce myself, explain that I'm playing in Tout Wars, the nation's toughest expert Rotisserie league, and that I've come to Florida to evaluate talent. I soften him up with a question about his recent Lasik surgery, then I jump right into the meaty stuff. "Some people think you're not very disciplined at the plate."

Baldelli stops cold, his apple suspended two inches from his face. His response isn't so much spoken as it is spat. "If I listened to what *Rotisserie* people had to say, I'd be out of the league by now." Dead silence. Interview over.

Instead of stopping to collect myself and refine my strategy, I decide to forge ahead. I ask rising star Aubrey Huff to explain the technical principles that guide his approach to hitting, and he says it's pretty simple: "See the ball, hit the ball." When I ask Devil Rays manager Lou Piniella whom he likes for the second half of the batting order, he mentions his new shortstop, Rey Sánchez, because "he's not afraid to bunt." I have a lively chat with general manager Chuck LaMar about the intangible benefits of having a bunch of track stars on your ballclub, and a ten-minute conversation with first baseman Tino Martinez, from which I glean the following: Tino has been doing a lot of sit-ups.

Four hours later, paging through my notebook in the parking lot, I realize that Rotisserie scouting is an elusive art form that requires practice, preparation, and some degree of tact. I've basically taken a mulligan on the Devil Rays.

Day Two: The Yankees

To be granted access to Legends Field, the forbidding Tampa campus of the Bronx Bombers, my official major-league press credential isn't sufficient. I have to show ID at the door and be *photographed,* too. On this particular morning, down in the Yankees clubhouse, at least twenty writers are milling around, including one columnist who's standing just outside the door, talking to his editor on a cellphone while covering his mouth in an apparent bid to frustrate any would-be lip-readers. Two dozen Japanese photographers are scattered around on the field awaiting the moment when Hideki Matsui bends over to touch his cleats.

My expectations could not be lower. Yankee superstars aren't very interesting in Rotisserie terms—they're all good, and they're all expensive. Given the number of reporters covering the team, it's next to impossible to get them to say anything you haven't already heard, and that's assuming you can *find* them. Derek Jeter and Mariano Rivera seem to be spending a great deal of time in the trainer's room.

My first priority is to talk to Gary Sheffield, the team's new, imported superstar right fielder, although I'm not holding my breath. Sheffield's name has just surfaced in connection with BALCO, a California laboratory under investigation for distributing anabolic steroids to athletes, and the morning jabber shows made it clear that this was the scandal *du jour.* It's hard to imagine Sheffield is going to be particularly chatty.

Nonetheless this news has actually made me more interested in picking up Sheffield for my Tout Wars team. Before leaving for Florida I'd called a handful of baseball medical types, granted them full anonymity, and asked them which players, in their educated opinion, were on the juice. Sheffield's name had come up a couple of times but only with a most emphatic "no."

In fantasyland, information like this is more valuable than gold bullion. The longer rumors about him persist, the more likely my Tout Wars opponents are to believe the notion that Gary Sheffield owes his success to steroids and that if he should stop taking them, he'll probably start sucking. If everybody in the competition takes this view, there's a good chance I'll be able to grab him for a discount.

When Sheffield arrives at his locker, he's wearing a tracksuit and an expression of pleasant calm, as if nothing unusual was happening. If he wasn't a ballplayer, Sheffield would probably volunteer to man a tank turret in Falluja. Still, no reporter wants to be the first to test the trip wire, so I swallow hard and go in. First I tell Sheffield what I'd heard, that people in the know have been standing up for him on the steroids question. "Thank you," he says, with a level gaze.

Now that the coast is clear, I ask him about a number that's been on my mind since I first saw it in Ron Shandler's book. After sixteen seasons in the majors and seven All-Star selections, Sheffield had actually raised his batting average against left-handed pitchers by 16 percent last season to a magnificent .341. This is exactly the kind of anomaly I'd come to spring training to investigate.

Sheffield is clearly delighted, if not a little surprised, to be talking about his craft. "A lot of lefties like to run in on you," he begins, brushing my chest with his hand to simulate the flight of a pitch. For years he'd focused on trying to hit those inside pitches, he says, a skill he'd largely mastered. But after watching himself on video, he noticed that when the reverse happened, when a lefthander pitched him outside, "I was doing them a favor by going after it." So in the off-season, during his countless hours of extracurricular practice, Sheffield had willed himself to lay off those outside pitches, even if they looked like strikes.

"How'd you do that?" I ask.

Sheffield smiles. Every time he stepped into the box and waggled his bat, he says, he just repeated a new mantra: "No lefty can get me out."

Soon, it was true.

This is not the kind of revelation that makes for sexy headlines, especially not today. Nonetheless, it's convinced me that this guy belongs on my Tout Wars team. Even after all he's accomplished, Gary Sheffield can still improve his game, just because he wants to. (Now that's something you won't read in the *Baseball Forecaster*.)

Day Three: The Tigers

Okay, be cool.

Inside the Tigers clubhouse in Lakeland on a gray and rainy morning, I'm having a hard time staying focused. Everywhere I look, there's another icon from the 1984 World Series team, just sitting on a couch or changing his socks or eating a corn muffin. The last time I saw Kirk Gibson, Lance Parrish, Alan Trammell, and Sweet Lou Whitaker this close together, they were taped in portraiture to my bedroom wall. Five minutes into my talk with Trammell, now Detroit's manager, I can no longer restrain my inner adolescent. "I was there when you hit those two home runs in Game Four!"

Trammell glances at my credential and cocks an eyebrow. He's accustomed to being fawned over but not by members of the press. "Good times," he says, warily.

No matter how badly I want to win Tout Wars, I've already made one concession to loyalty: My team must include at least one Tiger. Trouble is, the Tigers weren't just the worst team in baseball the season before, they finished one loss shy of joining the 1962 Mets as the lousiest team in baseball's modern era. This locker room is not exactly a Rotisserie candy store.

My leading candidate is cleanup hitter Dmitri Young, who, even on a punchless team, hit .297 with 29 home runs and 85 RBI. Dave Dombrowski, the Tigers GM, is a generally cool and reserved character, but when I brought up Dmitri Young during a visit to his office earlier this morning, he brightened. "He's our standout hitter," he said. "If you look at the lineup around him, it's amazing that he put up the numbers he did." If there was any knock on the guy, Dombrowski added, it's that the worse things got, the more he tried to win games by himself. "He struck out more than he normally does and he was chasing more pitches."

Heading back to the clubhouse with my nose in the *Forecaster*, I'm getting good vibrations about Young. Last year, if he wasn't taking one of 58 walks, he was forced to swing at borderline crap because that's all he was given. Opposing teams had the luxury of pitching around Young in order to face all the feebs who came up next in the order. But in the off-season, Dombrowski added a few dangerous bats to the lineup, which should put an end to that nonsense. And if Young could hit lousy pitches as well as he did, imagine what he'd be able to do with fat ones!

Young is kicked back in a chair when I find him, reading the sports section. He's a bull of a guy with cornrows and a shaggy beatnik beard that comes to a point. As I launch into my standard spiel about Tout Wars, he flips down his newspaper to listen politely. Everything seems fine until I get to the words "Rotisserie team."

At this, Young's eyes narrow to slits. "This is my livelihood," he grumps. "I don't give a crap about your Rotisserie team."

I *love* this guy.

Day Four: The Blue Jays

The first thing that strikes you about Blue Jays camp in Dunedin is what you don't see: reporters. Other than a couple of news cameras and a tiny clutch of beat writers, this team might as well be practicing in secret. If the Toronto Maple Leafs weren't in town for a hockey game, I'm not sure anyone would have turned up.

Do I care? Of course not.

In fact, for a few minutes this morning I find myself in a state of unspoiled Rotisserie scouting nirvana. The Blue Jays were a very good team last year, winning eighty-six games in a division where they were wildly outspent. And thirty minutes before practice, there are two dozen of these overachievers hanging out in the locker room, awaiting questions from the media—or in this case, *me*.

Making my rounds at a leisurely pace, I learn that Ted Lilly has a bum wrist, Vernon Wells has lost twenty pounds, Orlando Hudson spent the winter working out with the team's hitting coach, Carlos Delgado showed up to camp early, and, for what it's worth, Justin Miller just got a new tattoo on his stomach. In the middle of explaining Tout Wars to third baseman Eric Hinske, he interrupts.

"I play fantasy football."

"Really?" I ask. "How'd your team do?"

"I had *two* teams last year."

For the next eight minutes, Hinske tells me about his shrewd pickup of Steve Smith and the mediocre season turned in by Curtis Martin, and offers a complete account of all the reasons he failed to make up twenty points in the final week of the season. I feel like I'm back at the winter meetings with Scott the intern.

The Blue Jay at the top of my target list is starting pitcher Miguel Batista, who just came over from the Diamondbacks. In our research Nando and I noticed something odd about Batista the season before. In general, the better the opponent, the better he pitched. Coming into a division that includes marquee teams like the Red Sox and Yankees, I have a feeling Batista may thrive.

More than this, Batista is undoubtedly one of baseball's quirkiest players. He doesn't hang his clothes in his locker; he folds them. He's not a Nike or Reebok endorser; he likes Puma. He doesn't just have three or four pitches; he has somewhere in the neighborhood of fifteen, only a handful of which he can fully control. When I saw that Nando had written, "Ask Batista about his novel," in the Toronto dossier, I assumed he was messing around. But when I sat down with him in the clubhouse, I asked anyhow.

"It's a detective story," he said.

Batista tells me some interesting things about his approach on the mound, but in the end it's not what he says about baseball that impresses me so much as the *way* he says it. Whether he's talking about shutting down the Yankees in the 2001 World Series or pitching out of the bullpen between starts, he does so clearly, forcefully, and persuasively while flashing the fierce green eyes of a charismatic. He approaches pitching the way prosecutors study homicides.

"Have you thought about law school?" I ask.

"Yes, I have."

Get this man a jersey!

Day Five: The Indians

In a normal year I can't think of anything, short of a ball-playing don-key, that would lure me to Winter Haven to see the lowly Cleveland Indians on their first full day of spring practice. Throw in today's chilly and dank weather, and even the donkey might not be sufficient. Inside the clubhouse, a clutch of local reporters stands to one side, making cracks about all the "high-priced talent" the frugal Indians have collected.

"Who's that guy?"

"Who knows?"

But this year I'm not only here first thing in the morning, I'm *excited* to be. To win a deep and treacherous Rotisserie league like Tout Wars, you need to find some quiet players who are poised to take off. Any dope can predict that Alex Rodriguez is going to have a good year, but it takes a champion to pick up on Jody Gerut, an obscure Cleveland rookie who hit twenty-two homers in 2003.

Outside at batting practice, I'm standing with Indians writer Paul Hoynes of the *Plain Dealer*. "What the hell's up with Matt Lawton?" I ask him, as the outfielder steps into the cage to take some hacks. Paul's face reddens. He lowers his voice to a whisper and points to the guy standing next to me.

"That's his dad."

Thankfully, Matt Lawton's father, who is also named Matt, is either hard of hearing or just exceedingly polite. When I work up the nerve to introduce myself, he's perfectly cordial. Lawton (the player) has been on a long skid. After landing a fat contract two years ago, he's been plagued by injuries and come to be viewed as a royal dud. "Underachiever" is Shandler's more diplomatic term. After selling for $27 at Tout Wars in 1999 (that's more than 10 percent of one team's entire budget), he dropped all the way to $16 last season and was projected at $11 this year.

But lurking in the ruins of Lawton's numbers, I found something bizarre. Throughout his career he's always been one of the most se-lective batters in the American League, swinging at only 14 percent of pitches outside the strike zone. And last season he'd actually lowered that percentage a bit. But for some inexplicable reason Lawton had also been striking out at a higher clip, which didn't make sense. Clearly he was just as good, if not better, at recognizing good pitches. So why were more of them escaping his bat?

When I put this question to the elder Lawton, he nods knowingly and explains that last year his son was recuperating from shoulder surgery, which limited his range of motion and kept him from working out. While he never told anyone, his shoulder was so weak he had trouble reaching pitches on the outside part of the plate. Sometimes he'd swing feebly and miss. Other times he just watched them slap the catcher's mitt for strike three. "He doesn't want to make excuses," Lawton's dad tells me, "but if you saw his X rays, you wouldn't believe he played at all." Now that he's back in shape, the elder Lawton continues, he doesn't just *want* to have a rebound year.

"He has to."

An hour later I'm sitting in the office of Cleveland general manager Mark Shapiro, who's reclining in his desk chair in blue jeans facing the mother of all magnetic player boards: a color-coded job the length of a Ford pickup. It's no secret that the Indians have often tried to trade Lawton, so I ask Shapiro to explain his reasoning.

"Overvalued contract," he says.

"Is that all?"

Shapiro nods, then leans over and clicks his mouse, calling up the team's menu of information on Lawton. "Everything," he says, his eyes darting across the computer screen, "the qualitative stuff, the scouts, the numbers, his on-base percentage . . . all of it tells you he's a good player." Shapiro leans back again and folds his arms. "He just has a contract from a time when the economics of the game were different."

Driving back to my hotel that night, I realize I've just experienced one of Rotisserie's greatest thrills: the moment you just *know* you've outwitted your leaguemates. Matt Lawton's skills had not eroded— even his boss agrees with that. If he can stay healthy and hit even a fraction of those outside pitches that eluded him last year, he's 100 percent guaranteed to improve. And if raw desire counts for any-thing, he's a tremendously smart buy.

Just ask his dad.

Day Six: The Red Sox

Kwok!

I'm standing outside a chain-link fence at Boston's training facil-ity in Fort Myers, watching the team's glamour boys take batting practice while a cluster of fans screams thoughtful comments like "Manny!" and "Nomah!" But the noise I've just heard, which sounded more like a gunshot, came from a forgotten cage behind me.

Kwok!

Wandering over, I check the uniform number against my roster. Then I check it a second time. The guy making all this racket is Wil-liam Richard Mueller, Boston's third baseman. If you've never seen him up close, the guy looks about as imposing as a popcorn vendor.

Kwok! Kwok! Kwak!

Bill Mueller is putting on a clinic. He's slicing balls into the corners, hitting frozen ropes to the outfield gaps, and swatting bombs over the center-field fence. Though he's not considered a power hitter, last sea-son Mueller became the first major-league player to hit a grand slam batting left-handed and a grand slam batting right-handed *in the same game.* He won the batting title, too, with a .326 average.

Nevertheless, Mueller is an afterthought to Red Sox fans. He doesn't stare down pitchers or do a little hop when he hits a home run. He's never been linked to a Hollywood starlet or thrown in jail with a passel of hookers. As he tells it, his whole major-league career is the result of a fluke. After the San Francisco Giants drafted him, he showed up for rookie ball to find three infielders ahead of him. By some bizarre coincidence, one twisted an ankle, another broke a jaw, a third was moved to shortstop, and all of a sudden he got to play. Mueller was a solid performer for the Giants but hardly a star. His stock-in-trade was—and still is—mastering the little things that help a ballclub win: defense, situational hitting, and baserunning. A typical Mueller quote is something like: "I put team way ahead of everything else."

Rule number one in Rotisserie baseball is whatever you do, *never* get infatuated with a player. Doing so is the antithesis of effective game theory, the enemy of science, and a prelude to crushing disappointment. It's also a maxim I promised Sig I would follow.

Kwok!

Or maybe not, I can't remember.

The Red Sox clubhouse is a drafty barracks with an aluminum roof. It's Photo Day, and the place is loud and loose, like a frat house on a football Saturday. Pinned to one wall is a postcard of an enormously fat woman lying on the beach with a caption that says, "Welcome to Florida, the food's great!" Her face has been cut out and replaced with a picture of backup catcher Doug Mirabelli.

Mueller isn't at his locker yet, so I decide to look for the first guy on my list of intriguing Red Sox talents, David Ortiz. Known to his teammates as "Big Papi," Ortiz, a slugging first baseman, stands 6'4" with a thick barrel chest that makes his arms and legs seem spindly by comparison. Everything about him is big, from his appetite and his booming laugh to the blinding diamond stud in his ear. He looks like Babe Ruth's long-lost Dominican brother.

Back in February, I placed a call to Inside Edge, a Minnesota company that does contract scouting work for major-league teams. Using a staff of former pro ballplayers, Inside Edge scouts every game and prepares fantastically detailed scouting reports that tell you, for instance, how often Nomar Garciaparra hits sliders for base hits with two strikes (26 percent of the time) or how often Josh Beckett throws changeups with runners on base (7 percent). Their reports, which cost teams forty thousand dollars a year, are dugout staples for ten managers, including Bobby Cox of the Atlanta Braves.

After some pleading on my part, cofounder Randy Istre agreed to slip me two proprietary stats that few people outside baseball ever see: "chase percentage," a measure of how often a batter swings at pitches outside the strike zone, and "well-hit average," a measure of how often a hitter drives the ball hard, even if it becomes an out. (When Sig saw this data for the first time, he nearly lost consciousness.)

The season before, Ortiz had led the American League in "balls well hit" with a garish .365 average, trailing only Barry Bonds for the overall best. But something strange had happened. At year's end Ortiz's batting average was nearly one hundred points *lower* than this, which was one of the largest discrepancies for any player. The obvious question: How can somebody hit the ball that hard that often and not come away with more hits?

When I find Ortiz, he's squatting on a cheap plastic folding chair that's about a quarter the size of his derriere. He looks at the data and breaks into a wide grin. He's not surprised. "I can't think of all the bombs I heet," he says, "goot balls, I mean balls I crushed, right at people."

"Bad luck?" I ask.

"Not essactly," he says.

Last season, Ortiz had moved from Minnesota to Boston, whose ballparks couldn't be more different. Balls that would be doubles in the spacious gaps of the Metrodome are flyouts at Fenway Park. And while he tried to adjust his swing, opposing outfielders had figured out how to exploit his tendencies. His goal at spring training, he says, is to work on mixing things up. "You'll see me heet to the opposite field, you'll see me pool the ball."

Now the gears are turning. By the law of averages, Ortiz is already liable to collect more base hits this year, and if he figures out how to redistribute the ball even slightly, he could have a fearsome season. Right here, once again, I'm sure I'm on the brink of another scouting coup. I ask Big Papi if he thinks his average will improve.

He swats me on the arm.

"You bess believe it!"

Pencil in David Ortiz.

Time is running short, so I decide to park myself at Bill Mueller's locker. On the top shelf, there's a hockey puck with the logo of the St. Louis Blues, Mueller's hometown team. Just below it someone has written, *the St. Louis Blues suck ass.*

Mueller walks up in shorts and an undershirt and drops down wearily in his chair. He's about to turn thirty-three, and his goatee is flecked with gray streaks. I rave about his batting-practice display and his numbers from the previous year, then ask if he thinks he can replicate them. "It remains to be seen," Mueller says calmly, peeling a soft brace from his right knee. "Things happen throughout the season healthwise, it's all about injuries." He pauses for a beat. "I just try to stay under the radar. I enjoy playing the game, going home and being with my family. I treat this like I'm just going to work like everyone else in America."

"Billlleeee!"

From the shower, I hear the affected falsetto of Mueller's next-door locker neighbor, Trot Nixon. "Come into the shower, Billleee. . . . I'll show you my Nerf ball!" Mueller laughs.

Maybe it was the wear and tear of six days on the road or the pressure of all those numbers pressing against my skull, but after a while I put away my notes, and then we were just two guys talking. Mueller says he just got a second dog, another St. Bernard. He explains how he always tapes his wrists before games to make his batting gloves fit tighter. Soon we're comparing the beer-can collections we had as kids and the various discount brews we drank in college. "My first beer was Schaefer," Mueller says, smiling at the memory. "My grandpa had a mug of it, and he gave me a sip."

"Billllleeee boy!"

It's Nixon again. Mueller smirks, pulls his bath towel off its hook, and slips on a pair of generic shower shoes. Sig's data sheet says Mueller probably got a bit lucky last year, and he's likely to revert to his lifetime .280 batting average. Given his long history of injuries, Nando writes, some caution might be warranted.

But after hearing those *Kwoks,* listening to him downplay his achievements, and shooting the shit with him about dogs and down-market beer, I don't so much care about Sabermetrics or even about Rotisserie's rule number one. I'm reminded of something Big Daddy Williams told me in New Orleans when I asked him how you can tell when a player is special. "The great ones," he said, "you just know."

"Hey," Mueller says, wheeling around in the aisle on his way to the shower, "if I don't see you, good luck with your team."

You mean *our* team.

Day Seven: The Twins

Some days everything just falls into place. Within six minutes of arriving at the Lee County Sports Complex, I stumble upon exactly what I came looking for. Walking along a chain-link fence, I hear the pop of a catcher's mitt and right there, standing on a practice mound five feet away, is Minnesota pitcher Brad Radke.

After calling Inside Edge, I'd contacted another baseball mercenary service, a Pennsylvania company called Baseball Info Solutions. For a few hundred bucks, BIS agreed to give me another trove of rare data: the average fastball velocity for every starting pitcher in the major leagues the season before, broken down by month and inning. When I showed my partners this spreadsheet, even Nando was thunderstruck. "I feel like Charlie in the chocolate factory," he said.

While I had bigger plans for this data, my first goal was to see if it could help me identify a few pitchers who might do a lot better than my Tout Wars opponents have projected. I came up with a crude formula: average fastball velocity times walk rate (BB/9) divided by strikeout rate (K/9). The idea was to identify a few unheralded pitchers who fan a lot of batters and walk very few, all while throwing the ball with less than optimum firepower.

If Bill James ever got a look at my math on this, I'm sure he'd choke on his English muffin. But as unsophisticated as my methodology was, my formula did yield one pleasant surprise. Coming in fifth, right below a group of elite pitchers like Mike Mussina and Pedro Martinez, who would probably cost $30 at Tout Wars, was a guy who might sell for half that: Brad Radke.

All I knew about Radke was that he was considered a "finesse" pitcher and that he gave up a few too many home runs, a problem Shandler likes to call "gopheritis." But the discrepancy between his score on my scale and his likely price at Tout Wars made me think there must be something unusual about him. Watching him work from this distance, it only takes four pitches to discover the answer. Every time Radke follows through, his left foot lands in precisely the same spot on the mound. And I mean *precisely*. There aren't more than four millimeters of slack on the shoeprint.

From then on I decide to become a Brad Radke stalker. At batting practice, while other Twins pitchers bounce curveballs in the dirt, Radke works at a quick tempo, wearing out hitters with one borderline strike after another. When somebody smacks a fly ball, he doesn't flinch or even turn around to see where it lands. He already knows. "Warning track," somebody says. The moment Radke's done, the groundskeeper runs over to hear his opinion on the height, slope, and overall grooming of the mound.

After practice, about ten minutes before my wrenching conversation with Jacque Jones, I catch Radke on his way out the clubhouse door in sandals and jean shorts, carrying his lunch in a neatly folded sack. When I show him his score on my "finesse" scale, he doesn't flinch. "There's a large number of guys who throw ninety-five or ninety-six in the major leagues," he says. "I'm more concerned with mixing my pitches and hitting my spots." The whole time Radke is talking, he hasn't moved his eyeballs. "They can hit it as hard as they want to, I don't care," he continues. "I'll take twenty-seven balls to the warning track."

As he turns to go, I'm certain I've made another proprietary discovery that nobody else in Tout Wars will know. Brad Radke is a good Rotisserie pick because he's actually a *robot*.

Day Eight: The Orioles

It's quarter to four on the first day of March, and I'm sitting in a Kentucky Fried Chicken not far from Fort Lauderdale Stadium, where I've just spent five hours scouting the Baltimore Orioles.

I had nice chats with the team's two general managers, Jim Beattie and Mike Flanagan. I met outfielder Jay Gibbons, who told me, unprompted, "I'm going to have a good year." I watched the newest Oriole, shortstop Miguel Tejada, smack five gigantic home runs to left-center field in a ballpark where the fences are twenty feet *deeper* than the fences in Baltimore. But nobody made a stronger impression than pitcher Sidney Ponson.

Since his debut in 1998 Ponson has consistently ranked near the top of the league in the category of rock-headed behavior. In one famous episode, he chartered a limo in New York with two teammates in order to attend a Metallica concert. Trouble was, Ponson was scheduled to pitch at Yankee Stadium the next day. And the concert was in *Baltimore*. When he took the mound, Ponson gave up six runs in less than two innings and was later disciplined by the team.

In 2003 Queen Beatrix, Aruba's reigning monarch, decided (for reasons that are not entirely clear) to induct Ponson—a native son—into the Order of the Dutch Royal House. When reporters asked him for a comment about his knighthood, he said, "You guys should have been calling me 'Sir' a long time ago."

Nevertheless, Ponson had managed to win seventeen games in 2003, and the Orioles, desperate for arms, rewarded him over the winter with a new $22.5 million contract. Ponson promptly showed his appreciation by ballooning to 266 pounds on a diet of beer and cholesterol and showing up to spring training struggling to do calisthenics. "I swim," Ponson said when I asked him about his winter conditioning program. "I swim in the ocean at my house."

Sitting here in KFC, slurping a Diet Pepsi, I'm relieved to say that Florida is officially done. The final haul is ninety-six players, nine general managers, twenty-one coaches, thirteen scouts, four trainers, and one video coordinator. I've collected hundreds of extraneous tips that make me inclined to like particular players, from the "power slider" that Minnesota pitcher Carlos Silva is throwing to the fact that Boston pitcher Bronson Arroyo plays in a grunge band. But I've also accumulated a list of players whom, for whatever reason, I won't be bidding on at Tout Wars. Whether it's Ted Lilly's achy wrist or Sidney Ponson's expanding waistline, the negative intelligence could prove to be just as useful.

Above all, my strategy seems to be working. Using a blend of numbers and human scouting, I've formed strong hunches about players based on observations I never could have gleaned from a computer alone. Nobody else at the Tout Wars auction will be aware of Bill Mueller's work ethic or Brad Radke's mechanical precision or the secret problem with Matt Lawton's plate coverage.

Three days from now I'll be flying to Arizona to repeat this process, and after that there's the small matter of sitting down before the draft and making sense of all these random observations. But right now, sitting here with a stack of eight plump notebooks, I'm feeling pretty unbeatable.

I *see,* therefore I win.

The Cactus League

March

Barry Morrow cowrote the screenplay for the movie Rain Man. *He also plays Rotisserie baseball, dating back to the days when you had to do the statistics by hand. So when he met Kim Peek, the inspiration for the title character—an autistic man with a preternatural gift for counting—he naturally tried to recruit him to serve as the league's statistician. They nearly had a deal until Kim Peek's father nixed the idea.*

"Too stressful," he said.

· · ·

After two days of what might be loosely described as "rest" in New York, I fatten up my suitcase once again and board a flight to Phoenix for spring training, the cactus sessions.

In Florida, my sole purpose was to interview ballplayers and their superiors. But here in Arizona (with the Tout Wars draft just three weeks away) the agenda is a little more crowded. In addition to visiting teams, I'll spend a pair of evenings watching both sides of another expert Rotisserie draft that's being held here, and I've made plans to spend time with two more of my opponents.

Sitting next to me on the Avis shuttle bus in Phoenix, clutching a threadbare garment bag, is Ferdinando "Bonecrusher" Di Fino, who has joined me for the first three days. The official reason I bought him a ticket was to have another set of eyes on this expert draft, but the truth is that I'm starting to worry about the guy. He hasn't been spotted outside the front office since Presidents Day.

As the bus lurches forward, Nando lowers his voice and motions toward my overstuffed wheelie bag.

"Don't forget to plug it in tonight," he says.

"Plug in what?"

"You know, the Stalker."

Ever since it arrived in a cardboard box a week earlier, the "Stalker" has become Nando's favorite object. Knowing that I would be spending much of my time in Arizona watching exhibition games, I decided to spend $250 to rent a piece of equipment to help me gather intelligence about pitchers, even when I wasn't talking to them. It's a Stalker Sport radar gun, the same model the pro scouts use. The only difficulty so far was getting it through airport security.

"Are you a cop?" asked the baggage screener.

"No, it's for baseball."

"So you're a scout?"

"Well, no, but . . ."

"Step this way, Sir."

Day One: Jason Grey

At two minutes past eight the next morning, Jason Grey, the defending Tout Wars champion, marches through the doors of the DoubleTree Guest Suites, pulling a briefcase on wheels.

He is, hands down, the palest Arizonan I have ever seen, a condition exacerbated by his jet-black hair, which is heavily gelled. He's wearing a gold watch, black tasseled loafers, beige dress slacks, and a Tommy Hilfiger polo shirt that looks as if it's been washed two hundred times. His wallet makes a giant bulge on his hip. If I didn't know who he was, I'd assume he was selling aluminum siding.

Today's plan is to pay a visit with Grey to the spring headquarters of the Kansas City Royals. On the phone, I'd proposed our meeting as a formal interview, a chance for me to chronicle a day in the life of the national champion. My real purpose, of course, is to eavesdrop on his conversations, steal his methods, and goad him into revealing more about his draft strategy than he probably should.

If oddsmakers put a line on Tout Wars, Grey would be favored at about four to one. After winning the last two titles and finishing third as a rookie, he owns the highest scoring average in the competition's history. Shandler calls him "the cream of the crop" and fellow titlist Lawr Michaels "the best Rotisserie player I have ever seen."

In 1996, while living in Chicago and working in corporate risk management, Grey won all three of his amateur Rotisserie leagues by at least fourteen points. Convinced he knew just as much as the reigning "experts," he slapped up a Web site called Mastersball and started dispensing advice. Three years later a producer for the *Sports Illustrated* Web site discovered his work and hired him to write a regular fantasy column. He earned his first invitation to Tout Wars two years later and in 2003 quit his job and moved to the Valley of the Sun with his wife and baby daughter to make fantasy baseball his sole occupation.

Inside his apartment in Scottsdale there's a satellite dish on the roof, a TiVo in the office, and three scattered VCRs that he uses to record hundreds of ballgames a year. While his readership is tiny compared to Ron Shandler's, his ambition is anything but. He's started charging $39.95 for a subscription to his site, which used to be free, and in a bid to create his own radio show, he recently converted one of the bays of his garage to a soundproof studio. By sidling up to Cactus League scouts, he's taught himself some rudiments of baseball physics, like whether a pitcher throws from a consistent arm slot. Lately he's determined to do a better job communicating with Latin players. "I bought some of those 'Spanish in twenty-four hours' tapes," he says. "Anything for an edge."

In my rental car on our way to Royals camp, I begin to see glimpses of one characteristic that makes Jason Grey a formidable Rotisserie player: He has the world's fastest metabolism. In the passenger's seat, his legs pound like jackhammers, and he keeps his hands in a state of perpetual motion, fiddling with the air vents, cracking his knuckles, checking the contents of the glove box, or taking rapid pulls from a water bottle.

Once we reach the door to the Royals locker room, Grey flips open his notebook with a purposeful flourish to check his list of targets. "Affeldt, May, Guiel, DeJesus," he says. Next, he reaches for a holster on his belt and unfastens something I've never seen in a clubhouse (or anywhere else, for that matter). It's an Audiovox Thera Pocket PC with a 206 MHz processor and 32 megabytes of RAM. It's a cellphone, a digital voice recorder, and a wireless Internet browser. It even has an external keyboard that allows him to file columns from the ballpark. As he wields it around the building, he looks like he's checking in rental cars at the airport.

When it comes to locker rooms, Grey operates by a few simple maxims. He rarely talks to coaches, he says, because "they don't tell you shit." He introduces himself as "Jason Grey from *Sports Illustrated*," omitting the "dot-com" part, and he *never* mentions that he writes a fantasy-baseball column. "I think it would color their answers," he explains.

As Grey works the clubhouse, I try to keep a curious distance. I've never been in the position of trying to report on a reporter before, and the players look baffled. "There's media covering the media now," someone says.

The first thing that strikes me is that Grey doesn't do a lot of preparation. He doesn't bring along reams of data or ask a lot of needling questions. He's mostly interested in issues of mechanics or playing time. "How's your swing?" he'll ask, or, "Have they talked to you about your role?"

His chief target today is Jeremy Affeldt, a young pitcher he's been touting for a couple of years. Affeldt struggled the prior season with a recurring blister on his pitching hand and had been demoted to the bullpen. Grey levels his Pocket PC just under Affeldt's chin and commences the interview.

"Any problems?" he asks.

"No, the finger blister is fine."

"Are you back in the rotation?"

"They haven't told me anything."

"Working on any new pitches?"

"I might work on a cutter."

"How's the curve?"

Hearing this, the other Royals start to chortle. Affeldt, an excitable sort, had apparently started calling his curveball "The Affy" and bragging to everyone about its befuddling powers. Leaning over, Royals closer Mike MacDougal launches into an impression. "Did you see that Affy? It *buckled!*"

Everybody laughs. Affeldt turns crimson.

"No, no," he says. "Don't write that!"

Grey, getting in on the joke, looks at MacDougal.

"Mike, how do you spell that?"

"A-f-f-y."

More laughter.

At this, Grey's work is done. He clips the Audiovox back on his belt and strides toward the door with a big smile plastered on his face. His armpits are damp with perspiration.

"Get anything good?" I ask.

"I'll tell you later."

It's pretty clear that Grey works his butt off. His player knowledge is deeper than Lake Baikal and he's been in upward of one hundred Rotisserie auctions. You don't win Tout Wars *twice* just by accident. It's entirely possible that he toned it down today because I was there, but other than asking a few innocuous questions, having a look at some guy's blister, and prompting a joke, he offered no Eureka! moments. Grey walked in with a set of assumptions about players and spent most of his time confirming them. As far as I can tell, he's no better in the clubhouse than I am.

Day Two: LABR

It's sundown on Saturday, and Nando and I are camped in the corner of a conference room at the downtown Phoenix headquarters of *The Arizona Republic*. Outside the window, the dusk is washing the mountains in a magnificent shade of purple.

Nobody cares.

In front of us there's a horseshoe of tables facing a dry-erase board. Sitting around it are a dozen people in various states of anxiety and caffeination, all poring over laptops, stacks of books, and reams of paper with rows of data packed in blindingly small margins.

The League of Alternative Baseball Reality (LABR) is the grand-daddy of expert Roto competitions. It was founded in 1994 by John Hunt, a fantasy-baseball columnist for *USA Today's Baseball Weekly*. Hunt had spent years listening to various "experts" brag about their abilities in the fields of auction strategy and player projection, and he wanted to find a way to shut them up. So he started issuing invitations.

The inaugural LABR competition was the Rotisserie equivalent of a *Vanity Fair* Oscar party. Bill James agreed to play, as did Glen Waggoner and Ron Shandler. Then-ESPN anchor Keith Olbermann not only signed on, he thought up the league's title and, once the season started, quickly earned a reputation for bombarding people with trade offers. He once called Hunt late at night to try to swing a deal, even though Hunt was, thanks to a case of strep throat, unable to speak. (Hunt's wife eventually hung up the phone.)

Bill James, playing in his first-ever Rotisserie league, was, by his own admission, hopeless. "I was never good at exploiting the cracks in the system," he tells me. "I was more inclined to complain about them." Besides, he adds, "I have no negotiating skill whatsoever." James finished eleventh and never played again.

Ron Shandler was in first place for eight weeks but dropped to third just before the players went on strike, ending the season and his title hopes. Still, he was thrilled by the exposure. The LABR participants, along with the names of their various publications, were written up in *Baseball Weekly*, the bible of the Rotisserie masses.

Today, LABR is no longer a pure "expert" league. While some of the nation's top players still compete, John Hunt wanted to make the game more egalitarian, so he began reserving spots for a group known as the "Regular Guys," mostly longtime readers who've won their local leagues and don't mind paying their way to Phoenix for the draft. While LABR still has more name recognition, Tout Wars has assumed the role of Rotisserie's *fin du tout*.

But between tonight's National League competition and the American League draft the evening before, I've learned a couple of important lessons. First, there are still quite a few baseball players I've never heard of.

"Who's J. J. Putz?" I asked.

"Seattle bullpen," Nando whispered.

Second, I learned that I'll not only have to know who these people are, I'll have to know immediately whether I want to have them on my team or not. And I mean *immediately*. In most amateur Roto leagues, the bidding is more regimented—each owner gets to weigh in on every player nominated, which makes it easy to stall for time. But in expert leagues, where it's assumed that everybody knows everything, the bidding process is a free-for-all. When a player is put on the block, anybody can holler out a bid at any moment until the auctioneer counts two beats and says "sold."

During the AL draft, I borrowed somebody's stopwatch. The moment Seattle infielder Bret Boone was nominated, I clicked *start*. If I'd been drafting for real, I'd have had to look up Boone's projections, check the list of remaining players at his position, calculate how much money I'd have left if I bought him, decide if he's a good fit for the current makeup of my team and, if so, how much I was willing to pay for him. When the bidding on Boone ended at $27, I clicked "stop." The whole exercise took seventeen seconds. This isn't Rotisserie baseball. It's *Jeopardy!*

Day Three: Steve Moyer

Short and stocky with bleached hair, thick muttonchops, and a pair of silver earrings, Tout Wars veteran Steve Moyer might pass for Johnny Rotten's older brother, which is, it turns out, precisely the look he's going for. Years ago, Moyer played bass guitar in a punk band called Follow Fashion Monkeys, whose climactic moment was taking a national van tour with an Italian hardcore group called Indigesti. These days, at forty-three with a wife and two daughters, he's graduated to playing country and western. But the cowboy boots stay in the closet.

I've met up with Moyer tonight at the ballpark in Peoria, where the Padres are hosting the Angels. Moyer has come to Phoenix to participate in the National League LABR draft and to drum up business for Baseball Info Solutions, the Allentown, Pennsylvania, company he runs. BIS is a statistical mercenary service with six major-league teams under contract. To Rotisserie players, it's best known as the outfit that publishes *The Bill James Handbook*, an annual statistical recap of the baseball season that serious players swear by. That Bill James lends his name to the book is no coincidence. He's a close friend of company founder John Dewan.

Though Moyer's never won Tout Wars in six tries, his baseball résumé is, hands down, the most intimidating of the group. He sells data to everyone from player agents and baseball-card companies to Ron Shandler and even me (he was the source for those pitcher velocity numbers). Through his years of work in baseball information, he's come to know dozens of executives, including Brian Cashman of the Yankees, and now, thanks to Bill James, the Red Sox have become the company's biggest client.

But for all the proprietary data at his fingertips, Moyer prefers to play Rotisserie baseball by the seat of his trousers. To him, the numbers are a smoke screen, and the entire tradition of expert leagues is pompous and a bit phony. At home he plays in a rowdy blue-collar league where beers are thrown, fistfights are narrowly averted, and, he assures me, winning is just as difficult. To Moyer, the beauty of Rotisserie is that a snowplow driver with good instincts can beat a Ph.D. statistician. "Expert leagues are so antiseptic," he says. "The only highlight is what stupid, nerdy strategy the winner uses." At LABR the night before, while everybody else pored over laptops and study aids, Moyer came with *nothing*. The morning of an expert draft, he rolls out of bed, rips the latest team rosters out of the newspaper, and shuffles out the door. All the information he needs is already stored in his head. "This is all I think about all day," he says.

As we take our eighteen-dollar seats in the first row above the dugout, I'm still trying to absorb what I've just heard. While I had been picturing Tout Wars as a monolithic contest between math lovers, Moyer approaches it like a night at the craps table. In an expert league where everybody knows what he's doing, he says, there's even less need to prepare. Since everybody values players about the same, the marketplace is efficient. "An idiot can win an expert league," he says. "I'm sure of it."

What a lot of experts seem to forget, Moyer continues, is that the point of this game is to win. Not to finish third or sixth but to smoke the field. To that end, Moyer is famous for spending liberally on a nucleus of aging superstars the Sabermetricians wouldn't touch and surrounding them with leftover scrubs who cost a buck. If most of his gambles pay off, he reasons, he'll whip the math nerds by a comfortable margin.

As you might expect, this attitude makes Moyer a bit of an iconoclast in Tout Wars, where he's uniformly liked but not exactly *feared*. His average finish is seventh. "Steve goes a lot by his gut," Ron Shandler says, "but he hasn't won much."

By the fifth inning there's a full yellow moon parked over right field. I ask Moyer, now halfway through a second beer, if he has a favorite ballclub. He showed up for the LABR draft in a Ken Griffey jersey, so I was expecting the Reds. "No," he says, "I found that shirt in a discount bin for five dollars." It's then that I notice the purple jacket at his feet with the Diamondbacks logo. "I got that for thirty bucks at Value City," he explains. Even the Yankees visor he bought betrays nothing. He picked it out for his dad.

The truth is that Moyer doesn't really have a favorite team. He considers himself a fan of baseball or, more accurately, baseball players. When he joined his first Rotisserie league in 1988, it was a revelation. Suddenly he didn't have to defend the dumb moves real executives make out of fealty to a uniform. He was free to cheer for Dwight

Gooden if it suited him. And best of all, he could shop for baseball gear by price rather than logo. "I'm a contrarian," he says.

Day Four: The White Sox

With Nando on a flight back east, I'm alone now at the mercy of my harebrained Cactus League schedule. I have eight teams to cover in eight days, starting this morning with the Chicago White Sox, down in Tucson.

It's here that I realize I'm going to have to change my work habits. Turns out it's a lot easier to talk to baseball players for long stretches at spring training when they aren't actually playing baseball games. By custom, most starters play the first few innings of spring games, then shower and go home. To catch them, you have to get up *early*. As it happens, by the time I reach the Sox clubhouse, I have time to talk to five players. Paul Konerko tells me he got married in the off-season and took up yoga. José Valentin says his goal is to hit .300. And when Joe Crede tells me he wants to be "more consistent on a consistent basis," I know it's not my day.

In the final minutes, I sit down with outfielder Aaron Rowand, whom I'd been eager to meet. During my scouting trip to Puerto Rico in late December, in the dugout of Hiram Bithorn Stadium in San Juan, I'd had a long talk with Wally Backman, the former New York Met who was Rowand's winter-league manager. With his leathery tan, peppery mustache, and husky Marlboro voice, Backman is the kind of baseball character who can talk a guy like me into almost anything. And that day, he was determined to make me a believer in Aaron Rowand. "There's thunder in his bat," he'd marveled.

Backman told me that he'd been forced several times to bodily drag Rowand out of the batting cage after he'd taken something like a thousand swings. He predicted that Rowand would hit twenty homers in the majors this season, easily.

Here in Tucson, the Sox brass agreed that Rowand had star potential, but only if he could be less of a kamikaze on and off the field. He'd missed part of last season after being badly injured in a dirt-bike accident. I have only a minute or two, so I ask Rowand if he's going to, you know, *tone it down*. He nods earnestly.

"I sold my dirt bike."

Over at Tucson Electric Park, as the White Sox game is about to begin, I take a seat directly behind home plate and unzip the black case that contains my pride and joy, the Stalker. No sooner have I attached the charger and powered it on than the Stalker reveals its first secret. In his first five pitches, Rich Harden of the visiting Oakland A's, an alleged fireballer, has posted no reading higher than 84 miles per hour. "Harden has lost velocity!" I write in my notebook, underlining and starring the words for emphasis. This goes on for a few minutes until one of the real scouts leans over.

"You need to set it to *peak hold*," he says.

Whoops!

Next pitch, 98.

Still, by the end of the game, the Stalker proves to be worth every dollar. Not just because it's absurdly fun to play with, but because it seems to give me a modicum of credibility. As scouts file in and take seats around me, they see me taking readings and assume I must have some tangential connection to the scouting fraternity. As a result, they talk freely about their impressions of players. As the days pass, I'll learn that Chicago's Billy Koch has lost all the "zip" on his fastball, José Guillen of the Angels swings the bat well even when he strikes out, and Clint Nageotte, a Seattle pitching prospect, is "going to be a real good major leaguer one day."

I'm in Rotisserie heaven.

Day Five: The Mariners

Signing in at the entrance to the Seattle clubhouse in Peoria, I notice a name on the line above mine that nearly causes me to drop my Croissan'wich.

John Benson.

Of all the legends of Rotisserie punditry, Benson is the most elusive. A former sales executive from Connecticut, he was one of the first people to establish himself as a Roto expert in the late 1980s. And though he's never accepted an invitation to play in an expert league (he believes he should be paid to do so), those who have played with him say he could be the greatest Rotisserie player of all time. "Benson is almost mythical," says Alex Patton, one of his earliest competitors, who's met him only once. "He's like Greta Garbo; he doesn't like to schmooze." Weeks ago, I tried to find a number for Benson but gave up in frustration. One of Benson's loyal customers, a former member of the National Security Council, once told him, "You're harder to get than the president."

Wheeling around, I see a man in his early fifties wearing a white dress shirt and a crisply pressed pair of khakis, staring back at me intently. In a decade of various beats in the newspaper business, I've interviewed George W. Bush, chatted with Michael Jordan, hit golf balls with Rudolph Giuliani, and sipped coffee with Walter Cronkite. But it took John Benson to make me gush like an idiot. "You're not John Benson, the Rotisserie John Benson, are you?"

"I am."

"I have your book in my car!"

After making quick work of my interviews with the Mariners, I join Benson for a late lunch at a nearby Cheesecake Factory. He's come to Arizona, he tells me, to gather intelligence for his Rotisserie clients and to collect anecdotes for a book of baseball wisdom. Benson orders a Coke with no ice, sucks it down, and then orders another. In a matter of minutes, he will excuse himself to go to the lavatory, telling me, "I've ingested a lot of fluids."

Benson is a meticulous guy. His silver hair is immaculately cropped at a military length. He's wearing a spotless and carefully ironed white short-sleeve dress shirt. He talks in a sententious monotone, considers his words carefully, and at times refers to himself in the third person. "I don't like to talk about myself," he explains.

Benson first made his mark in 1989, when he published one of the first books of player analysis aimed at serious Rotisserie buffs. Later he opened a hotline where Roto players could call and ask him questions for $2.50 per minute. It became so popular that the moment he hung up the phone, it would ring again. He also developed one of the first draft-simulation software programs.

Over time other more aggressive pundits have overtaken Benson in stature. While he still publishes an annual player guide and recently came out with an updated version of his software, his 900 number no longer exists. Today he limits his consultancy to a select group of loyal followers who pay $150 *an hour* for his counsel. He's hired his son to manage the Rotisserie business while he pursues another goal: earning a master's from the Yale School of Divinity.

To Benson, these two pursuits are not dissimilar. Baseball, he believes, is an amalgam of many disciplines—politics, religion, philosophy, and art. "Pregame infield practice," he says, "is one of the most spiritually cleansing things to watch."

As another Coke comes and goes, the subject turns to my quixotic bid to compete in Tout Wars. Speaking between long, thoughtful pauses, Benson lays out his bedrock Rotisserie axioms: "Look for healthy, improving starting players in secure roles," and "Try to relax at the draft; don't make faces," and "Run out of money; it forces you to use your knowledge." After scribbling all this down, I ask him for some scouting pointers. As one of the first Rotisserie experts to ever trawl clubhouses for information, much as I'm trying to do, Benson is uniquely qualified to offer guidance. When talking to managers, he says, by way of example, don't just ask them who their closer is going to be; it's better to take a general approach like, "Tell me about your bullpen." Listen when they talk, he adds, "and you will hear unstated things."

As the sun begins to set on Peoria, I pay the check, and the two of us head out to the parking lot. Benson can tell that I'm a little intimidated by Tout Wars, so he offers me one last parting word of advice. "If you've never played golf before, your ball is going to go all over the place," he says. "If you pick up a violin, it isn't going to be perfect or beautiful in the beginning." He pauses to let his words sink in.

"You have to practice."

Day Six: The Royals

Since I already canvassed the Kansas City clubhouse a few days earlier with Jason Grey, I decide to focus on watching the game and taking readings from the Stalker. This yields exactly one interesting result. When Brian Anderson throws a changeup, the display says 74. That's the slowest pitch I've recorded.

Between innings, as I'm standing in the aisle behind home plate, there's a tap on my shoulder. It's former Negro Leagues star Buck O'Neil, who's still sharp and spry at ninety-two. He's seen my radar gun and come down to ask me what the reading was on Brian Anderson's changeup. I tell him. We laugh.

Soon O'Neil and I are sharing a bag of peanuts. He's telling me what it sounded like when the great Josh Gibson hit a home run. Not the roar of the crowd, but the mighty howl of his bat. "Never heard that sound since," he says.

After the game, I realize it's been a nice day at the ballpark but a fruitless one in Rotisserie terms. I head back to the clubhouse, which is nearly empty now except for Kansas City manager Tony Pena, who tells me he has time for one question. It takes me exactly two seconds to figure out what to say.

"Tell me about your bullpen."

Day Seven: The Angels

My trip to the locker room at Tempe Diablo Stadium begins with a sight I cannot explain: Anaheim reliever Ben Weber, alone at his locker, doing an impression of Beavis, or possibly Butthead.

"Bungholio!" he says.

After scratching Weber off my list, I start filling my notebook with random bits. Second baseman Adam Kennedy is eating a tunafish sandwich, reliever Francisco Rodriguez has a weak handshake, and pitching prospect Bobby Jenks tells me he's working on a new "out" pitch, which he calls "one-oh-three." When I ask injury-prone veteran Tim Salmon if he's stepped up his off-season conditioning program, he says: "I go hiking twice a week with my wife. As you get older, it's important to stay active."

So much for the Angels.

Out in the stands as the game begins, the sun is beating down, and the metal bleachers are frying the backs of my legs. I'm sitting behind home plate with the newly arrived Sig Mejdal, who has, in a matter of minutes, developed an inseparable fondness for the Stalker. I'd hoped this would happen, that a little high technology would give him at least some appreciation for what scouts do.

The last time Sig played Rotisserie was nearly ten years ago, when he worked in the satellite operations unit at Onizuka Air Force Station in Sunnyvale, California. His office was inside a building called the Blue Cube, a communications nerve center from which all satellite transmissions are routed. It has no windows, and you can't get within a thousand feet of the place without a security clearance. For years he worked an occasional graveyard shift, which was dreadful in every respect but one. Most nights he would race through his work in about ninety minutes, leaving him seven hours to pursue his real passion. "I was responsible for billion-dollar satellites," he says, "and all I wanted to use the computer power for was baseball."

Sig was commissioner of the Blue Cube Rotisserie League, whose members were, in every sense of the word, rocket scientists. Some of the best players were the engineers responsible for calculating the geosynchronous orbit of satellites. Just as they measured the paths of objects in space, these people constructed mathematical models to predict the career trajectories of ballplayers. "The orbit analysts!" Sig says, shaking his head exhaustedly. "They were tough."

On the ballfield now, Anaheim pitcher Bartolo Colón has just rung up Arizona's Richie Sexson on a nasty changeup, and I'm wondering how much Tabasco he took off the pitch.

"What's the reading?" I ask Sig.

"I didn't get it," he says.

I look over and see that Sig is training the gun on a tractor trailer on the highway, miles in the distance. He notices me and turns the gun back on Colón, who is now walking toward the dugout. "There we go!" he says, holding the display under my nose. "Colón is walking to the dugout at three miles per hour."

Over the next five innings, Sig will measure the swings of batters in the on-deck circle, the velocity of a bird flying over the park, and the foot speed of a hot-dog vendor.

"This thing is *great!*" he says.

Ever since I picked up Sig at the airport this morning, we've been bickering like Cinderella's stepsisters. The gist of the argument is this: I'm convinced that he's been blinded by science, while he considers me a member of the Flat Earth Society. Now, watching him gleefully violate the dignity of the Stalker, I've had enough. "Let me get this straight," I say. "You don't think there's *any* use in scouting Colón, even though he might go for twenty-five dollars in Tout Wars?"

Sig lets the gun fall to his side with a tired sigh. His general view, he says, is that the best place to scout talent during spring training is any nightclub frequented by coeds from Arizona State. To him, it's profoundly silly to make judgments about one tiny sample of a player's career when he's got results from thousands of *real* games on his hard drive. "Spring training has only a loose correlation to the regular season," he says. "You're not going to see anything here you can really believe in." If there's any Rotisserie value to be had down here, he adds, it's in talking to managers about the only variables a computer can't predict: plate appearances, save opportunities, and innings pitched.

Everything else is bullshit.

As my chief statistician, of course, Sig is only doing his job, trying to muscle me over to the quantitative side. But after two weeks on the road and hundreds of interviews, I'm not in the mood to hear that my efforts have been misguided.

In my defense, I mention my talk with Matt Lawton's dad and how he'd helped explain that anomaly in his son's strikeout numbers. "You talked to his dad, that's perfect!" Sig says. "We drafted him because his *dad* said he was going to have a good year."

Fine, I say. What about Seattle closer Eddie Guardado, who'd told me that Oakland's Mark Ellis is one of the most underrated hitters in the game? Sig pulls down the brim of his cap. "Unless the rules of baseball change and Mark Ellis only hits against Eddie Guardado, that's meaningless."

Just three hours ago, thanks to the supreme generosity of the Angels media-relations staff, Sig Mejdal had draped a credential around his neck and stepped inside his first major-league clubhouse. Last week, when the Royals extended the same courtesy to Nando, he'd frozen up so completely that I had to put a notebook in his hand to keep him from scaring people.

But once inside the carpeted sanctum, Sig, the Ph.D. candidate, calmly unzipped his backpack, pulled out a sheet of graph paper, and breezed over to ask Angels pitcher Jarrod Washburn why his "opponent batting average" is so much lower for the first hitter he faces in an inning than for subsequent ones.

In other words, he was about to get beat up.

Watching anxiously from the corner of my eye, I saw Sig sketch some figures on the paper. Washburn looked at them, then dropped his head and stared at the carpet for a few seconds. "What's the matter?" Sig finally asked. "Is it something I said?"

Washburn glanced up at him briefly. "No," he replied, smiling slightly to indicate that no offense was taken. "Now you've got me thinking. Man, this will be on my mind all week."

As a last salvo in our argument, I remind Sig of his chat with Washburn, which had gone on for fifteen minutes and covered a panoply of statistical topics. "You didn't learn *anything* from that?" I ask.

"No, I did," he says.

"What?"

"Humans are funny."

Day Eight: The A's

Billy Beane, the general manager of the Oakland A's, stands at the edge of a green carpet near the showers in the team's clubhouse at

Phoenix Municipal Stadium. He's wearing cargo shorts, black Mizuno flip-flops, and a pink-checked buttondown with short sleeves. He looks as if he's been grilling bratwurst by the pool.

Since the publication of *Moneyball*, he's become the most famous baseball executive since Branch Rickey and the game's most divisive figure. He's been besieged by requests for his time, which makes it all the more surprising to see him down here holding court with reporters.

At this point there are two teams left on my spring-training agenda, and I'm feeling a profound sense of urgency. Arizona hasn't produced nearly as many epiphanies as Florida did, so I'm counting on this visit to help close the gap. Before we left the hotel I'd arranged to get Sig a press pass, written up a list of target players, and split it down the middle. Sig had rolled his eyes but promised to ask my little questions anyhow.

"There's Beane," I say, turning to see what sort of Pavlovian response this generates from Sig, but it's too late. He's already walked away and planted himself behind the pack of reporters to listen to Beane with the sort of expression last seen in the Kool-Aid line at Jonestown. It's pretty clear he won't be talking to any ballplayers this evening.

During my trip to Puerto Rico, I spoke with Minnesota Twins bench coach Steve Liddle, a former teammate of Beane in the minor leagues, who told me that Beane used to play Strat-O-Matic or some other baseball board game on road trips—and, given his statistical bent, I have a hunch Beane has either tried Rotisserie or learned enough about it to venture an opinion.

By now I'd asked most of the GMs in the American League about their Roto experiences. Brian Cashman said the only fantasy baseball he'd ever played was Atari. Baltimore's Mike Flanagan hasn't indulged, but he does frequent Rotisserie sites like RotoWire. Terry Ryan said his son plays "that stuff," while Tampa Bay's Chuck LaMar said he gets questions at cocktail parties. The only GM who'd copped to playing Rotisserie was Boston's Theo Epstein, who said he tried it in high school but quit after one season. "It took away from the game," he said. "Your starting pitcher would be playing your team, and you'd have mixed loyalties." As a lifelong Red Sox fan, Epstein explained, he'd suffered enough already.

As the local writers peel off, the mob around Beane has come down to me and a bronze statue formerly known as Sig. The moment I tell Beane about Tout Wars and the existence of national "expert" leagues, it's clear my suspicions were correct.

"That's pretty cool," he says.

Beane hasn't just played fantasy baseball, he's tried just about every variety. As a kid he tore through Strat-O-Matic and grew to love another tabletop game, *Sports Illustrated*'s All-Time All-Star Baseball. "I used to platoon Rudy York," he says, "and he'd hit as many home runs as Babe Ruth." In the early 1980s, just as Rotisserie was catching on, Beane invented a simplified form of the game with categories like runs and errors and recruited some of his teammates in the Mets system to join him.

And a few years ago, Beane started a fantasy league in the A's front office with several employees including his assistant, Paul DePodesta, who's now the GM of the Los Angeles Dodgers. It was a different format than Tout Wars: Rosters consisted of a batting lineup and three pitchers. Every player in the majors was eligible at the draft, and the categories were more along the lines of the stats Beane prizes most, like OPS, or "on base plus slugging."

"I had McGwire, Maddux, Bonds, and Belle, back when Belle was still good," he says, smiling at the memory. "I've always had a passion for creating teams." At this point, Sig, snapping out of his reverie, asks Beane if his experiences with these games helped him when he became a baseball executive. Beane laughs. "Some would say it hurt me. I went from being a ballplayer to a geek."

My next question, naturally, is whether he has any advice on running a Roto team. "Look for value, like you're running a business," he says. "Take an actuarial approach. Be dispassionate and always trust your paradigm." (I feel Sig's eyes burning a hole in the side of my head.) "Even if you know the deck is stacked in your favor," Beane continues, "you still have to have the discipline to trust the math and the cojones to go to the ATM. The more unemotional you are, the more actuarial, the better."

It's almost game time, and as I prepare to leave the clubhouse, I notice Sig madly digging through his backpack. A few seconds later, he's pressing something into Beane's hands. It's the Sig brochure.

Beane flips through it quickly, finds the quotes, and is suddenly engrossed. He loves quotes. Desperate to salvage *something* from the flaming wreckage of all my arguments with Sig, something that will convince him that scouting ballplayers is more than just a waste of time, I ask Beane if there's something in particular he looks for when evaluating players at spring training.

"Not really," he says matter-of-factly, his eyes still roaming the brochure. "Spring training doesn't mean anything."

Day Nine: The Rangers

Slept in. Drank beer by the pool.

Boot Camp

March 21–25

Donald Haworth wasn't much of a Rotisserie player—until he had a heart attack. Forced by law to take six months off, the Florida air-traffic controller bought every book and magazine, crisscrossed the state to watch spring-training games, and spent seventy hours a week preparing scouting reports. In the end, he drafted forty-one teams. "I don't think I'm a junkie," he says. "Just above average."

· · ·

When you're drafting a team in an expert Rotisserie league where the results are posted on the Internet and dissected by fans in a live chatroom, it's not enough just to plop down at the table and start chucking out bids.

You need a plan.

As much as Rotisserie is a game of baseball smarts, it's also a contest of economics, mathematics, and game theory. Knowing which players are likely to overachieve is meaningless unless you can figure out a way to exploit the draft to acquire them for less than they're worth. So over the years, Tout Wars contestants have learned to think like villains in a James Bond movie. Every spring they come to the auction armed with strategies that are, at least in their minds, equal parts brilliant, befuddling, and diabolical.

When these gimmicks succeed, they become part of the Rotisserie lexicon. In addition to Shandler's classic LIMA Plan, any serious player has heard of Stars and Scrubs, where you compensate for a shortage of medium talent by splitting your roster between expensive players and dollar specials. The Sweeney Gambit calls for eschewing overpriced sluggers to focus on hitters with high averages, and the Labadini Plan advocates spending only nine dollars, the bare minimum, for your nine pitchers. The goal of the Sandra Bernhard Strategy is to form a team that finishes fourth in every statistical category, producing a winning roster that is, in the words of creator Mike Vogel, "so ugly it's kind of beautiful."

It's now March 21, and after three solid months of research and a bumpy flight home from Phoenix, I have one week left to prepare for the auction and, most important, to come up with a plan of my own, something that'll make Dr. No look like a garden-variety tax cheat.

To minimize distractions and promote obsessiveness, I've kidnapped Sig and Nando and driven them to an undisclosed location two hours from Manhattan for five days of growing beards and running numbers, the Rotisserie equivalent of basic training at Camp Lejeune. It was, as you can imagine, a rather awkward concept to explain to my wife. "You're leaving to do *what?*"

Ten hours into the exercise, the three of us are gathered at a table that's covered by power cords, cellphones, pocket calculators, books, magazines, and greasy paper plates. With no takeout for miles, our meals consist of burgers and more burgers, punctuated only by Bonecrusher's signature dish, scrambled eggs with mystery spices.

After a period of mutual suspicion, Sig and Nando have set aside their ideological differences and become accommodating teammates, if not friends. When Sig launches into a riff about Markov modeling or something else that might make an old scout choke on his Copenhagen, Nando calmly turns his ballcap backward and disappears behind his computer screen. When Nando gets to talking about how Juan Gonzalez bought a pharmacy in Puerto Rico or Rocco Baldelli's little brother is allergic to peanuts, Sig politely excuses himself and heads to the kitchen for a beer. Four months ago I didn't know either of these guys, but now I have a pretty good idea what they're going to say before they form the words.

In a few weeks I will approach my first major-league ballplayer and say, in all seriousness, "Dude, you're on my Rotisserie team." But at this moment, what's even harder for me to fathom is that we're not alone. Across the country, from the tip of Long Island to the shores of Malibu, thousands maybe even millions of schmucks just like us are trying to untie the same Gordian knot: how to predict *everything* that's going to happen in the upcoming baseball season, down to the last run scored, and use this knowledge to humiliate others.

Rotisserie baseball may be the most ridiculous duplication of effort in the history of human affairs, but that's hardly a concern. For the next four days our universe begins with Paul Abbott and ends with Alec Zumwalt.

———

Before we start formulating a draft plan, there's another small job on our agenda: determining the precise value, in Rotisserie terms, of every player who may set foot in an AL dugout.

Considering that each of the twelve Tout Wars teams will purchase twenty-three players for its active roster and another six reserves in a separate draft, that's 348 people, all of whom we'll have to be ready to make lightning judgments about. But when you add in all the other players who are eligible to be chosen, that's another two hundred at least. To tackle the job, we've assembled two very different analytical systems: Zoladex, Sig's player-projection and auction-management machine, and something called Hunchmaster, a system for grading players intuitively that Nando's been tinkering with for two months. Nobody's going home until they're both off the gurney.

Our first priority is Zoladex, which is already weighing in at a healthy two megabytes. With its systems fully synched and its numbers calibrated to the thousandth of a decimal point, it's just as sophisticated as anything you'll find in the average major-league front office. But in the context of Tout Wars, it's still inferior equipment. After two months of work, Sig's attempt to match the predictive accuracy of the guys who build these things professionally has come up short. When he ran last season's results through Zoladex, the other mathematicians had him beat by a margin of about 6 percent. Sig took the defeat hard. He's not accustomed to being stumped by the best minds at NASA, let alone a bunch of Rotisserie hacks. "Someday I'll get there," he vows.

In the meantime, we decide to cannibalize. After studying their methodologies, Sig proposes that we take the fundamental algorithm used in Tom Tippett's Diamond Mind Baseball and the playing time projections from Nate Silver's PECOTA to form a hybrid. After a full day of maniacal mouse clicking, he's essentially lifted the drive train from one system and the chassis from the other, and soon we have a spreadsheet with the likely stats for every American League player translated into Rotisserie dollars. Sig considers his job done.

"Anybody want a beer?" he says.

On the long drive from the city, I'd thought about trying to prepare Sig for what was about to happen to Zoladex: that I might want to make a few tweaks to his numbers, based on some theories I developed at spring training. But I'd chickened out. Ever since that day in Arizona when I dared to question the scientific method, Sig has been awfully hard to argue with. In fact, he's taken it upon himself to examine and then critique everything I've ever done: from refinancing my mortgage to cutting back on carbohydrates. "I should show you an article I have in *Scientific American* about what science knows about a good diet," he said. So when Sig returns from the kitchen with a Michelob, I try to break the news as gingerly as possible. "I want to make a few little changes, nothing major."

At the loudest point of the ensuing shouting match, Sig slaps both hands on the table and tells me, in essence, that my head is lodged so far up my ass that I might as well be talking to my pancreas. "PECOTA and Diamond Mind have a proven track record," he snorts. "There's no reason to think *you* can do better." Just as I'm about to pull Nando into the argument for backup, he shrewdly grabs the sports section and slinks off to the bathroom.

Ours is the same battle going on right now between the old scouts and the Sabermetricians. I'm convinced that my intuition is valuable, while Sig would rather swallow a carrot peeler than mess with the best data. At the end of the day, I'm a humanist and Sig is a techno-crat, and neither of us is eager to change.

The trouble is that right now, Sig holds all the cards. To make our blended approach work, I've already embraced the numbers to a de-gree that I never imagined I could. Now it's Sig's turn to take a few steps in the direction of the old scouts. If he does, we'll be halfway to glory. If he refuses, I'll be left to fend for myself and he'll be walking back to Manhattan.

When the hollering subsides, Sig sits still for a few beats, trying to simmer down. He takes a pull on his beer, sets it down gently, and then claps his hands. "Okay," he says, smiling. "I'll do whatever you want. Just make sure you register my opposition."

Adjustment 1: Playing Time

To predict a ballplayer's performance before the season, you must know precisely how much he's going to play. There are dozens of variables that go into this, from injuries to slumps to whether or not his manager eats a balanced nutritional breakfast on any given morn-ing. You can't divine these numbers from a laptop; they have to be eyeballed.

At Baseball Prospectus, this is an annual chore that requires every staff writer to take four teams and, through whatever means possible, estimate how many innings each pitcher will throw and how many times every position player will come to bat. The results are dumped into PECOTA and treated as gospel.

While they've clearly done a fine job, I'm convinced that in some cases the information I picked up at spring training is better. While BP says that Kansas City's Tony Graffanino will get 250 at-bats this season, Allard Baird, the team's GM, told me the likely number is closer to 350. And given what I learned in Florida about Boston's David Ortiz, I have no trouble giving him an additional 50 AB on top of the Prospectus estimate of 453. In the end, we tweak the numbers for about fifty hitters.

Adjustment 2: Injuries

Each year, an insurance company that underwrites baseball contracts performs an exhaustive study, commissioned by the league, on player injuries. The results are printed in a book with a red cover and sent to each front office. But by order of the commissioner's office, it's never distributed to the press.

After making a few calls, several pages of the "Red Book" are burbling through the fax at the undisclosed location. Most of this data isn't relevant to Rotisserie, but there's one feature that is: an actuarial table that shows the likelihood of injury for all players by age and position. It tells you, for instance, that a left-handed twenty-three-year-old starting pitcher has a 20 percent better chance of landing on the disabled list than a catcher in his late thirties.

Using this table, we rank every ballplayer by his relative risk of injury. Then we take the fifty biggest "ifs" and dock them the equivalent of ten days' work. Among the losers by this measure: Kevin Brown, Derek Jeter, and Nomar Garciaparra.

Adjustment 3: Steroids

Just after the 2003 World Series, word came out that 5 to 7 percent of the survey drug tests given to major leaguers had turned up positive for steroids. The s-word was suddenly on everybody's lips, including those of President Bush, who'd railed against it in his State of the Union address.

Most Rotisserie players cope with the steroids question the only way they know how: They ignore it. And from a statistical perspective, it's hard to blame them. Even if you suspect a ballplayer is taking performance-enhancing drugs, it's usually impossible to know for certain. Even if you do know, it doesn't become a statistical issue unless you're also certain he's stopped. And even in that case, how many home runs do you dock?

During spring training, I committed myself to getting an off-the-record education on this subject. I learned about all the diuretics and masking agents that players take to beat the tests and got a rundown of people who are widely considered to be users. But time and again I heard two surprising things. First, that contrary to public perception, muscle-bound power hitters weren't the only ones using these drugs. In fact, they might be just as prevalent among *pitchers*. To hit a lot of homers, I was told, you have to be a pretty good hitter in the first place. But for pitchers, the difference between the majors and oblivion can be as simple as a fastball clocked at 92 versus one at 88 or the ability to pitch every day rather than once in every five. In some cases, pitchers were using steroids to close the gap.

The second surprise was the consensus opinion that a majority of players who'd been taking steroids had quit. If that's true, I thought, baseball could have a new problem on its hands: an epidemic of pitchers losing velocity and suddenly getting stormed like the Bastille. My goal, then, was to find a way to protect myself at Tout Wars by drafting pitchers who rely more on guile than gas.

To do this, Sig helps me come up with a more sophisticated twist on my crude "finesse" scale from spring training. Dipping into our exclusive data, we take each pitcher's average fastball velocity from the season before and multiply it by his "well hit average," or the percentage of hard-hit balls he gave up. Then we divide that figure by his "chase rate," or the percentage of his pitches hitters swung at outside the strike zone. The point was to identify those pitchers who fool hitters into swinging at garbage and induce a lot of weak hits without necessarily throwing very hard.

At the top of the scale, to nobody's surprise, was Boston knuckleballer Tim Wakefield, who rarely tops 77 on the radar gun. He was followed by pitchers like Curt Schilling, Miguel Batista, and Brad Radke, each of whom got a healthy boost in Zoladex value.

Adjustment 4: Pitch Efficiency

This idea came to me back in Florida during my conversation with Miguel Batista, the budding novelist and litigator of the Toronto Blue Jays. Batista had impressed me with his opinion on the topic of strikeouts, which he considers vastly overrated. "A perfect game isn't twenty-seven straight outs," he said, "it's twenty-seven *pitches*."

For at least a decade, baseball has been suffering from something I'll call the Nolan Ryan syndrome, the idea that the true measure of a pitcher's manhood is how many batters he rings up. The problem with this way of thinking, according to several pitching coaches, is that strikeouts are a poor use of pitches. If given a choice between a pitcher who throws three blazing fastballs to get an out and a guy who throws one lazy sinker that's bounced harmlessly to the short-stop, they all said they'd prefer the latter. While the result is the same, the pitcher with the sinker has cut his workload by two pitches, or 67 percent. If he keeps that up, he might be able to pitch a complete game instead of hitting the showers after six innings.

As a group, pitchers are rather like thoroughbred horses: ex-tremely expensive and, in many cases, too strong for their own bod-ies. The shoulder rotation of a big-league pitcher may be the fastest motion in sports. Scientists say that if a pitcher could hold his peak speed for two full seconds rather than a fraction of one, his arm would make *fifty* full revolutions. It's little wonder, then, that pitchers get injured more often than do other players and cost teams hundreds of millions in blown salary. Teaching pitchers to be more efficient makes good economic sense.

As I made my rounds in spring training, I got the feeling pitchers across the league were being told to ease up on the unhittable smoke and throw more sinkers, cutters, and breaking balls to induce quick outs. But it was Baltimore GM Mike Flanagan who swayed me for good. By teaching starters to be more efficient, he said, the Orioles hoped to someday lower the number of pitchers on the roster from twelve to nine.

To put this information to use in Tout Wars, Sig, skeptical as he was, performed a clever bit of quantitative gymnastics. He generated a list of the American League starters who'd thrown the most pitches per batter—in other words, the ones who'd been the least efficient. If pitchers were, indeed, under orders to cut workloads, it stood to rea-son that these pitchers were the ones who'd benefit most from the change. They would pitch more innings and, if all went well, shave a few points from their ERAs.

To all the names at the top of the list—Javier Vazquez, Rich Harden, Johan Santana, and C. C. Sabathia, among others—we gave a 10 percent innings bonus, making them all a bit more valuable on the Zoladex dollar scale.

———

Hunchmaster, our private database of the wholly unscientific, has two intellectual fathers.

The first is something called DiamondView, an internal computer system the Cleveland Indians built. In Florida, Mark Shapiro waved me over to his PC to have a look, clicked his mouse, and *poof!* up came an old scouting report on shortstop prospect Brandon Phillips that said he's "not maintaining consistent power." Another click and *pow!* a log of 2001 trade discussions with the New York Mets about José Reyes. For every player in baseball since 1984 the system has scouting reports, psychological profiles, detailed injury reports, and, as soon as they can get it synched up, digital video. As far as I know, it's the world's richest bank of subjective baseball data.

The next model was something Nando stumbled across in the archives of the Baseball Hall of Fame. In 1938, Philip K. Wrigley, the owner of the Chicago Cubs, hired a psychologist named Coleman Griffith to spend two years following the team and analyzing the psyches of the players. Griffith, who's widely regarded as the father of modern sports psychology, started something called the Chicago National League Ball Club Experimental Laboratories and began issuing the results of his studies—some of which were a bit naïve. (He blamed the rampant "chasing of women" on the large meals ballplayers eat after games.) But he also hit on an interesting concept: giving each player a numerical "grade" for each of fourteen traits including mental quickness, courage, loyalty, and emotional balance.

The basic principle of both these systems was roughly the same: to create the fullest possible picture of a ballplayer by collecting and ranking subjective data the way statisticians did the numbers.

After three months of slavish work, Nando's player knowledge borders on the medically inadvisable. As a consequence he's developed almost as many hunches about players as I have. Some of these ideas are shrewd and others totally irrational, but rather than let them flit away I wanted to find a way to preserve them like the Indians do and, if possible, to grade them the way Griffith did.

Enter Hunchmaster. There are thirty Hunchmaster categories in all, from sensible stuff like the private opinions of major-league scouts I talked to, to purely superficial judgments like whether a guy seems to have "maturity" or "intensity." If a player fares well in a category, he gets a few points. If he doesn't, points are deducted.

Our first challenge is figuring out how to value all the information we've collected. By scouring clips and public records, Nando has compiled some unusual lists: which players are single, which ones have kids (and how many), which ones have been arrested and when, which ones are devout Christians, and which ones have recently seen their salaries more than double. While we want to use these traits as Hunchmaster categories, we have no idea what to make of them. Does a guy get bonus points for getting married or demerits? And does finding God make you a star?

For help on this, we naturally turn to Sig, who's been sitting across from us trying to depersonalize. To talk us out of it, he says that any research he might do on these questions would be compromised by a small data sample.

Nando and I nod absently.

"You don't care, do you?"

We shake our heads.

Sighing heavily, Sig makes a copy of a spreadsheet on his laptop that contains the complete stats for every major leaguer since 1950, broken down by year. He instructs us to take every player on one of our lists, find his name, then enter the exact date of each major life event, from marriages and arrests to moments of religious conversion. While we're doing this, Sig works up a program to compare each player's statistics before and after these milestones.

The results, unscientific as they may be, are nonetheless fascinating. Marriage has *no* impact on performance. Players who double their salaries play only slightly better the following season. Those who are arrested for drugs, guns, or lewd conduct show no appreciable change, but anyone who commits assault sees a performance dip. Having a first or second child isn't significant, but 80 percent of the players who had a *third* child saw their statistics decline more than a typical player of similar age. As for the impact of religion, Sig's analysis yielded a troubling conclusion: "Turning to God," he says, "costs you 2.5 runs a season."

Once we'd finished incorporating all this information into Hunchmaster, Nando and I turned to the final and most unconventional category. Back in February, while trawling for any and all forms of baseball knowledge, Bonecrusher had Googled the term "baseball astrology" just to see what would happen.

There was a match.

Andrea Mallis lives in Berkeley. She's been an astrologer since 1989. Her fee is ninety dollars per hour, and her specialty is reading the charts of major-league ballplayers. "With four planets in Virgo, I'm a rather analytical soul, dedicated and serious about my craft," she wrote by way of introduction. "I do a lot of research and number crunching myself, as astrology is a metaphysical science. I'm not a psychic that gets information from thin air. . . . Not that there's anything wrong with that :)." Right then and there, we added a new category to Hunchmaster called "Zodiac."

I've hired Andrea Mallis to run charts on twelve players we've had trouble making judgments about. Since Mallis gets up in the afternoon and works through the night, we made arrangements to talk late on Wednesday, and at the appointed hour she picks up the phone, cheerful and full of spunk, ready to interpret the planets.

Yankee pitcher Kevin Brown, with his Mars in Virgo, should have an excellent year, she tells me, gaining strength in August and September. On the other hand, Seattle closer Eddie Guardado seems likely to struggle with a cycle of low energy. Cleveland's C. C. Sabathia, with Jupiter nine degrees Virgo, was a good bet to pitch well until late June, when he might suffer a setback. In a bid to engage Sig in this process, I decided to ask Andrea Mallis about Jarrod Washburn, the Angels pitcher he'd cornered at spring training. Mallis says Washburn will be fine for the first two months.

"Then what?" I ask.

"Then Neptune gets in the picture."

After I hang up, Nando opens Hunchmaster and we begin trying to assign Zodiac "scores" to these players. This results in a lengthy conversation about the relative merits of a favorable Mars cycle versus the potentially deleterious effects of a Saturn return.

Pfffft.

Sig opens beer number five.

———

With our player evaluations squared away, it's time to come up with the Plan.

As a general rule, the best way to build a successful Rotisserie draft strategy is to zig when everybody else is zagging, to find some small inefficiency in the player market that's invisible to everyone else. After much thought, I'm convinced the key to dominating this year's draft is coming up with a clever approach to pitching.

To statisticians, pitchers are a predictive nuisance. While hitters' performances can be projected with 70 percent accuracy, pitchers are so skittish and fragile that even the best mathematicians are happy if their predictions are only half right. As a result, my Tout Wars opponents, math majors that they are, tend to look at pitchers as if they were New York taxicabs: The only question when you hire one is how much it's going to stink. And if it's too putrid, there's usually another one right down the block. Jason Grey's success has only reinforced the idea that pitchers are interchangeable commodities: He's won the last two titles by spending less on arms than anyone else.

But this year, there's a pretty good argument for spending *more* on pitching. In the off-season, some of the better starting pitchers in the National League—stars like Schilling, Brown, and Vazquez—defected to the AL, which suggests the league's overall quality has improved at the high end. If my opponents continue their miserly ways, we might be able to pick up a few stellar arms for a lot less than they're worth.

The established standard for Rotisserie auctions is that you should spend 70 percent of your budget on your fourteen hitters and 30 percent on your nine pitchers. This ratio is so ingrained that most auctions, Tout Wars included, automatically fall within a single percentage point of it. The problem is, I have no idea who came up with this ratio or how they did the math.

Looking for answers, I dig out John Benson's 2003 Rotisserie guidebook, where he writes that a good Roto team is like a conservative investment portfolio: "You don't want risk." To Benson, predictability has value, the same way blue-chip stocks often sell for more than the calculated value of the company's underlying assets and cash flows. Nothing derails a ballclub, real or imaginary, like an expensive flop, he continues, so it makes sense to pay a premium for security. Therefore, he writes, Roto players generally spend more on hitting and less on pitching.

But when it comes time to explain the mathematical justification for the 70/30 split, Benson reveals something stunning. There isn't one. "Someday someone (probably an insurance underwriter by profession) will give us the correct calculations to discount pitcher values and enhance hitter value," he writes, "but no one has done it yet."

After reading this aloud to Sig and Nando, the three of us stare at one another, blinking in confusion. Basically, Benson is saying that the only reason Rotisserie players stick to this spending pattern is because that's just *what you do.* My Tout Wars rivals, for all their statistical savvy, were operating their drafts in a market where prices were governed by some arbitrary standard that nobody had apparently bothered to research. "Just out of curiosity," I say, glancing at Sig, "what would happen if we spent 50 percent of our money on pitchers?"

By now, Sig's conditioned response to any big idea of mine is to flail at it as if it were a flying cockroach. But after a few abortive attempts, he seems to be thinking out loud. "There are five pitching and five hitting categories, so exactly half the points come from pitching. Of course, only nine of the twenty-three players on a team are pitchers, so that's 39 percent of the players. But if the experts only pay 30 percent for them, that puts an additional constraint on the bidding process."

I'm not sure where Sig is going, but I sense momentum. He grabs the Benson book and reads the passage over again. "That's all wrong," he says after pondering a while. "When you buy stock, you don't want risk, you'll pay to have stability. But in a league where the only goal is to win, that's not the case." If there's no prize for finishing second in Tout Wars, he continues, you actually want to *embrace* risk and variation. "You'll have trouble sleeping at night if you have risky stocks," Sig says, "but in Rotisserie you may have trouble sleeping if you're stuck with a bunch of boring-ass players." The best way to win, he says, is to draft risky players and hope, in the end, that they all hit the high end of their potential. And what could be riskier than investing in pitchers?

Right then, with the smell of mystery spices lingering in the air, three months of exhaustive research starts to jell. While the other Touts continue to treat pitchers as unremarkable taxis, we would come to the auction ready to commandeer all the limousines. Since the best pitchers are generally nominated in the first two rounds of the auction, we could scoop up three or four of these plush Lincolns before anybody realizes what we're doing. And if we value them correctly, we'll surely get them for less than they're worth. Sig's goofy grin has returned from a long hibernation, and Nando is actually laughing. "It's brilliant!" he says.

The more we think, the more sense it makes. If we build a staff that dominates every pitching category, we'll generate such a fat lead that by midseason, we can trade some of our pitching for offense without losing any ranking points. The plan also makes sense in a season when there's a lot of uncertainty about steroids. If it's true that most players have stopped taking them, it's safe to say that a few expensive power hitters won't earn their salaries this season. So by waiting a few months to trade pitching for offense, we'll have a chance to see for ourselves which sluggers are legitimate.

Nando, who's been hunched over scrawling numbers, holds up a sheet of scratch paper. By his calculation this "paradigm," as Billy Beane would call it, should give us 55 ranking points in pitching, and if we managed to finish only seventh in every offensive category we'd still have 80 points, which would all but guarantee us a finish in the top two or three.

"Game over," he says.

———

Two sheets of paper.

As we pack up to leave the undisclosed location (it was a beach house on the north fork of Long Island), the sum total of everything I've learned about major-league ballplayers in three months fits on two alphabetical lists, one for hitters and one for pitchers, that take up 360 square inches. Next to each name there's a Zoladex dollar value from zero to forty-five and a Hunchmaster grade from A to F.

There are 650 names in all.

To produce them, I've spent $7,400 on scouting trips to Arizona, Florida, New Orleans, and Puerto Rico, another $1,800 on computer components and software upgrades, and $895 on books, magazines, encyclopedias, and subscriptions to every Roto Web site that accepted my credit card. Sig's and Nando's salaries and expenses amount to another $3,000 a month, and considering all the extras, from the Stalker to my astrology bill, these two pieces of paper are worth about $19,500, which is roughly the cost of a nicely equipped Subaru Legacy. For the record, the official Tout Wars entry fee is $75.

Admiring our handiwork I see that the most valuable player on Zoladex is Red Sox ace Pedro Martinez at $45, followed by Mariano Rivera and Alex Rodriguez at $38 and Curt Schilling, Javier Vazquez, and Boston closer Keith Foulke at $37. On Hunchmaster, the top five are Schilling, David Ortiz, Miguel Tejada, Kevin Brown, and Gary Sheffield. So, according to my combination of cold numbers, gut hunches, and old-fashioned scouting, the most valuable player in the American League is Boston's Schilling, who cracked both top fives.

If he sucks this year, I'll be a dope.

On the Long Island Expressway bound for Manhattan and my own bed, which I've slept in exactly twice this month, it dawns on me that the Tout Wars draft is now forty-eight hours away. I have never worked harder on any one project, and from the haggard looks on their faces I think I can say the same for my employees. Sig is sprawled across the backseat, snoring like a night watchman.

From the passenger's seat, Nando turns around to have a look at him and starts to smirk.

"What?" I say.

"I can't wait to see the look on his face when you take Kevin Brown just because of the astrologer."

We laugh.

Glancing in the rearview mirror, I see Sig's eyes pop open. It takes him a moment to realize that he wasn't dreaming, then a few more beats to realize that Nando was only kidding. "Don't worry about it," he finally says, settling back down to resume his nap. "I'm going to be on sedatives."

The Cloak of Camaraderie

March 26

When Sandra and Jock Thompson decided to join the same Rotisserie league, their wedding vows were all but forgotten. While Jock was on a business trip and nowhere near a computer, Sandra tried to trade him a pitcher who'd just been demoted to the bullpen. And when Jock wanted to make a trade, he followed Sandra around the house for seven days and even blocked the door to the shower stall while she was still inside.

In the end, she relented. "It's called wearing down your trading partner," he says.

· · ·

If you subscribe to the notion that the hippest Friday-night party scenes in New York are the ones that haven't been discovered yet, there may be no place more avant garde than the Wyndham Garden hotel at LaGuardia Airport.

By eight o'clock, there's a row of budget business travelers at the lobby bar, their tie loops yanked open, talking to a waitress with a pencil in her hair bun. Hovering near a neglected jukebox is the city's least ambitious barfly, a gawky woman well north of forty in a leather miniskirt. A disclaimer on the restaurant menu says, "The Wyndham LaGuardia is not associated in any way with the Wyndham Manhattan."

Roger that.

Tonight, however, unbeknownst to the other guests, the Wyndham is playing host to the world's greatest concentration of Rotisserie baseball starpower. Nine of my eleven Tout Wars opponents are here, the only exceptions being Steve Moyer, who's driving in from Pennsylvania in the morning, and the famously elusive Mat Olkin of *USA Today*, whose whereabouts are unknown. In fourteen hours, these men will meet in a downstairs ballroom to match wits in the 2004 American League Tout Wars draft. Until then, they will shun the temptations of Manhattan to smush five tables together and drink Pepsi.

After taking our seats among them, Sig, Nando, and I settle in to listen. Our goal is to gather as much intelligence as possible without mentioning *anything* about the scope of our own preparations. None of these guys has any idea how much work we've done, and we're determined to keep it that way. The topic under discussion when we arrive is an obscure Texas backup catcher named Rod Barajas. "Am I right," asks Jason Grey, just in from Arizona, "that we're going to get in a bidding war tomorrow for Rod Barajas?"

"Yes, yes. Barajas!" somebody says.

"My boy Barajas!"

"A toast to Rod Barajas."

Pepsi mugs clink.

It's safe to say that collectively the men at this table know more about Rod Barajas than Barajas knows about himself. They've studied his BPV and his VORP, his rising BB% and his promisingly low G/F ratio. They've talked to scouts about his struggles with right-handed pitching and monitored his recovery from wrist surgery. The idea of a bidding war is only a joke—Barajas is a $1 player at best. The real point of the exercise is to revel in the fact that within this unusual circle, a third-string Texas catcher with a funny name needs absolutely no introduction. "To me," says Matthew Berry, a Hollywood screenwriter and Rotisserie columnist just in from the West Coast, "the great thing about fantasy baseball is that you've got to know who the fuck Rod Barajas *is*."

But for a bunch of hobbyists who've known one another for years, the vibe at the table is surprisingly awkward, the conversation halting. Every time someone speaks, all heads turn. At first I just assumed these guys were a bunch of social klutzes, but after a few minutes I realized the problem. For five months, to the exclusion of everything else in their lives, these men have spent every spare moment predicting the future performance of major leaguers—and now, on the eve of the auction, nobody wants to betray even the slightest prejudice. With the topic of ballplayers off the table, nobody has much of anything to say.

Since I left him in Arizona, Jason Grey has grown the sort of goatee favored by ballplayers. He's sitting at the center of the table in a white polo shirt with a Mastersball logo, clearly savoring his role as the man to beat. Last year's victory was anything but flashy. After what he considered a miserable draft, Grey began upending his Tout Wars roster with his trademark relentlessness: juggling pitchers, making bold trades, and scouring clubhouses for tips on free agents. By the final day of the season, he was clinging to a tiny lead over Rick Fogel of USA Stats that, according to Grey's calculations, could have been erased by a single home run. He hadn't clinched the title until the eighth inning of the final game.

By custom, the defending Tout Wars champion is also the auction's primary target. Every time Grey bids on a player tomorrow, it's almost guaranteed that the other Touts will gang up on him to drive up the price. "My whole strategy is to screw Jason Grey," Matt Berry acknowledges. For his part, Grey seems thoroughly unfazed. After hearing Berry's wisecrack, he picks up my tape recorder and holds it to his chin. "I will beat Matt Berry," he says.

Pale and balding with the puffy eyes of a haphazard sleeper, Berry, thirty-four, writes a prominent column for Rotoworld and operates his own Web site under his nom de plume, the Talented Mr. Roto. Berry favors a wardrobe that runs to L.A. grunge, if there is such a thing: all jeans, sneakers, and T-shirts. In Hollywood, he's got television credits ranging from hits like *Married . . . with Children* to unmitigated bombs like *Kirk*. His signature credit is having collaborated on the screenplay for *Crocodile Dundee in Los Angeles*, the third installment of the Paul Hogan trilogy, which grossed a respectable twenty-five million dollars. His Hollywood career is a classic study in feast and famine. "Every spring for the last ten years I've had to look for a job," he says. "I've basically slept my way to the middle."

Berry wasn't formally invited to Tout Wars. He's basically a gate-crasher or, as he puts it, "a weasel." When a Rotoworld colleague backed out at the last minute in 2003, Berry swooped in and claimed the spot. Though he's been playing Rotisserie since he was fourteen and recently won a title in a second-tier expert league, he's the first to admit that his technical expertise is not the deepest. "I'm not going to outstat a guy like Shandler," he says. "I'm not going to outscout Jason Grey, either."

What he can do, better than anyone else at this table, is talk. After years of experience in Hollywood, Berry knows how to work a room: setting the tone, reading the flow, projecting confidence, and, when necessary, picking somebody apart with a clever barb. The result is an arsenal of draft-table trash talk that, even when tinged with humor, can be highly effective at crucial moments. "I've been in auctions where people have been, like, 'Shut up,' " he says. "The minute they say that, I know I've gotten to them."

At the moment, Berry's favored target is Jeff Erickson of Roto-Wire, Rotoworld's chief competitor. Tall and trim with a neatly clipped goatee, Erickson, thirty-two, bears a passing resemblance to Ben Affleck. He finished dead last the season before with a cautiously constructed team that, to Berry, was a nearly perfect reflection of the man who assembled it.

"Virulently boring," he says.

Erickson endures Berry's taunts by turning a shade of crimson and scooching farther down in his vinyl booth. Born in Indianapolis and one of three Touts with law degrees, he's earnest, conservative, and businesslike, or as he likes to say, "risk averse." Erickson's idea of a ribald story is the time he cut short a weekend in Las Vegas to drive home to L.A. to settle a traffic ticket. "I wouldn't make a good character in a fictional novel," he concedes.

As a Rotisserie player, Erickson favors hitters with plate discipline, even though walks are not a Tout Wars category. He rarely makes trades, and when he talks about his auction strategy he likes to use the word "nuances." In five tries at Tout, he's finished in the bottom half all but once.

In the Rotisserie business, however, Erickson may be the biggest swashbuckler at the table. RotoWire, the Los Angeles–based Rotisserie news site he helped launch with some college friends, sells something in the neighborhood of ten thousand subscriptions a year, making it larger than even Ron Shandler's online empire.

Since last year's drubbing, Erickson has spent the off-season simmering with an uncharacteristic intensity. "I probably dropped an F bomb or two," he says. To get psyched up for tomorrow's draft, he's been watching Derek Jeter's 2003 Opening Day shoulder injury on video as many times as he can stand it. This season, he tells me, "there's a definite need for redemption."

At the head of the table is Trace Wood, thirty-nine, the competition's resident intellectual. With an upturned chin, a pair of round spectacles, and a taste in literature that runs from Joyce and Voltaire to Douglas Hofstadter's *Gödel, Escher, Bach*, he observes the proceedings with the bemused expression of a man who's entirely comfortable with his own convictions. His personal baseball blog, the Long Gandhi, was named in honor of his hero, former Brooklyn Dodgers owner Branch Rickey, who used to be called "the Mahatma." Wood lives in northern Virginia with his wife and daughter, where he makes a living managing rental properties—a job that leaves him free to spend twenty hours a week watching baseball, contributing to Roto magazines and Web sites, and working as an Internet "datacaster" at Baltimore Orioles games.

At the auction, Wood likes to target inexpensive players who, in his opinion, have been mismanaged or unlucky or underestimated, a strategy he calls the Tao of Boring. While his Orioles job comes with a press credential, he rarely talks to players because, he believes, getting to know them would only cloud his objectivity. "I don't care about players, only about winning."

Joining Wood at the quiet end of the table is Dean Peterson, a

Chicago computer engineer who, if a roll call was taken, might be marked absent. With his strong chin, light-brown eyes, and brown hair graying at the temples, he's as forgettably pleasant as a nightly news anchor. He wears jeans, sneakers, a White Sox golf shirt, and the perfectly benign expression of a conversational voyeur. It seems only fitting that Peterson spent thirteen years at Northrop Grumman, where he helped build a radar jammer for the F-15 fighter jet.

Today, Peterson is manager of technical operations for a suburban Chicago sports data–collection company called STATS, Inc. His office there is a few paces from a chamber called the newsroom, where a dozen or so young, underpaid sports nuts slouch over terminals like stockbrokers, recording every imaginable event that occurs in every ballgame. There are five faxes, seventeen television monitors, and, in the back room, a knot of mainframes and servers that contains the entire corpus of baseball data from the last two decades. If there's a trade or an injury or a bit of press-box scuttlebutt, Peterson hears about it instantly.

Married for only a short time after college, Peterson has since become a gleeful bachelor. "I'm forty-three, but I act twenty-two," he says. He sleeps five hours a night, plays on two softball teams, eats chocolate crepes for breakfast, and plays in so many different fantasy baseball leagues he's lost track. "I've been telling people it's nine," he says. (It's actually *thirteen*.) After finishing no better than fifth in three tries at Tout Wars, he's chosen this year to craft a new draft strategy that suits him to a tee.

The other Windy City representative is Dean Peterson's polar twin. Striding into the Wyndham restaurant in a University of Illinois baseball jersey, 2003 Tout Wars runner-up Rick Fogel is all smiles, handshakes, and howeryadoins delivered with a distinctive *Chicawgo* accent. With his longish locks, sharp features, and fashionable tan, Fogel, forty-eight, might be mistaken for an aging folk rocker. He's not terribly analytical—for seventeen years he's prepared for drafts by simply ranking the players he wants on a legal pad. Instead of generating spreadsheets on summer nights, you'll find him at Wrigley Field, where he attends about twenty Chicago Cubs games a season.

But Fogel is no pushover. By day he's a bankruptcy trustee, a job that requires him to scour the assets of insolvent companies to squeeze out every last dollar—a process that isn't demonstrably different from the way a good Rotisserie player studies the auction pool. In his rookie season he displayed a freakish talent for finding value. "It's all about figuring out how to slice up pies," he says.

Unfortunately he also found more than his share of controversy. After being handpicked to represent a Rotisserie "commissioner" service called USA Stats, Fogel arrived at last year's draft in Chicago to become the first pure living-room player in Tout Wars history. And while he was thrilled to be in the company of the legends he'd been reading about for years, some of the Touts were less than happy to have an amateur in their midst. "None of them knew who I was or cared," Fogel says. When the draft was finished, Fogel turned to the Tout next to him, who'd been tracking bids on a homemade software program, to ask the guy for a critique of his roster. "You're going to finish tenth," the guy said.

But after Fogel ascended slowly into contention ("I could win!" he remembers telling himself), Jason Grey and Lawr Michaels cut a blockbuster deal at the Tout Wars trade deadline that, in his opinion, was an obvious ploy to keep an outsider from winning. Fogel made a stink about it in the league chatroom. "Collusion" was his term for it; "sour grapes" was Grey's response. By the end of the season, Fogel conceded that the trade wasn't *that* lopsided, but he's still not over it. "In my heart of hearts, I felt that was the difference."

The only other Tout Wars rookie, besides me, is Joe Sheehan of Baseball Prospectus, who has dragged his chair away from the table to watch college basketball. Short and round with a stubbly scalp, a rumpled suit, and an incongruously high voice, Sheehan, thirty-three, looks like a lovable bulldog. But beneath this exterior, he's a hypercompetitive native New Yorker with an opinion for every occasion and a temper to behold. His comportment during regular Friday golf outings with friends in Los Angeles has earned him the nickname "The Volcano." While most of the Touts cover baseball exclusively from a Roto perspective, Sheehan's regular column is a running critique of major-league managers and executives that rarely, if ever, ventures into fantasy talk. But even though Tout Wars will be his first expert Rotisserie competition, he's hardly lacking in confidence. "I'm not intimidated," he told me, hotly, when we met the night before. "I'm intimidated when I have to call Billy Beane and talk baseball."

Sheehan's employer, Baseball Prospectus, began as a group of baseball wonks who met in an antediluvian Internet chatroom to plot baseball's quantitative revolution. As such, it's always been a shoestring operation. Even today, with a subscriber base in the thousands, the company has no physical address, and Sheehan is one of only three full-time staffers. In the early days, he mailed out the first of BP's annual books from his apartment while working days as managing editor of *Law Office Computing*.

But with their brash tone and unapologetic passion for the power of advanced statistics, Sheehan and his colleagues have, for better or worse, bullied their way into the consciousness of baseball executives. "I know Joe," Billy Beane said when I ran through a list of my Tout Wars opponents. "His stuff is outstanding."

In the main, BP writers consider themselves "serious" Sabermetric purists who resent Rotisserie baseball, not just for the outdated statistics it uses but because they believe its dorky image has colored the entire analytical movement. In other words, they're the kind of analysts who thumb their noses at "fantasy guys" like Ron Shandler. "We have some fantasy snobs on the staff," Sheehan concedes.

For this, BP has long been viewed in Rotisserie circles with a combination of fear and contempt. And now that BP is starting to market products for fantasy players, the animosity is barely contained. "Baseball Prospectus will rot your brain," Lawr Michaels told me privately. "They're so friggin' arrogant," Ron Shandler said. "Joe Sheehan is one of the only guys over there I have any respect for."

In the middle of the table, smiling subversively, is Lawr Michaels, the 2001 Tout Wars champion who is, at fifty-one, the contest's elder statesman. Tall and lanky with lazy eyelids and a jutting nose that's perpetually red at the tip, Lawr wears his hair in a frizzy mullet that flows from his bald spot down to his shoulders. He has a gristly beard and a diamond earring, and he rarely leaves home in anything but red or black Converse high-tops. The day before, he showed up for a business lunch in Manhattan in a multicolored knit sweater and a black-and-gold Arabian scarf with matching sunglasses. He looked like a cross between Mick Jagger and Natalie Wood.

Michaels has the type of brain that, as he puts it, "makes you walk around the block to get to the house next door." Ask him a simple question, like how he does pitcher projections, and he'll start with a Homer Simpson reference, move on to an anecdote about Zatoichi the blind samurai, then segue into a rant about the Saudis. This will remind him that there are three players in major-league history named Ivan, "not one of whom was Eastern European." By the time he's run out of new tangents, he's forgotten the question.

Michaels has a master's in English with a concentration in nineteenth-century British literature. *Jane Eyre* and *The Mill on the Floss* are two of his favorites and he's written a Dickensian novel about a character who's obsessed with Laundromats. On his fantasy-advice site, CREATiVESPORTS, Michaels writes as many as five columns per week. When he's not doing that, he's playing the guitar in local garage bands with names like Midlife Crisis and Strictly Olga, or typing up existential treatises about baseball or politics or philosophy and sending them to friends. "Lawr," a recipient once reminded him, "there's no Nobel Prize for e-mail."

To pay the bills, Michaels works fifty hours a week for telecom giant SBC, where for many years his job was to step in whenever some enormous system implementation sent all the MBAs and computer scientists scrambling up a tree. It was a job for which he had no formal training, other than a preternatural ability to tolerate chaos. Every time an SBC customer in one of thirteen states signs up for Internet service, the order is processed through a labyrinthine system implemented by Lawr Michaels. "I'm pretty sure I've made them hundreds of millions of dollars," he says. Nevertheless, whenever the techies come to his office to ask him, for example, how far back to set the stubs when the MT goes down, he'll point two thumbs at his chest. "English, dude. Liberal arts."

Michaels considers himself the Zen master of Rotisserie baseball. After absorbing all the data, he tries to view everything through a metaphysical "third eye." In one section of his brain, he says, he's able to store, identify, and compartmentalize numbers for every player in the majors. Then, working from the other side, he looks at a player's circumstances and intuits which direction these numbers will go.

"I can just *feel* it," he says.

Where most Touts come to the auction with at least some sense of what they want to accomplish, Michaels likes to empty his mind and let his subconscious guide him, even if the result looks a bit messy. In his rookie year, he shocked the table by confusing two pitchers with the same name and drafting three catchers, rather than the usual two, which sent the other Touts into peals of laughter. As a result, he doesn't have much credibility. "Kind of a hippie-dippy type," Shandler says. Steve Moyer, never one to mince words, has only this to say: "Lawr Michaels is an idiot."

Truth be told, Michaels is shrewder than he seems. The red sneakers, the wild hair, the strange draft moves, and the fondness for the word "groovin' " are all genuine bits of Lawr, but they're also part of a calculated plan. In his opinion, there's no better strategy in Tout Wars than to be dismissed. If everyone thinks you're a weirdo, he told me, they'll be more inclined to let you do whatever you want. The zany outfits? The player mix-ups? The crazy bids? It's all *deliberate.* "I want to be underestimated," he says. "If somebody underestimates me, I'll cream them every time."

———

For a bunch of intense competitors, the Touts are a pretty incestuous group. Steve Moyer used to work for Jeff Erickson, who does business with Shandler, who buys his statistics from Moyer and is joining a new venture with Matt Berry. Trace Wood has written for Grey and Michaels, and Olkin writes blurbs for just about everybody.

In fact, the impression the Touts like to convey to outsiders is that above all they *like* one another. If Rotisserie is, at bottom, an elaborate excuse to hang out with your buddies, it stands to reason that Rotisserie professionals ought to be role models in this regard, too. "I love everyone in this industry," Erickson says during the evening. "So many great guys!" raves Jason Grey.

Nonetheless, the more successful their businesses become, the more this cloak of camaraderie begins to fray. When you get these entrepreneurs alone, the tone is not nearly so chummy. In fact, there's one guy in the group who's holding back enough grudges and smoldering resentments to fill ten episodes of *The Young and the Restless*. His name is Ron Shandler.

As he sits at the far end of the table following the conversation in a floppy Cardinals cap, Shandler, the Bearded One, looks like an exasperated father wondering how he could have been so indulgent. While he invested almost two decades building his business from scratch, all some of these guys had to do was slap together a Web site and start touting players. "The post-Internet crowd," he calls them. But the real root of Shandler's discontent is something nobody in the elite ranks of Rotisserie could have imagined five years ago, and something no one at this table has the temerity to mention.

Shandler is in a slump.

Back in 1997, after four years of playing in LABR, Shandler was fed up with the event. It bugged him to no end that *USA Today* wouldn't pay travel expenses for the contestants and that the organizers had once asked him to chip in twenty dollars to help pay for a photographer. He thought the league was poorly promoted, overly autocratic, and, since the LABR draft takes place at the beginning of March before major-league teams have any idea what their final rosters will be, not especially meaningful as a pricing guide for the Rotisserie public. When coordinator John Hunt started inviting "regular guys" to the auction table, Shandler thought it dumbed-down the level of play. "It's a concept I absolutely hate," he says.

In Shandler's opinion, there were only about a dozen true Rotisserie experts—legitimate *Touts* who'd played the game for more than a decade and been published to some extent. If he could gather these people together himself, he thought, he could create the ultimate Rotisserie league, a true national championship. And with some advertising and a little promotional razzle-dazzle, it might become a major spectacle, not to mention a brilliant marketing tool for the participants. Shandler organized the first draft in 1998 at the All-Star Café in Manhattan, where seating was provided for a few hundred spectators. Each owner was given a fluorescent Tout Wars polo shirt to wear, and former Texas Rangers outfielder Billy Sample was retained as a celebrity auctioneer. When the bidding finally began, Shandler could barely contain himself.

Now *this* is an expert league!

Back then, part of being a serious Rotisserie pundit was having a shtick. There was the garrulous Gene McCaffrey of Wise Guy Baseball, the grandson of a crooked New York cop with a gambler's stomach for risk taking. There was Irwin Zwilling, the Manhattan CPA and master auction strategist, who could name nineteen players he wanted before the draft and then walk out owning every single one of them. There was the urbane John Coleman, a Cleveland tobacconist and the king of the free-agent pool, who liked to draft with a beer at the ready and a cigar flapping in his lips.

Colorful as they were, these experts weren't the most enthusiastic statisticians. Among them, Shandler played the role of the bespectacled math professor who used his formulas to pick all kinds of crazy players. Early on, by using his own advanced statistical models and picking up all those "crappy" pitchers, Shandler nearly ran the table, winning three titles in three years.

But in 2001 Shandler decided to freshen up Tout Wars by inviting more of the major Rotisserie companies to send representatives. In doing so, he opened the door for a new breed of Rotisserie expert who, he'd soon discover, didn't care the least bit about shtick. These guys were quantitative, coldly practical, and, since most of them had been reading the *Forecaster* for years, completely unashamed to ape his methods. Some, like Jason Grey, had even developed potent LIMA hybrids. All of a sudden, nearly half the contestants in Tout Wars were locking horns for the same unheralded players.

For Shandler, baseball's quantitative revolution was, at once, the best thing and the worst thing that could have happened. While it validated what he'd been doing for twenty years and kicked open the door to a job with the Cardinals, it also robbed him of his Rotisserie advantage. Before all these new kids showed up, he was baseball's great undiscovered genius, the only sane man in an insane world. But by 2001 he was just another baritone in the popular chorus. That year he finished seventh in Tout, and the following year second to last. As he sits here at the Wyndham tonight, Shandler's last title is four years old.

To the new breed of Touts, Shandler is a lion in winter. Jason Grey told me in Arizona that the LIMA Plan "is a little past its sell date," and Trace Wood wrote that its usefulness "may be on the wane." Jeff Erickson calls Shandler "a victim of his own success," while Lawr Michaels thinks the Bearded One may be too wedded to his numbers: "If he played a little more intuitively, he'd do better."

After finishing a disappointing fourth in 2003, Shandler spent a few long days in Roanoke, moping around in his basement. The LIMA Plan clearly had to be modified, if not scrapped, and in darker moods he wondered if he ought to resign from Tout Wars altogether. But during a jog around the neighborhood on a cool autumn morning, Shandler stopped, pulled out the pad of paper he keeps in his shorts in the event of a cognitive emergency, and started scribbling.

A few weeks later, he would decline his standing invitation to LABR for the first time in ten years to focus all his energies on Tout Wars. There, on the stage where he once felt the brightest spotlight, Shandler would try to make a comeback.

Tomorrow, then, he plans to unveil a new draft strategy he envisioned on that jog, one that will, if all goes well, become the biggest thing in Rotisserie baseball since the LIMA Plan. The only thing he's revealed so far is what he's decided to call it.

The *RIMA* Plan.

———

It's now midnight at the Wyndham. A party from one of the downstairs ballrooms has spilled into the bar, where four enormous women, intoxicated to the point of wobbliness, have locked arms to sing "Let's Stay Together." For the tireless Wyndham barfly this is the evening's most exciting development. Wearing an oversized pair of sunglasses now, she claps along to the music.

As the Touts begin to peel off, I'm comfortable that Nando, Sig, and I have accomplished our main objective: conveying the idea that we're in this up to our chins. I get the feeling nobody knows what to make of the members of my team or, for that matter, me. All I've given them to work with are some vague lines like, "I'm not sure what I'm going to do tomorrow" and "I hope I don't screw up."

Back in my room, I fasten the deadbolt, hook the door chain, and fish out my draft materials from behind the dresser where I'd hidden them, just in case of a burglary attempt. To my great relief, my value sheets are inside the manila folder where I left them. Weeks ago, Lawr Michaels told me a story about one expert player who showed up to a draft with his numbers locked in a metal briefcase. At the time, I figured the guy was bonkers. Not anymore.

After laying out my clothes for tomorrow—a comfy old pair of corduroys and my lucky charcoal sweater—I place the folder on the desk with other essentials: notebook, reading glasses, calculator, bottle of Excedrin, and my bedraggled copy of the *Forecaster*. Once I've set the alarm clock for ten minutes to eight and placed it on the floor five paces from the bed to make sure I don't just roll over and whack the snooze button, I call the front desk to arrange a separate wake-up call ten minutes later. After taking a gulp from a bottle of NyQuil (the sleep aid of champions), I call the desk a second time to quiz the night clerk on what time my wake-up call is set for.

"Eight o'clock," he says with a huff.

Lying in the dark, I can feel the exhaustion of the last four months in every limb. Tomorrow I'll have a Rotisserie team to manage and an entirely new set of challenges, but right now I'm oddly content. If nothing else, I've absorbed a lifetime's worth of baseball information and managed to find a pair of assistants who've taught me things I never could have learned on my own. And while the matter at hand is serious to me, I have to admit I've had a pretty good time running around North America chasing major-league ballplayers, even if I'm doing it on my own dime.

Back in college at Michigan, one of my English professors once told me that sometimes, at crucial moments in life, he likes to tap into his subconscious to see what's lurking there. The best way to do this, he said, is to suspend all thought and just blurt out the first thing that comes to mind. Whatever emerges from your lips at that instant, he suggested, would be profoundly truthful and revelatory. As the NyQuil starts to kick in, I decide to give it a try.

For the record, the entire contents of my subconscious consists of a single word: *Barajas*.

The 2004 American League Tout Wars Roster

		Titles	Average Finish
1.	Jason Grey, Mastersball	2	1.7
2.	Rick Fogel, USA Stats	0	2
3.	Ron Shandler, Baseball HQ	3	5.3
4.	Trace Wood, The Long Gandhi	0	6
4.	Lawr Michaels, CREATiVESPORTS	1	6
6.	Steve Moyer, Baseball Info Solutions	0	6.1
7.	Mat Olkin, *USA Today Sports Weekly*	1	6.4
8.	Dean Peterson, STATS, Inc.	0	7.5
9.	Jeff Erickson, RotoWire	0	9.4
10.	Matt Berry, Rotoworld	0	11
11.	Joe Sheehan, Baseball Prospectus		Rookie
12.	Sam Walker, *The Wall Street Journal*		Rookie

The Auction

March 27

Chicago commodities trader Danny Stern arrived at his first Rotisserie draft prepared to dominate. Since he was new, the members of the Highland Park League allowed him to call out the first player, but "Barry Bonds" was met with laughter. When a flustered Stern called out Bonds again, one of his leaguemates explained the problem.

This was an American League *draft.*

• • •

Christine Price is an actress, a yoga instructor, a good friend of mine, and, by virtue of being a tall brunette with green eyes and curves in all the right places, the kind of woman who causes sidewalk collisions.

On the morning of the Tout Wars draft, she's wearing a black midriff top with a plunging neckline and low-hipped jeans that show off the tattoo on the small of her back. She sashays into the conference room just before ten o'clock, and all eyes follow. "Are you Sam?" she asks, extending a hand.

"You must be Christine."

Over the years, my opponents have written chapter and verse on the subject of draft-day psychology. They talk about the art of mastering your facial expressions or tossing out comments designed to fill opponents with indecision at critical moments. But as far as I'm concerned, all these suggestions lack one important element: *perfume.*

151

Christine has agreed to put her acting skills to work for me today in the improvisational role of a videographer I've hired, at random, to tape the first few rounds of the draft for research purposes. After a ten-minute tutorial two days earlier, she's already wielding my camcorder with the élan of a professional. Within seconds, Dean Peterson trips over sheepishly to introduce himself, and I have to sip my coffee to keep from laughing.

Her real purpose at the auction is to help us execute our draft strategy, which in deference to Ron Shandler's mysterious RIMA Plan, we've decided to call Really Expensive Mound Aces, or REMA. If draft-day tradition holds, the superstar pitchers we've targeted will be some of the first players nominated, and for REMA to work I'll need to grab three of them at significant discounts. Of course once I start picking up elite pitchers, I'm going to make a spectacle of myself, especially in a roomful of people who make a living telling amateur players *not* to do this. Should one of my opponents realize what I'm up to and see the inherent brilliance of the idea, all he'd have to do is make one comment to the table, and the other Touts would gang up on me, bidding these pitchers up to the point where they're no longer bargains.

REMA, then, will have to be executed like a smash-and-grab job at a crowded jewelry store, where nobody is really sure what happened until the burglars are halfway to Hackensack. This is where Christine comes in—she's the decoy, the coquettish distraction. I'm betting the guys at the table will be too mesmerized by her cleavage in the early going to realize I'm robbing them blind.

"Fellas," I say, clinking a water glass. "This is Christine. She's a videographer who's working with me today. If you don't mind, she'd like to take you outside one by one and ask you a few questions on tape, just for my records."

There are hoots, whistles.

"I promise she won't hurt you."

Just as I suspected, there is nothing more emasculating than standing in front of a camera and talking to a beautiful woman about your lifelong fascination with fantasy baseball. It's an affront to natural selection.

One by one, Christine slowly drains my opponents of their excess testosterone: complimenting Steve Moyer on his tan, asking Lawr Michaels if he'd like to play some air guitar, and panning in tightly on a visibly irritated Ron Shandler. "I like to think I know what I'm doing a little bit," says a suddenly modest Matt Berry. "I certainly know I'm not one of the sharks today," Joe Sheehan confesses. "I'm a little guppy swimming through the water, and I'm going to get eaten before the day's out."

"No, no," Christine purrs. "Repeat after me: 'I'm going to be a shark!'" Sheehan blushes, waits a few beats. "I'm going to be a shark!" he says.

"There you go!"

———

The conference room is windowless and overlit. Three skinny tables covered in white cloths have been arranged in a horseshoe to face a screen, where the auction results will be projected. In one corner of the room, a technical team prepares to broadcast the draft live on the Internet and to moderate a fan chatroom.

There will be very few spectators. If the Touts learned anything from that first draft in 1998 at the All-Star Café, it's that there's really no sense in promoting the auction as a public event. Despite all the media buys, only two dozen people showed up. "The bottom line," Shandler says, "is that watching a six-hour draft is not a spectator sport."

To my relief, Tout Wars has no rule forbidding posses, and mine isn't even the largest. Erickson has brought along three RotoWire stringers to sit behind him and whisper in his ear like Senate staffers. In all, there are twenty-five people in the room, including draft lieutenants, the auctioneer, and a few fans. The auction is still twenty minutes off, but Sig and Nando are already at their battle stations, crouched over their notes with tongues poking out like a couple of second-graders. Since my serendipitous lunch with John Benson, we've heeded his advice and practiced for this moment ad nauseam. Each of us has a defined role, a choreographed series of buttons to push, calculations to make, and lists to check every time a player is purchased. We're as tightly organized as a NASCAR pit crew.

To keep tabs on our progress, Sig has rigged Zoladex with a special feature: After each player is sold, he'll pop into his new owner's column next to a color bar based on his purchase price. If he sold for less than our projected value, he'll be marked with varying grades of hot colors like red and orange, while an overpayment will carry cool shades of blue. At a glance, even a moron will be able to see how efficiently all the teams are bidding. "That's nice, Sig," I said when he first showed it to me. "Bringing technology down to my level."

As the Touts find their seats, Christine has taken a conspicuous spot along the wall behind me. I open the manila folder that contains my draft sheets, arranging them on the table for quick viewing. On the bottom of each page, Sig has added the Tout Wars logo and, just below it, a helpful caption that says, "Trust the Paradigm." Exactly half the Touts are using laptops, including Lawr Michaels and Jason Grey, while the "gut" players like Moyer and Fogel go without. Shandler, in a nod to his analog roots, is strictly paper, too.

Brian Feldman, the auctioneer, is a New York sales executive and Rotisserie nut who performs on the side as an actor in dinner-theater productions. He may be the only man in America who can pronounce the names of hundreds of obscure minor leaguers with perfect Shakespearean diction. Taking the floor, Feldman delivers the ground rules and establishes his cadence, "Going once, going twice, sold." As the nomination order is announced, I'm not so much nervous as numb. By all accounts, the auction is the most crucial moment of the season. "You can't win Tout Wars on draft day," Jason Grey likes to say, "but you can definitely lose it." I'm aware that thousands of lifelong Rotisserie players would happily run me over with a lawn tractor for a chance to take my place at this table, even though there's exactly *zero* prize money.

But on the whole, I'm eerily confident. I believe in our plan, and I'm convinced that nobody in this room has worked harder than we have. For all I care, there could be two million dollars on the line to-day. I wouldn't have prepared any differently.

———

At twenty-one minutes past eleven on March 27, 2004, Brian Feld-man, a glass of ice water in hand, opens the American League Tout Wars draft with three words.

"Is everybody ready?"

As defending champion, Jason Grey is allowed to nominate the first player for bidding, and as he peers intently at his laptop screen, I begin muttering a silent REMA prayer, *Pitcher, pitcher, pitcher.*

"Mariano Rivera for fifteen dollars."

This is *excellent.* Rivera, the Yankee closer, is one of my top five REMA targets and the second-most valuable pitcher on Zoladex. That Grey called him out first isn't much of a surprise. The season be-fore, nearly 60 percent of major-league closers lost their jobs after Opening Day, which made saves the most volatile and unpredictable Rotisserie category. Rivera is one of the few bankable stars at the po-sition, which makes him more valuable than ever. And since Grey likes to ignore saves at the draft and trade for them later, throwing out Rivera is a ploy to make someone else spend a chunk of his $260 on a player that Grey doesn't need.

My competitors for Rivera's services are the contrarian Steve Moyer, who pushes the bidding to $24, and the unassuming Dean Pe-terson, who raises it to $26. Zoladex has Rivera valued at $38, so there's no doubt that I'm going higher. The only question is whether one more bid will do it. I wait a few beats, trying to seem conflicted. "Twenty-seven," I say, and the table is silent.

Just like that, it's over. Rivera, the first player nominated, belongs to me!

"So much for those opening-bid jitters," Grey says, opening up a wave of good-natured heckling. "You know about the elbow, right?" Sheehan jokes. "By the way, you just set a new Tout Wars record," Berry adds. "No one's ever fucked their draft after the *first* player."

The room cracks up.

Smiling, I steal glances at Sig and Nando. All the ribbing was pretty innocent, so the coast is still clear. We now have one third of the REMA Plan completed, and nobody's the wiser. Christine, who's been briefed on the sensitivity of the first two rounds, walks to the center of the room like a runway model, panning from face to face. Lawr Michaels has the floor now, and I'm holding my breath again. *Pitcher, pitcher, pitcher.*

"Curt Schilling for ten," he says.

Next to me, Nando freezes, his fists clenched at his temples, afraid that by moving he might betray his ecstasy. It's not just that Schilling is one of my Five Kings of REMA, he is, by our calculations, the most valuable player in the American League. Zoladex has him at $37, and Hunchmaster, Nando's database of the purely subjective, gave him an A+.

Laying low, I let six bids fly by before I step in at $26. If somebody else is planning to go heavy on pitching, this would clearly be the moment to strike. The leading candidate is the conservative Jeff Erickson, who dusts off an old trick and bumps the bidding to $29. Before the auction, Grey told me that bids ending in nine had an uncanny knack for ending things.

Facing us from across the room, two of Erickson's posse members, a heavy guy in suspenders and a skinny dude in a turtleneck, glower in our direction like something out of *West Side Story*. This is a little more than I'd hoped to pay, and if Erickson is willing to go higher, it could be curtains for REMA. "Thirty," I say, gritting my teeth.

At this, Erickson drops his pencil. "I'm out," he says.

Schilling is mine.

Now that I've taken the first *two* players, tongues are really wagging. "Sam, do you have an appointment or something?" Grey asks. He sounds more amused than anything.

"I'm just going to take the first twenty-three players," I say, trying to keep the mood light.

Then, like a warning shot, Ron Shandler speaks. "It's the anti-LIMA," he says, without looking up from his draft sheets.

"Yeah," Grey adds, "LIMA's out the window now."

Before anybody else can join this potentially calamitous discussion of my strategy, I am saved by, of all people, Matt Berry. "Rivera and Schilling!" he chirps, doing his best Jason Grey impersonation. "It'll be *column fodder*!" At this, brilliantly, Christine breaks into giggles, causing heads to turn. From then on, every guy in the room wants to be her favorite comedian.

REMA has now entered what Sig would call the "mission critical" phase. I'd expected to have to sit through at least fifteen players before getting the nucleus of my pitching staff together, but now I'm just one ace short. I glance over at Shandler, and we lock eyes. If he hasn't figured me out already, he's surely getting close. Sheehan, up next, nominates Boston closer Keith Foulke, who is useless to us now that we have Rivera. I exhale. Peterson grabs him for $24, which was also a nice discount. "That's good!" Sig whispers, a little too loudly.

Mat Olkin, the *Sports Weekly* fantasy-baseball columnist, is up next. He's staring into space, scratching his elbow, and waiting for his cue. He has the twitchy look of a man who's about to pull something, and in short order he does: nominating Javier Vazquez of the Yankees for $28. When Sig looks up Vazquez on Zoladex and realizes he's the third name on our list of REMA Kings, I see his jaw slowly drop.

"Oh, my God," Nando says.

If this was, in fact, a jewelry-store robbery attempt, Olkin would be the bumbling clerk who accidentally shuts off the lights in the middle of the chaos. His $28 callout is a tactic he's used before—it's known in Rotisserie circles as a "freeze bid," the idea being to toss out a player you covet for such a big number that nobody else will dare to top it. But for us it's an unbelievable stroke of luck. By the time anybody at the table realizes we're gunning for Vazquez and that we're clearly trying to corner the market on stud pitchers, they will have to pony up $30 to stop us.

Olkin's eyes rove the table, while his head remains perfectly still. He wants Vazquez in the worst way, and he must think he's going to get him. "Vazquez at twenty-eight," Feldman says, pacing the room like Iago. Sig is getting antsy. Nando is silent. Christine, sensing the tension, leans conspicuously over a chair.

My hands are shaking.

"Twenty-nine," I say.

The room is now quiet enough that I can hear the *ping* of an e-mail arriving on someone's laptop. As the blood rushes to my cheeks, I drop my head and shuffle papers like a news anchor, trying to look unperturbed. Brian Feldman, as surprised as anybody, takes his time before beginning his countdown.

"Going once," he says. Olkin is staring at me as if I just kicked his puppy. "Going twice." There's no trash talk of any sort.

"Sold to Walker."

With trembling fingers, I write "Vazquez" below Rivera and Schilling on my roster sheet. In four minutes and twenty-seven seconds, I have purchased three elite pitchers at a gaudy 23 percent discount from their Zoladex values and executed REMA to the letter. Nando is beaming like a Girl Scout with a bulk cookie order. Under the table, where only I can see, he flashes a thumbs-up. Zoladex is glowing red and orange like a lava lamp, and Christine is panning the faces of my opponents, taking an inventory of shock and awe.

Lawr Michaels rubs his eyes and does a double take. Joe Sheehan points at me and makes words without sound. Hollywood Matt Berry shakes his head, speechless for once, and Trace Wood wrinkles his chin sardonically.

"Can you believe that?" someone whispers. "That's one way to do it, I guess," says somebody else. I catch Christine's eye for a millisecond, and she crinkles her nose.

This is *too easy.*

—

By the seventh round, tendencies have begun to emerge. Moyer, as expected, is boldly larding up on fading superstars like Juan Gonzalez and Rafael Palmeiro. When Rocco Baldelli's name comes up, Dean Peterson seems to want him so badly that his lips twitch. The moment Trace Wood's favorite player hits the block, Minnesota pitcher Johan Santana, he nervously pushes the bridge of his glasses. Lawr Michaels, true to form, has arrived in full nincompoop camouflage: red sneakers, ripped jeans, and a black John Lennon T-shirt with the sleeves hacked off. The Zen master augments his wardrobe with bursts of flaky behavior, from contorting himself in a predraft stretching ritual to flapping his arms and squawking like a seagull after picking up Oakland pitcher Mark Mulder.

Shandler is the toughest to read. All of Christine's vampish moves—stretching luxuriantly in front of the room, bending over to retrieve dropped pencils, and making "incidental" contact as she cranes for close-ups, are having no effect on him. He sits quietly, one leg drawn up on the other, chewing the cap of a beige pen, and keeping a scholarly eye on his papers. That morning, as I dipped into my scrambled eggs in the lobby restaurant, Shandler had shuffled in, looking more irritated than usual.

"How'd you sleep?" I'd asked him.

"Not well," he winced, rubbing his temples. "I woke up at three A.M. with a pounding headache. I think it's a migraine."

The last I'd seen of Shandler before the draft, he was heading upstairs with Michaels, the unofficial Tout Wars pharmacist, to fetch a Tylenol with codeine. This was cause for rejoicing. The Bearded One would have to begin the most important draft of his Rotisserie career under the influence of a narcotic.

So far Shandler has filled only three blanks on his roster, and in the Tout Wars chatroom, his minions are growing restless. One of the posts I saw during the first bathroom break said, "What's Shandler waiting for?" Before the draft, there was speculation about what RIMA stands for, but so far nobody has any idea. The best guess comes from Steve Moyer, who suggests that it means "Shandler's gonna ream your ass."

But there's one strategy that Shandler isn't trying to hide—his desire to make Jason Grey, the defending champion, miserable. First, Shandler baited him by calling out Angel Berroa, Grey's favorite shortstop, and helping to jack up the price. And when Grey made a play for Seattle's Randy Winn, Shandler bid him up to $21 before Erickson jumped in to drive him higher. Feeling the heat, the hyperkinetic Grey is working a full range of nervous twitches, stroking his goatee, crunching mouthfuls of ice, and rubbing his hands together like a hypothermic. In the end, he takes Winn off the table for $25. "How much did you just pay?" Berry asks him.

"Too much."

Meanwhile, I'm not the only rookie making waves. The volcanic Joe Sheehan of Baseball Prospectus has unveiled an approach that couldn't be more different than mine but is no less dramatic. Already he's spent an outrageous 62 percent of his $260 budget on four big bats, including Carlos Beltran, Magglio Ordóñez, and Alfonso Soriano. When he bought Alex Rodriguez for $45, the other Touts literally gasped. Sheehan glanced at Christine almost apologetically, like a man who's lost control.

"Turn the camera off," he squeaked.

"You can't see it," Berry said to the lens, "but Sheehan just unbuckled his pants." There was laughter at Joe's expense. "A new strategy," Moyer added, "superstars and super scrubs." At this, Sheehan, reddening and flustered, makes a crack he'd later regret. "Hey, I have $251 to spend on hitters."

By now, the initial good humor about my pitching spree has been replaced by a murmur of hostility. Once I'd scooped up three of the top aces, my opponents were left to haggle over the second tier of pitchers, like Roy Halladay, Mike Mussina, and Kevin Brown, who, according to our Zoladex values, all sold at close to full retail.

As for the other members of Team Walker, they're a model of efficiency. Nando is calmer than the Swiss Navy. Sig and I have managed to maintain détente. And Christine, her mission undeniably accomplished, has stayed in character flawlessly, even as she's packing to leave. "It's been a fantasy of *mine* to be in a room with so many men!" she purrs. Once the door closes, the comments come.

"All the air just left the room."

"Did you see the tattoo?"

"I should have asked her for a massage."

"Where'd you find *her*?"

"Yellow Pages," I say, shrugging.

After nine of the twenty-three rounds are in the books, all the bona-fide stars, the top sirloin of the American League, have been gobbled up, with Sheehan's bids for Rodriguez ($45) and Alfonso Soriano ($43) topping the charts by a fair margin. The next four hours will be devoted to carving up the potatoes and lima beans. I begin by wrapping up Blue Jays pitcher Miguel Batista for a dollar below his projected value and stealing the robotic Brad Radke for another 26 percent discount, a pair of buys that seems to make the other Touts cranky. "You need hitters, too," Moyer scolds.

It's my turn to nominate a player now, and I'm scanning my list of candidates. The most common practice in a Rotisserie draft is to call out a valuable player you either don't want or don't need, to force your opponents to drain their savings. Now that my pitching staff is solid, I'm looking for a high-priced pitcher I've identified as a turkey, a choke artist, or a surefire flop.

Seconds later, I have my man: Sidney Ponson.

The last time I saw him, Ponson was parked in Baltimore's clubhouse in Fort Lauderdale, plump as a jelly doughnut, explaining how he'd spent the off-season splashing around off the coast of Aruba.

But in addition to packing on pounds, Ponson had given me another reason to avoid him. Looking at my secret data from last year, when Ponson managed to win seventeen games, I'd noticed that hitters were chasing more of his pitches outside the strike zone and making weaker contact. When I asked him about this, Ponson had a ready answer: He'd been pitching around people. In other words, when tough batters came up, he tried to retire them by throwing garbage and hoping they'd flail away. Not only was this a dubious strategy, it was a dramatically dumb thing to admit to a guy with a tape recorder. When hitters finally caught on to him, Ponson would start walking more people than a pack of leader dogs.

Nevertheless, on the strength of his seventeen wins some Rotisserie pundits had valued Ponson as high as $19, and I have to believe that somebody, even at *this* table, is foolish enough to pay it.

"Sidney Ponson for twelve dollars," I say.

It might have been five seconds, but it felt like an hour. As I sat there, waiting for somebody to venture a bid, the room was quiet enough to hear insects—a phenomenon known as "crickets."

Suddenly everybody is peeking out from behind their laptops. Shandler's head is swiveling like a tennis fan at center court. Even the retreating Dean Peterson is observing me like Jane Goodall.

"Twelve dollars is the bid," Feldman says, gravely.

More crickets.

One of the worst mistakes you can make in a Rotisserie auction is to call out a player you don't want for more than anyone else is willing to pay. Under the rules, if nobody else bids, he belongs to you.

I have no idea why I nominated Ponson at an opening price of $12, but it probably had something to do with peer pressure. In Tout Wars, where everyone is supposed to know what they're doing, it's considered churlish to throw out a relatively valuable player for a buck. So in a nod to looking like a pro, I'd actually *overestimated* the market for Sidney Ponson. Turns out everybody in the room knows about Ponson's shortcomings, too.

"The fat hobbit," Jeff Erickson calls him.

I'm starting to feel the telltale symptoms of panic. Dry mouth, sweaty palms, tightness in the shoulders. I unclench my fists and wipe my hands across the pockets of my corduroys. Scanning the table, it appears that my best hope is Mat Olkin. He's staring at the auctioneer as if there's something on his lips, possibly a bid.

Come on, say it!

"Twelve dollars going once."

"ELEVEN!"

The wisecrack comes from the likeliest suspect, Hollywood Matt Berry. As much as his comment is meant to provoke laughter, it's also designed to alert the room to the fact that I've just made a classic rookie mistake. "Let him have the guy," Berry continues, his tone more serious. "Make him fill in his pitching."

Translated, this means I was about to get my REMA comeuppance: Regardless of whether Ponson was worth $12 or not, Berry and the other Touts wanted to force me out of the pitching market, which I'd been screwing up all day. For Olkin, the social pressure to avoid bidding on Ponson couldn't be greater. He looks befuddled.

"Ponson going once."

In the next five seconds, I see Olkin lean forward, unblinking, holding the corners of his draft paper with thumbs and forefingers. He looks at Shandler and back at me. He's clearly thinking about it.

"Ponson going twice," Feldman says.

Come on, Olkin!

"Sold."

My response to this horrible development is to clench a fist and shout "Yes!" as if I had just matched three apples on a scratch-off lottery ticket. There was no sense in moping. If I ever wanted to trade Ponson, I had to create the impression for the table that owning him is a kick in the pants. You should try it! For their part, Nando and Sig seem to have been cast in copper. Two players are nominated and sold before any of us regains his composure. Nobody has to tell me that mistakes like this can torpedo a season.

————

Hitters—I need them, too.

So far, my only conscripts are two of my spring-training favorites, Minnesota right fielder Jacque Jones and Boston slugger David Ortiz, both of whom cost a few bucks more than I'd hoped to pay. Earlier, I'd gaped in horror as another apple of my eye, Gary Sheffield, sold for $5 *more* than his Zoladex value, despite the steroids whispers and some ominous reports about his injured thumb.

Joe Sheehan's spending spree was clearly part of the problem. By driving up the prices of top hitters, he'd forced the other Touts to bid up the subsequent guys, jarring the market the same way I'd done with pitchers. But some of this was the force of habit. Even in a year when pitching had clearly improved in the AL and steroids were casting real doubts about the reliability of power hitters, the Touts were spending money as if it were the other way around. The bidding was so inefficient that Sig's color-coded Zoladex program was all but useless. Every pitcher was a red bargain, every hitter a blue dud. Our numbers hadn't accounted for this level of prejudice.

I'd been told that the key to success at a Rotisserie auction is to roll with the punches and adjust, and it was clear that I'd have to start spending a little more money on hitters. For most of the draft I'd been biding my time, waiting for a few bats to fall into my lap at bargain prices. The last player I'd bought was Josh Phelps, the Toronto designated hitter, who'd been sitting there for the taking, seven dollars below his projected price. I hadn't met Phelps in Florida or heard a single rave. In fact, I wouldn't have bought him at all if Sig hadn't jabbed me in the shoulder with his mechanical pencil and whispered "Value!"

But after caving in on Phelps, I felt a wave of regret. The last thing I want to do is fill my roster with whatever players the market forgot. It was time to disregard the numbers and start going after *my* guys.

Right on cue, the next nomination is Bill Mueller.

It's been a month since I watched the Boston third baseman put on that batting-practice artillery exhibition in Florida, but time has done nothing to discourage my crush. Zoladex gives Mueller a raw value of $18, and he earned a solid A on Hunchmaster. As the bidding begins, I jump in calmly at $7.

Thirteen seconds later, it's pandemonium. Ron Shandler has matched my five bids with five of his own, driving Mueller's price all the way to $20 before either of us can catch a breath. All of a sudden I'm trading haymakers with the master in the hottest bidding war of the afternoon. Mueller's price is already two dollars above our Zoladex target, but with Phelps still fresh in mind (and Nando nudging me with his elbow) I don't care.

"Twenty-one," I say.

I'm not surprised that Shandler shares my ardor for Mueller. In a column, he once calculated that Mueller is one of the better pure hitters in the majors, and last season he'd been the only analyst to predict his surge in home runs. But I also know that Shandler thinks Mueller is, at best, a $20 player, and the bidding is already beyond that. Feldman is starting his countdown, and I'm fully expecting him to back down.

"Twenty-two."

Shandler's voice is pouty and strained. Even after a dose of codeine, he looks like he's passing a kidney stone. For the first time this afternoon, I feel the internal conflict between my mind and my gut, the competing tugs of intuition and cold analysis. I know that another bid would be a gross overpayment for Mueller and a clear violation of the paradigm. But here, in the heat of battle, I decide to trust my own basic nature.

"Twenty-three," I say.

Shandler sinks into his chair as if popped by a pin. He's out.

As I add Mueller's name to my lineup, Sig takes off his glasses and rubs his eyes, as if he can't believe what he's seeing. Looking at my roster, I realize what I've done. Bill Mueller, a guy with the physique of a crossing guard, is now my most expensive hitter.

––––

If anything separates the Rotisserie men from the boys, it's the endgame, the final moments of the auction when the whole table is nearly broke and most players sell for $1 to the person who nominates them. It's the Rotisserie equivalent of hitting with two strikes. Thanks to my rash purchases in the middle rounds, I have $12 left to fill nine spots, and I'm learning some hard lessons about money management. I watch helplessly as Matt Lawton, one of my spring-training babies, sells for less than expected but more than I can afford to pay. Two full rounds pass before I manage to obtain my next player, Minnesota pitcher Carlos Silva, who costs $2.

"Sam, you're still here?" Grey asks.

My only consolation is that the other rookie, Joe Sheehan of Baseball Prospectus, is drawing most of the fire. His earlier comment about spending $251 on hitters was astonishingly boneheaded. He'd basically tipped his hand that he was planning to try the old Labadini Plan, where you spend $9, the bare minimum, on pitchers. What he didn't realize is how many people at the table were drooling at the idea of making the guy from Baseball Prospectus look like a gorilla and how easily this could be accomplished.

Every time Sheehan tries to take a pitcher for $1, somebody outbids him. Not because they really want that particular guy but because they know it will stoke the Volcano. When he finally decides to abandon the Labadini and bid $2 for Boston reliever Scott Williamson, Shandler jumps in at $3 to foil him, letting off a wicked cackle. After Trace Wood outbids him for Jon Lieber, Sheehan snaps.

"Just get out of my way!" he huffs.

Rather than enjoying Sheehan's flameout, I'm focused on one last goal: obtaining Chicago's Aaron Rowand, the player I'd heard raves about in Puerto Rico. Trouble is, the most I can pay for him is $3, which would be a steal for a starting center fielder. One of the keys to success in the endgame is to keep tabs on how much money the other contestants have and what positions they need to fill. At Tout Wars, this information is beamed on the projection screen at the front of the room, and looking it over, I see that my only competition is Mat Olkin, who has $8 remaining to spend on an outfielder and an infielder. Scratching some figures on my draft sheet, I realize that if Olkin spends $5 or more on an infielder, Rowand is mine. So when it's Olkin's turn to nominate a player, I clench my fists.

Infielder, infielder, infielder.

"Aaron Rowand for seven dollars," he says.

Foiled again.

From then on, the auction becomes an exercise in throwing darts, filling in roster spots with the dregs of the American League. The last open spot on my roster is shortstop, and my choice is Rey Sánchez of the Devil Rays who, in thirteen years in the major leagues, has hit, on average, exactly one home run per season.

"Welcome to Roto, Sam," Matt Berry says.

"We've all done it once," adds Grey.

Once every team has filled its active roster, it's time for the last bit of torture, the reserve draft, in which everybody picks six bench players they can rotate into the lineup during the season as need be. This isn't an auction but a classic draft where everybody is allowed, in turn, to select whichever leftover major-league player or minor-league sensation they want. Because the minor leagues are involved, the knowledge curve is steep and scary. Nando is my point man, and he's ready to go now, his lucky pencil jammed behind his ear. He's set his sights on a list of minor-league sleepers, mostly hitters.

Sig has other ideas. Ever since the Mueller debacle, he's been quietly seething, and now, after six hours, he's determined to push the pendulum back in a quantitative direction. At some woozy moment during boot camp, he'd apparently extracted a promise from me that in the reserve draft we'd load up on leftover starting pitchers. Sig's rationale is this: When a bad starting pitcher is scheduled to pitch twice in one week, he is, by the numbers, likely to produce more value than a fair-to-middling pitcher who only takes the mound once. By rotating these two-start guys into the lineup every week, he says, we'll get more for our money.

I have no idea why I agreed to this or even if I did, but after I take one of Nando's minor leaguers with the first pick, the tension begins building. When our second turn comes around, Nando urges me to grab a Cleveland shortstop prospect he loves, while Sig has his eye on pitcher Paul Abbott, another famous Rotisserie dud who'd found new life in Tampa Bay. I turn to Nando to hear his argument. "Our offense sucks!" he says, glaring at Sig.

"Yes," Sig replies hotly, "but we're not going to improve it with these guys."

Now I'm completely brain-locked. I can feel the eyes of the room.

"Somebody tell me what to do!" I plead.

Nando points at the name of his pet prospect, Brandon Phillips. Sig, no longer bothering to whisper, crowds over me like an overbearing T-ball coach. "Abbott is more valuable than any minor leaguer!"

We look like the Three Stooges.

"Do you have a selection?" Feldman prods.

As I pretend to ignore him, I see something I have never seen before and will not likely see again. The ruthlessly polite Nando turns beet red and blows his stack, right there in the basement of the Wyndham LaGuardia.

"That's a joke, Sig!" he snorts.

I freeze. Sig freezes. The whole room is watching, and I'm wondering why we let Christine go home early. This would be a perfect moment for her to trip and fall into somebody's lap.

In the end, the embarrassment defeats me. For the sake of balance, I decide to overrule my gut instincts this time and give Sig and his numbers their due.

"I'll take Paul Abbott."

———

The Tout Wars afterparty at Donovan's Pub in Queens is mostly a haze to me, drowned out with pints of Guinness and forkfuls of shepherd's pie. After six hours of high anxiety, I'm running on fumes. I haven't been able to divine the substance of Ron Shandler's RIMA Plan or Dean Peterson's stealthy strategy, or the fine points of Michaels's Zen approach. Spring-training crushes like Sheffield and Lawton somehow belong to other people, and I'm still not sure how Minnesota first baseman Doug Mientkiewicz wound up on my squad. Sig has nearly passed out trying to pronounce the guy's name.

"It's 'ment-KAY-vich,' " I say.

" 'MIN-a-keech'?"

"Forget it."

As the beers arrive, Jason Grey, still operating at Mach 2, calls up the Tout Wars site on his Pocket PC and starts reading the rosters aloud. The consensus is that Dean Peterson's team is the strongest, although nobody is about to give him the trophy yet. "There wasn't one team that I thought was totally screwed," Matt Berry says.

If there's a bête noire at the table, it's Joe Sheehan, who, in addition to fumbling the Labadini Plan, somehow managed to leave $19 on the table. "I think Sheehan kicked himself in the balls," Nando says. Nonetheless, his strategy is a huge boost to my own chances. His team's surplus of power hitters and my team's overstuffed menagerie of top pitchers makes us natural trading partners. On the way out the door, Sheehan presses his thumb and pinky to the side of his face—the international symbol for "call me."

Other than labeling my squad "a little weak in offense," the reviews are mostly positive. "Sam's team isn't looking *that* bad," says

Trace Wood. After I explain all of REMA's theoretical underpinnings to Mat Olkin, he seems genuinely impressed. Maybe a lot of Rotisserie experts are just like typical baseball executives, he postulates: They, too, latch on to superstitions for which there is no evidence. Maybe the dim view of pitchers in Tout Wars was just another example of the lazy following the ignorant.

Mat Olkin is a smart guy.

After a couple of hours, the Touts separate into various rental cars to fan out to points across the United States. They will not assemble again until October, after a winner is decided. From this moment forward, Tout Wars becomes a battle conducted over phone lines and in the digital ether, with each combatant hunkered down in his den or office or dimly lit basement. The euphoria of unwrapping a new team will soon fade, replaced by the long grind of playing a chess match that takes six months.

Back at the Wyndham that night, Team Walker assembles in my room for our auction postmortem. Nando has now apologized, at least five times, for calling Sig's ideas about the reserve round a "joke." Clearly Sig wasn't the least bit offended. There's nothing he likes more than arguing about mathematical theories and postulates, and as he runs our team through Zoladex he's actually *pleased* by the result. "We were a lot more efficient than I expected!" he says.

There's a lot to be thankful for. We executed REMA to the letter— spending exactly 50 percent of our budget on a pitching staff anchored by three of baseball's greatest arms. And dumb as it was to get stuck with Sidney Ponson, we still bought him for $6 less than the cold numbers say he's worth. "Maybe he'll turn out to be a big success this year," Sig says, "the accidental pitcher." Meanwhile, on the other side of the room, Nando is happy, too. Despite Ponson's D grade, our team's Hunchmaster average is a B, and we scooped up six A players. Once Sig has loaded all the Tout Wars teams into Zoladex, he announces that our team, as constructed, should score 72 points, which would put us in the top four. But with a decent trade or two of pitching for hitting at midseason, he says, there's no reason we can't win. "Look how *terrible* our offense is!" he says delightedly.

By the time my shoes meet the pavement in Manhattan, it's well past midnight. As I'm staggering home down Bethune Street, something on the sidewalk catches my eye. It's scuffed and cracked and frayed at the seams, and probably not even made of leather, but nonetheless it's a baseball. On a damp and chilly night at the end of March, I step into the middle of the cobblestone street and, after checking for cabs, wheelchairs, dogs, bicyclists, and beat cops, I fix the ball in my fingers with a two-seam grip and take the sign.

Then I set, kick, and deliver.

The ball bounces under the glow of streetlights, skitters on a manhole cover, and ricochets off the front tire of a Toyota. The real major-league season doesn't start for a few days, but *mine* begins right now. One of the advantages of owning a Rotisserie team is the inalienable right to throw out your own first pitch.

I decide to call my Tout Wars team the Streetwalkers.

The Streetwalkers Baseball Club, in draft order:

	Player	Team	Position	Price
1.	Mariano Rivera	NY	P	$27
2.	Curt Schilling	BOS	P	$30
3.	Javier Vazquez	NY	P	$29
4.	David Ortiz	BOS	1B	$21
5.	Miguel Batista	TOR	P	$14
6.	Doug Mientkiewicz	MIN	1B	$12
7.	Brad Radke	MIN	P	$11
8.	Sidney Ponson	BAL	P	$12
9.	Jacque Jones	MIN	OF	$22
10.	Josh Phelps	TOR	DH	$15
11.	Bill Mueller	BOS	3B	$23
12.	Dmitri Young	DET	OF	$17
13.	Orlando Hudson	TOR	2B	$12
14.	Bronson Arroyo	BOS	P	$3
15.	Carlos Silva	MIN	P	$2
16.	Dan Wilson	SEA	C	$1

Player	Team	Position	Price
17. Kevin Cash	TOR	C	$1
18. B. J. Surhoff	BAL	OF	$1
19. Mark Ellis	OAK	2B	$2
20. Brendan Donnelly	ANA	P	$1
21. Ruben Sierra	NY	OF	$1
22. Ryan Ludwick	CLE	OF	$1
23. Rey Sánchez	TAM	SS	$1

RESERVE

Player	Team	Position
1. Jack Cust	BAL	DH
2. Paul Abbott	TAM	P
3. Adrian Gonzalez	TEX	1B
4. Kevin Appier	KC	P
5. Nick Punto	MIN	2B
6. Jason Grilli	CHI	P

Total: $259
Pitching: 50%
Hitting: 50%

Tout Wars overall:
Pitching: 29%
Hitting: 71%

THE SEASON

"Get Somebody Loose!"

April

In a summer when three separate hurricanes threatened the mainland of central Florida, Jim Mastropietro knew that precautions had to be taken. He laid down sandbags, boarded up windows, stockpiled nonperishables, and, of course, created a set of emergency provisions for his Rotisserie league in case of a power loss at the transaction deadline. Though Mastropietro had his roof torn off, and other owners had trees fall on their homes, not a single transaction was missed.

"We made it through," he says.

• • •

In the introduction to their 1984 book, the founders of Rotisserie baseball issued a warning: "It can be a wrenching experience, this transition from routine rooting to the burdens of ownership, and it has been known to bring on an intense sense of dislocation." When I first read this I had no idea what they meant.

I'm about to find out.

The first official game of the 2004 baseball season is a March 30 showdown between the Yankees and Devil Rays that's being broadcast live from Tokyo at five o'clock in the morning. If Halley's Comet, the space shuttle, and the first sunrise of the millennium weren't momentous enough to lure me out of bed before dawn, I was fairly certain that Rey Sánchez couldn't do the job.

But that morning, lying wide awake in bed at two minutes to five, I decide to revise my original position. And in the third inning, when Sánchez cracks a single and puts my Rotisserie team on the board for the first time, I grab Louise, my semiconscious long-haired dachshund, and hoist her above my head like the Stanley Cup.

I used to think of baseball in April as something like a movie trailer—a montage of short scenes, perhaps significant or perhaps not, that tell you next to nothing about the plot. In any other year, nothing short of chicken pox could have compelled me to watch six games before May. But in the first full week of this season, I'm frustrated that I can't watch six games *simultaneously*.

Too fidgety for the sofa, I begin parking myself on a wicker stool four feet from the TV, where I'm able to "interact" with the broadcast. When Matt Lawton steps to the plate and rips Brad Radke's first pitch for a base hit, *Whap!*, the Samsung buys it. When Jacque Jones whiffs on three pitches with runners at the corners, I unload a barbaric howl that sends my wife retreating to the bedroom with a book.

"You're so *loud* all of a sudden," she says.

For as much baseball as I'm watching in these early days, I don't have the slightest idea what the standings are, nor do I care. For the first time in my baseball fanhood, they're irrelevant. The *Times* and the *Journal* begin to pile up at the door while I spend most of my "news" time logged on to RotoWire and Rotoworld, the only media outlets one can depend on for saturation coverage of Mark Ellis and his torn labrum.

I have a new set of pet peeves: late games on the West Coast, broadcasters who mispronounce player names, highlights from the National League (who cares!), and most of all the whole cowardly tradition of bunting. Quite often I can't figure out whether to cheer or boo. If Sidney Ponson strikes out David Ortiz, is that good? Some of my oldest prejudices shift out of whack. Most of the time, I fear and despise the Yankees as much as always, but every time my closer, Mariano Rivera, comes into the game, I might as well be Vinnie from the Bronx: "Go Bombahs!"

The Tout Wars standings are maintained and continuously updated by USA Stats. On the Tout Wars home page, there's a grid where each team's live stats are displayed in all ten statistical categories and their overall point totals ranked in descending order. At this early point in the season, the rankings are so volatile that a single save can cause a mind-boggling fluctuation. In the space of an hour, the Streetwalkers vault from eighth place to fourth and back down to ninth. It's like watching the equalizer display on your stereo while listening to *A Chipmunk Christmas*.

Bill Meyer, the evil genius who founded USA Stats, tells me his average customer spends nineteen minutes on the site, which is a pretty remarkable total for cyberspace. Still, I'm convinced he's being modest. My average is closer to nineteen *hours*.

My social life is in rigor mortis. Phone messages are piling up, dinner dates are being scheduled only for nights when I don't have any pitchers on the hill, and I'm already getting puzzled looks from the uninitiated. Picking up takeout one evening, I bump into Ian, my upstairs neighbor. We talk for a few seconds, then I excuse myself, telling him that I'm anxious to get back to the Orioles game.

"I didn't know you were an Orioles fan," he says.

"I'm not."

If the first full week of my first Rotisserie season was defined by one image, it was the sight of Dmitri Young, my $17 cleanup hitter and the only Tiger on my team, writhing in agony on the Astroturf in Toronto. On the replay I see that Young had tried to avoid a tag at second base while running at full steam. This is a pretty ambitious piece of ballet for any ballplayer, let alone a guy who weighs 240 pounds, and Young executed it with all the grace of a Clydesdale on roller skates. He collapsed under his own weight and broke his fibula.

He's out for six weeks.

One of the competitive disadvantages of being a Rotisserie rookie is the inability to maintain perspective. Before the season, I'd been told a thousand times that at some point I would be *tested*. But watching the replays of Young's grisly flop, I'm not sure if this is the fulfillment of that prophecy or just a minor setback. Six weeks would put him back on the field in May, which doesn't sound so dire.

I sit down calmly at my computer to see what other Young owners are saying in the Rotisserie chatrooms, and the response is nearly uniform. They're about to drink hemlock. "When you lose Dmitri on the second day of baseball, that does make for some troubling times," says one post. "This always happens to me!" moans another.

Checking my messages, the condolences are rolling in. "Sorry about Dmitri," says my friend Hal. "Tough break with Dmitri— pardon the pun," writes Rick Fogel. I get a message from Lawr Michaels, the Zen master. "Breathe. Relax," he says. "If you make a move out of panic, you will create problems for yourself."

The phone rings. "What do you think?" Nando asks.

"I think we're *doomed*."

The following day, Nando and I are running around the front office under a code orange. I decide to deal with the situation by making eight trade offers, all of them rash, and several of them dangerously stupid. Under the Tout Wars rules, deals can be made at any moment until the trading deadline at the end of August. Once two parties come to an agreement, all they have to do is send an e-mail to the league's volunteer commissioner, Rob Liebowitz, another expert player. If a deal seems woefully unfair and detrimental to the "expert" image of Tout Wars, he's empowered to reject it. But for the most part, I'm operating without a safety net.

Given that it's only the third day of the season, none of my opponents is much in the mood for deal making. Mat Olkin says he'll trade Aaron Rowand but only for two hitters in return. Lawr Michaels says it's too early for him to consider any trade that isn't "totally lopsided," and the cautious Jeff Erickson answers my tentative offer for Gary Sheffield by saying he'll "sleep on it." The only serious bite is from the intellectual Trace Wood, who seems intrigued by a deal that would send Josh Phelps to his team in exchange for Matt Lawton. Hearing this, I dial Sig in California to run the idea by him, and after taking a moment to load Zoladex, he's ready with a typically measured response. "NO, NO, NO! That would be catastrophic!"

Ever since he prodded me to buy Phelps, the Toronto DH has become the flashpoint for our different philosophies. To Sig, Phelps was a stunning $6 bargain at the draft and therefore a shining achievement in game theory. He was so pleased with Phelps, in fact, that he actually broke his scientific code of objectivity and Googled the guy. When he found an old interview in which Phelps said his favorite subject in high school was *algebra,* Sig was hopelessly besotted. "We can't get rid of Phelps," he says. "He likes math!"

After ten minutes of hollering at each other, Sig and I hang up in a deadlock. All of my scouting tells me Lawton is more valuable than Phelps, but my statistician has planted a seed of doubt. That night, before I can make up my mind, Lawton settles the matter by collecting two hits and a home run, prompting Trace Wood to pass on the deal. Josh Phelps, the algebra whiz, is officially staying put.

Now that I've exhausted all trade avenues, there's only one place to go to replace Dmitri Young: the market for free agents. In fantasyland, "free agency" doesn't connote the same glamour it does in the big leagues. Here, most of the signable players are minor leaguers who've just been called up or leftover scrubs who weren't claimed at the draft. The only time a bona-fide superstar winds up in this pool is if he's traded over from the National League.

At the beginning of the season, every Tout Wars team gets a $100 "free-agent acquisition budget" for unaffiliated players. The auction takes place once a week on Fridays, and since the bidding is blind and everyone has the same $100 to play with, logic takes a back seat. Rather than calculating a ballplayer's precise value and pricing him accordingly, the challenge is to guess what the stupidest, most grossly irrational bid is likely to be and then to determine whether you're manly enough to top it. If you're not careful, it's possible to bid $20 on a player only to discover that you could have had him for a buck. The process is known as FAAB, an acronym that can be used as an adjective, a verb, and, more often than anything, an expletive.

When I call up the list of available free agents on USA Stats, I learn another rookie lesson. There are so many pitchers to choose from that they seem sort of like, well, taxicabs. Before the season, I'd been told that one of the reasons pitchers go so cheaply in Tout Wars is because there's always a ton of them available as free agents every week, but until now I'd never seen it with my own eyes.

After scrolling past all the arms for hire, I reach the list of available outfielders, which, in addition to its alarming brevity, reads like a list of cabin assignments at a camp for fat kids.

Mendy Lopez
Simon Pond
Bubba Crosby

Lopez, of Kansas City, is quickly eliminated. Though he hit a home run on Opening Day, he's all but certainly headed to the minors. The next name, Toronto's Pond, is a mystery to me. All I know is that he put up some decent power numbers in winter ball. The third candidate, Crosby of the Yankees, is the most familiar, only because I'd been reading about him in the New York papers. After six long years in the minors, Bubba caught the attention of Yankees manager Joe Torre by hitting .357 at spring training and covering center field like a water spider. He'd been the last guy to make the team. Trouble was, Bubba hadn't played yet, and when a couple of injured teammates returned he was likely to be dropped.

The next day, forty hours after Dmitri Young broke his leg and one day before the first weekly FAAB deadline, I'm standing next to Bubba Crosby in the Yankees locker room. The first thing you notice about Crosby, other than the fact that there's not a grain of dirt on his uniform, is that he looks like somebody's lost kid brother. He might well be 5'11" as the program states, but only in spikes.

Now that he's made the major-league team, Crosby tells me, he's trying to shorten his swing to focus on making contact and getting base hits. He's determined to make things happen by taking walks, stealing bases, and scoring runs, rather than crushing the baseball into powder. If anything, he's given up on the idea of hitting a home run, which is exactly what we need until Young comes back. "I'm not gonna make any money in deep center field," he says.

The next day, with exactly one hour left to submit my free-agent bids, I still can't decide. Sig has no meaningful data on these subjects.

Nando likes Crosby because of his torrid spring, but I'm leaning toward Simon Pond, only because he seems at least physically capable of hitting home runs.

To break the stalemate, I pick up the phone and call Joe Housey, a former pitcher who's now working as a scout for the Chicago Cubs. Built like a lumberjack with a gruff sense of humor, he's the kind of guy who slaps you on the back and nearly knocks you over. I know that he covers Florida, where he'd surely seen both Pond and Crosby at spring training. When I reach him, he's on the golf course.

"Not now," he says, "I'm on the tee."

"Ten seconds?"

"Okay, go ahead."

"What do you think of Simon Pond?"

"He *stinks*."

"What about Bubba Crosby?"

"He's better."

"Thanks, Joe."

Hanging up, I type an e-mail to Commissioner Liebowitz and bid $1 of my $100 budget for Bubba Crosby. Minutes later, Crosby is a member of the Streetwalkers. Mine was the only bid.

About two hours later on Friday evening, the White Sox are thumping the Yankees in the Bronx. In the ninth inning, with the outcome all but certain, manager Joe Torre sends our man Bubba Crosby out for his first swing as a Yankee. With teammate Hideki Matsui on second base, Crosby shuffles to the plate, looking as if he'd just finished breathing into a paper bag. With one ball and two strikes, he uncoils his bat and belts a fly ball to right field that, to the surprise of everybody on earth, clears the fence.

Home run, *Bubba*.

He's not the first Yankee to homer on his first trip to the plate, but he's got to be the most unlikely. Circling the bases, Crosby runs so fast he nearly slams into Matsui's back. "I was just trying to calm myself down," he tells reporters after the game. "Being a rookie and playing in New York, my heart was racing." *SportsCenter* features a highlight of Bubba's blast, followed by a graphic comparing his relatively paltry $301,000 salary to the millions earned by teammates Jeter, Giambi, and Rodriguez.

As a reward for Crosby's Friday miracle, Torre puts him in the lineup on Sunday. It's his first start in pinstripes, and when he jogs out to center field the bleacher bums begin chanting his name. Inspired, Crosby makes a pair of spectacular catches, hurling himself against the outfield wall with abandon.

After grounding out on his first trip to the plate, Crosby comes to bat in the fourth inning with two runners on. He takes two balls from Chicago's Danny Wright and then, with a swing that nearly topples him, drives a ball through the damp April air that bounces off the facade of the *upper deck* in right field. Right before my eyes, the unwanted free-agent outfielder I picked up for one lousy FAAB dollar is taking a curtain call at Yankee Stadium.

The next morning, I buy all the papers. The *Times* puts the story on the front of the sports section. The Bergen County *Record* calls Bubba an "instant sensation," and a New York *Post* headline shouts: "Hubba Bubba!" Gary Sheffield calls Bubba a "throwback." White Sox manager Ozzie Guillen describes him as "the new Babe Ruth in town," and Torre raves like a proud papa. "It seemed like every other inning I was tipping my cap," Crosby said. "This day's pretty much tattooed in my mind."

Crosby is the toast of Tout Wars, too. Hollywood Matt Berry praises my pickup in his nightly blog, and Lawr Michaels gives me props in a column on CREATiVESPORTS. "Keep up the good work!" says Rick Fogel. More important, Crosby's three-run home run vaults me up two places in the standings to seventh.

I'm quite aware Crosby isn't going to hit a home run in every game, let alone as many as a healthy Dmitri Young. There's still a chance he'll be back in the minors by the end of the month. But he's already given me something more important than a statistical boost: a new infusion of confidence. I'm going to be good at this game, because I know people.

———

In the pantheon of great sporting events, Red Sox at Blue Jays on April 22, 2004, would rank somewhere between lawn-mower racing and the featherweight championship of the world. At game time, the SkyDome is two-thirds empty.

Here in New York, it's one of the first glorious spring evenings. There are buds on the trees, tables outside the cafés, joggers on the sidewalks, and, for some reason, the faint smell of smoke. (It's an odd night for a fire.)

Nevertheless, I've canceled my dinner plans, turned off the cell-phone, shut down the computer, and taken a seat on my wicker stool. In a first for my Tout Wars season, I have seven players starting in this game, including both pitchers, Curt Schilling and Miguel Batista. For me, this is appointment television.

By the fifth inning, Boston has a 3–1 lead, and the game is playing out swimmingly. Curt Schilling is cruising toward a win, and after a rocky start, Batista has gathered himself to retire ten Red Sox in a row. Better yet, every run that's crossed the plate was scored by one of my guys. As I watch Schilling ring up Toronto journeyman Howie Clark, I'm starting to think these pitching duels aren't so excruciating after all.

Just then, I hear a clamor on the sidewalk and, after a few minutes of trying to ignore it, run downstairs reluctantly to see what's the matter. When I return, Batista has been chased from the game, Schilling has just induced a fly ball to end the seventh inning, and the score is . . . *tied?*

In pitching duels, tie games are the ultimate nightmare scenario. If neither of your pitchers leaves the game with a lead, neither one gets the win, and by virtue of their scarcity wins are second only to saves in the Rotisserie food chain.

With Batista in the showers, Schilling is my only hope for a victory, which means that I should want to see him back on the mound when the game resumes. But now that he's already given up ten hits, I'm worried that he could be on the verge of imploding and dragging down my team's cumulative WHIP and ERA. Before I can come to any conclusion, there's a tight shot on the screen of Schilling, standing on the mound.

Ten minutes later, the bases are loaded, and seven of the last ten Toronto batters have reached safely. Schilling has given up twelve hits, only two shy of his career high, and Boston has two relievers getting loose in the bullpen. "That's gotta be it," I mumble to the television.

The camera pans to Boston manager Terry Francona, who's sucking on a wad of sunflower seeds and clearly thinking about skipping up the dugout steps to yank Schilling.

"Dude, get up!"

It's no use.

The only bright spot here is that the next Blue Jay to the plate is Chris Gomez, a guy who hit only one home run last season in fifty-eight games. Even in his depleted state, Schilling should be able to get this joker out. As I watch, I'm crouched on my stool, leaning forward, and gripping two clumps of hair. It might as well be Gossage against Gibson in Game Five of the 1984 World Series.

Gomez works the count to one and one, and the sparse crowd in Toronto rises to its feet. Schilling looks whipped. He sets, kicks, and delivers a splitter that hangs up in the strike zone like a necktie.

CRACK.

Lawr Michaels once told me a story about the first time he played Rotisserie baseball, long before his Tout Wars title year. He was riding in the car with his second wife, Ava, listening to a game involving one of his pitchers, Kansas City's Mark Gubicza, who had walked a couple of batters with two outs. First there was an error, then somebody hit a single, and the runs started trickling in. "Get somebody loose!" he snapped. On cue, the announcer said the Royals didn't have anybody warming in the bullpen. "Fucking assholes!" he screamed, pounding the dashboard with his fist. "You don't have somebody warming, and it's the sixth fucking inning? You fucking assholes!"

Ava had never seen anything like this. The man she married was a gentle soul, a pot-smoking hippie with flowing locks and a taste for

Middlemarch. "Lawr," she suggested softly, as he sizzled like a plate of fajitas, "maybe you need an outlet."

"This *is* my fucking outlet!"

I'd like to think my reaction to the Chris Gomez grand slam off Curt Schilling on April 22, 2004, was not quite so Paleolithic. As I try to stand up, preparing to do something violent to the television, my butt skids off the back of the stool and I land on the floor. With the SkyDome crowd screaming like a convention of mental patients, I fumble for the mute button and wrap my arms around the stool, hugging it while moaning. Outside in the street, meanwhile, there are three fire trucks, eighty gawkers, and a torrent of water rushing down the gutters from an open hydrant.

That earlier commotion outside was the response to a kitchen fire in the building next door. The moment the squad leader told me they had it under control, I'd whistled to my dog, headed back up-stairs, waved the mist of smoke away from the television with a towel, and turned up the volume.

My wife, having just arrived home to witness the chaos out front, opens the apartment door and sees me crumpled on the floor, clutch-ing my stool.

"Oh, my God, what happened?" she asks.

I raise my head long enough to say four words.

"Francona is an *idiot.*"

———

Three weeks have passed since the "fire" incident, and I now consider myself a recovering Rotisserie maniac. I've had some time to reflect on my behavior on the evening of April 22 and to appreciate the mis-application of priorities it demonstrated. I have returned to watching games quietly on the sofa. I have stopped smacking the television and promised my wife to call the fire department the next time our apart-ment walls are warm to the touch.

At the moment, I'm holding down a café table at Newark Airport eating a breakfast burrito and reading the box scores before catching a flight. In my peripheral vision I have just noticed a thin man in a blue shirt standing twenty feet to my left, taking an inventory of the slim pickings at the food court. After making eye contact with the guy, I have to force myself to turn away. The surest sign that you've had too much Rotisserie baseball is when you start "seeing" your players in the faces of random people in public. And this guy looks a little bit like Mariano Rivera.

Shaking it off, I return to the box scores where I see, to my great relief, that the Yankees are opening a series in Anaheim tonight, clear across the country. I glance back to see the guy who looks like Rivera walking down the terminal hallway, dragging his own black rolling bag. "Man, I need a shrink," I say.

About two minutes later, the incident all but forgotten, I hear an announcement over the terminal loudspeaker that makes me drop my tortilla. "In a few minutes we'll begin boarding flight 287 with service to Orange County."

Abandoning my coffee and burrito at the table, I am suddenly run-walking as fast as my wheelie bag will allow. The Orange County gate is packed with passengers but no thin guy in blue. Then, sitting alone on the other side of the concourse, there he is. I watch him pull out a sleek cellphone and dial a number with movements that are so impossibly elegant, and an expression that's so unflappably cool, there's no longer any doubt.

In seven years of covering sports, I've seen Mo Rivera in person about thirty times. Next week, if I wanted to, I could sit down with him in the Yankees clubhouse and read him my favorite recipes for fifteen minutes. Of all the people in this terminal, I should be the least starstruck. But in the last six weeks Rivera has become a significant figure in my life. He was the first member of my first Roto team and the first player selected in the Tout Wars auction. He's been working hard for me, nobly chipping away at his $27 auction price.

I wait politely for Rivera to finish his phone conversation, trying to look nonchalant while standing in the middle of the concourse and blocking traffic for no apparent reason. I'm not sure what to do, although it's hard to ignore the rush of adrenaline.

When he's off the phone, Rivera notices me. He's famous enough that he knows when he's been spotted by a baseball whacko, and he nods at me in a manner that's neither inviting nor rude. I could have introduced myself and reminded him that we've met before. I could have asked him how much movement he's getting on his cut fastball or just told him that he was doing a nice job for my Rotisserie team. But the sentence that comes out of my mouth is something I've never said to an athlete or, for that matter, anybody.

"Hey, Mariano. Can I get your autograph?"

The Cinquo de Mayo Massacre

April 26–May 8

Ken Raskin had his friend Mick Kirven over a barrel. Mick had just set eyes on Fiona, the fetching friend of Ken's fiancée, and was prepared to do any-thing for her phone number. Since the two men played in the same Rotis-serie league, Ken agreed to give it to him but only in exchange for a rookie outfielder named Vince Coleman. The ballplayer went on to steal 110 bases and was named rookie of the year. Mick's seduction of Fiona was some-what less productive.

"We went out a couple of times platonically," he says.

$\cdot$ $\cdot$ $\cdot$

By the end of April I'm feeling impatient. It's not that I'm entirely un-happy with fifth place, but I seem to be tethered there in the middle of a pack.

My pitching is not the problem. REMA has been a roaring success. Curt Schilling, grand slam and all, has thirty-nine strikeouts in a little over thirty-five innings. Mariano Rivera leads the league in saves, and Javier Vazquez has an ERA below 3.00.

But other than Jacque Jones, who's batting .329 with half my team's stolen bases and nearly a quarter of its home runs, the rest of my offense looks like a reflection in a funhouse mirror. Kevin Cash, my $1 catcher, has hit two home runs, which is better than Josh Phelps, who has more strikeouts than base hits. My other bargain catcher, Dan Wilson of the Mariners, is hitting .315, while Bill Mueller, the defending batting champ, is hovering at .267. Ever since his unlikely curtain call in the Bronx, Bubba Crosby hasn't hit anything but the Yankees showers, and, just as I feared, he's being sent back to Columbus in a couple of days. With Dmitri Young recuperating, I still need to fill that hole in my outfield.

The knock on expert Rotisserie leagues is that they're too cerebral, too respectful, and altogether too dull. Unbridled displays of enthusiasm are frowned upon, and nobody burps without consulting a spreadsheet. But if there's any exception to this rule in Tout Wars, it's Rick Fogel, the gregarious Chicago lawyer. Last season, as the first pure amateur to enter the competition, Fogel felt like a fish out of water. The other Touts were so cautious he was unable to make a single trade, which bugged him to no end. "I'd rather spend time talking trade than almost anything!" he says. I've started to suspect that Fogel might be itching to make a deal just for the sake of making a deal and that if I can catch him at a weak moment, I might be able to get the fatter end of it. In fact, just a few days earlier, he'd written a line in a message that I had to read twice to believe.

I do like Ponson.

In two of his last four outings, Sir Sidney Ponson has given up seven runs and looked every bit like the candied ham I'd imagined him to be. But by some miracle he'd also pitched a complete game against Tampa Bay and eked out two wins, which was just enough to create the illusion that he might be worth acquiring. If I'm going to dump him, it's clearly now or never.

After checking to make sure Fogel is really interested in Ponson (he is!), Nando and I meet in the front office on April 26 to study his roster. We identify four players we'd like to acquire:

José Guillen
Jason Johnson
Pokey Reese
Alex Rios

Our primary target is José Guillen, the starting left fielder for the Angels, who would shore up our depleted outfield. He's been so rotten this April that Fogel seems to regret every penny of the $15 he paid for the guy. "I'm sick of José," he tells me.

One of the principles of making a baseball trade, whether real or imaginary, is to always remember the old Wall Street axiom, *Buy low.* With a miserable .250 average and only one home run, Guillen's stock is basically trading in fractions.

Nevertheless, the mention of Guillen's name makes Nando dance like a circus bear. The year before, he tells me, Guillen played with a broken bone in his left hand. "The guy's tough as nails," he gushes. Nando had also discovered that this isn't the first time Guillen has started slowly. His career batting average in April is .265. While I hadn't met Guillen in Arizona, I'd overheard one scout say that he always swings the bat well, even when he strikes out. Besides, if the price is Ponson, we're basically getting him for nothing.

If we do manage to trade Ponson, we'll still need another starting pitcher to take his spot, and Jason Johnson of the Detroit Tigers seems a fine candidate. At spring training, Tigers pitching coach Bob Cluck told me that when Baltimore didn't tender Johnson a contract after the 2003 season, "I was thrilled." He thinks that Johnson, with the confidence of a new $7 million contract behind him, has a chance to become a dominant ace.

So far this season, however, Johnson has given up six runs in two of his first four starts and has been blaming his struggles on a blister. Trivial as this may sound, a blister can force a pitcher to change his grip on the ball, alter his throwing mechanics, and, in some cases, abandon a pitch or two. From a speakerphone in the front office, Sig tells us that last year, Johnson relied almost exclusively on two pitches: a fastball that tops out at about 94 and a big, looping curve. In fact, he'd thrown one or the other a staggering 93 percent of the time. If that blister stops Johnson from throwing his curve, he'll be forced to throw nothing but fastballs and an occasional changeup. In the major leagues, that's sort of like showing up for a gunfight with a pickle fork.

To settle the issue I rummage through my notes from Florida, dig out Bob Cluck's e-mail address, and dash off a note asking him for an update on Johnson. His response arrives the next day.

"Sam—the blister is fine. Get J. J."

The next name on our target list, Red Sox second baseman Pokey Reese, requires no further study. Less than twenty-four hours earlier, after watching Boston sweep the Yankees in their second series of the season, I boarded a D train in the Bronx bound for Manhattan. Sitting across from me was a grandmotherly woman in sneakers and a white cap with the Olympics logo. She noticed the press credential dangling from my neck.

"Four police cars!" she said bemusedly. "That's what it took to get the Boston bus out of there."

"Crazy," I said, returning the smile.

Seated to my right on the crowded train was a trim African-American man of about fifty wearing an impeccable gray suit with a butter tie. "They're in a hurry," he offered, matter-of-factly. "They have to catch a five-thirty train downtown."

The Olympics lady and I exchanged a curious glance. She asked the guy in the butter tie if he worked for the Yankees at the ballpark or something, and he smiled bashfully.

"No, my son plays for the Red Sox."

"Sam Walker," I said, extending a hand.

"Calvin Reese."

We shook.

"Pokey, right?"

"That's correct."

Thanks to my preseason immersion in American League baseball, I knew more than I probably should about Pokey Reese. I knew that his dad, the guy sitting next to me, was a legend in South Carolina, a semipro shortstop whose gymnastics with the glove had earned him the nickname Slick. I also remembered, for some reason, that Pokey has a sister named Peaches. (Nando would be proud.)

In Rotisserie terms, Reese had the potential to be one of the league's more valuable second basemen. He'd been known to steal a few bases, and figured to score a lot of runs in Boston's prolific lineup. The only issue was his health. So far this season, Reese was hitting an anemic .200, and in Florida during batting practice, I'd watched him hit a sad mélange of grounders and weak pop-ups. "Seems to have a slow bat," I'd written.

I asked Calvin why his son was off to a slow start.

"Well, he was injured last year, you know. Tore his ulnar collateral ligament, you know, the thumb." On the roaring and jostling train, Calvin stood up and crouched like a hitter at the plate. "To keep pressure off the thumb, he'd been keeping his right shoulder up too high, like this." He pantomimed a swing. "He needs some time to get back in the flow, you know. He didn't swing a bat all winter, but he'll be fine, just you wait and see."

As the doors flew open at Calvin's stop, he turned to say good-bye. "Give my best to Pokey," I said. "Maybe I'll try and pick him up for my Rotisserie team." Calvin shook my hand, glanced at my credential, and gave me a puzzled look. "You do that," he said, stepping onto the platform. "He's going to be fine."

When Pokey's name comes up in our front-office summit, I already know that I want him. The only question is how to sneak him past Sig. Any sentence that begins "His dad told me" is sure to make him boil over like a pot of linguine. So when Sig asks me why I'm so high on the guy, I tell him somebody in the know had beseeched me to get him.

"Who?" Sig asks.

"Billy Beane."

Welcome aboard, Pokey.

The final target on our list is Alex Rios, a minor leaguer in the Toronto system. To the fun-loving Rick Fogel, Rios is merely a toss-in, but as far as I'm concerned he's the linchpin of the deal.

Back in December, of course, my wife and I had flown to Puerto Rico for a "vacation" that would serve both our purposes. She could loll around on the beach with a frozen daiquiri while I spent my afternoons scouting ballplayers.

The day after Christmas, I drove to Estadio Hiram Bithorn in San

Juan to see my first game, a clash between the Carolina Giants and the Santurce Crabbers. There was a credential waiting for me at the league office—a blue plastic card that said "Prensa"—but I hardly needed it. In a few minutes, without showing it to a soul, I was standing behind the batting cage with Wally Backman, the Santurce manager. Backman was leaning against the netting watching his players take their warm-up hacks. His eyes brightened at the rare sight of a reporter from the mainland.

The moment I told Backman what I was up to and asked him for some advice on players, I learned one of the fundamental laws of the 2004 Puerto Rican League: No conversation lasts more than fifty seconds without somebody mentioning the name Rios, followed by a bunch of flowery superlatives.

Rios, who was playing right field for the Caguas Creoles this season, had all the raw skills of a superstar, Backman said. He hit for power and average, stole bases, fielded his position adequately, and had an arm that nobody challenged. The only way to neutralize him at the plate was to pitch him high and tight and hope he hit a pop-up. "But if you throw him a breaking ball for a strike," Backman said, leveling his eyes, "somebody's going to get hurt out there." When major-league pitchers try to work Rios inside as they usually do with rookies, he added, "he's going to fucking drive the ball *hard*."

Three days later I arrived at the hilltop ballyard in the southern town of Caguas to see the Creoles play the Ponce Lions. When Alexis Israel Rios jogged in from right field, I could see, instantly, what the fuss was all about. His red-and-white Caguas uniform hung off him a bit, and he wore his pants pulled down to his cleats, making him look even skinnier. But at 6'5" he had the basic shape of a young Alex Rodriguez. And with an easy smile, extortionate good looks, and a glinty diamond in one ear, he oozed charisma. Rios had what the scouts like to call "the good face."

In his first trip to the plate, he promptly ripped the second pitch up the middle for a single and, once on base, attempted to steal second. When the throw arrived from the catcher, Rios was already dusting his pants and chatting amicably with the umpire.

When the game ended, I wandered into the office of Caguas manager Mako Oliveras, who was poring over some box scores at his desk while a member of his coaching staff sat nearby, pounding on a set of bongos. I introduced myself and asked if he had a second to talk about Rios.

"REE-vers?" he said.

"No, Rios."

"REE-vas?"

I hadn't prepared for the possibility that Oliveras, a former major-league coach, didn't speak English. "Thanks anyway," I said, turning to leave.

"Wait, I'm just fucking with you."

Oliveras signaled to the bongo player to knock it off and motioned for me to sit.

"Did you see the way he battled out there?" he said. "He's got a great approach at the plate; he's the whole package." Oliveras dropped the box scores and leaned forward in his chair. "He goes strong to the opposite field. The ball jumps off his bat, and he's only twenty-two years old. I'm superstitious about talking up one of my players too much, but I can't think of anything, other than injury, that could keep him out of the big leagues. He should be in the majors by the end of the season."

Back in the front office, as I page through my notebook from Puerto Rico, a scrap of newspaper falls out. It's an article I'd ripped out of a Spanish newspaper at the San Juan airport. Rios had finished the winter season hitting .348 with twelve homers and was elected the league's MVP by unanimous vote.

I've *got* to have him.

On Wednesday, April 28, Rick Fogel answers one of Nando's deal offers with a counterproposal that's too good to be true. He would take Ponson, Ruben Sierra, injured reliever Brendan Donnelly, Minnesota backup second baseman Nick Punto, and one of our $1 catchers for Guillen, Reese, Johnson, Rios, and Kansas City backup catcher Kelly Stinnett. Not only would this deal give us everyone we wanted, it would be the largest in Tout Wars history.

The front office kicks into high gear. Nando feeds the deal through Hunchmaster, and just as I'd expected it's a massacre: 49 points coming in and only 18 going out. My next call is to Sig, who runs the trade through Zoladex and, true to form, comes up with the opposite conclusion. By his calculation, we'd be sending out 18 Rotisserie value points and getting 15 back in return. Once again, the chasm between the scouting and the data is wide as can be.

I respect Sig's opinion. I have no doubt (nor does he) that if he ran this team by his own principles it might do perfectly well. But from the beginning my approach has been to weigh the numbers and the scouting in equal measure and, when they don't agree, to follow my better judgment. This time, it's not even close. In my view, the scouting beats the statistics hands down.

No sooner have I decided to overrule Sig than the following day a new challenge presents itself: Rick Fogel is getting cold feet. Just to be prudent, he writes, he'd like to see Ponson pitch one more time before making the trade. It sounds reasonable enough, but given what we know about Ponson it's probably a deal killer.

The one trait that separates great baseball executives from the also-rans is the ability to manipulate a sensitive negotiation. The best of the best have such an uncanny human radar that they can talk any opponent into doing the stupidest thing he's capable of, without having to tell a single lie. Seeing as this is the first trade of my Rotisserie career, I decide to keep it simple and try the crudest tactic in the book.

The horseshit backup offer.

Our straw man for this exercise is fellow rookie Joe Sheehan of Baseball Prospectus, who's starting to realize that his pitching staff shares a lot in common with the Ford Pinto. Sheehan says he's willing to trade us one of his underperforming outfielders, Baltimore's Luis Matos, in return for Brad Radke and somebody else. It's not a deal we like one bit, but right now that's not a concern. All we need from him is a live offer we can use to bludgeon Rick Fogel.

That evening, fewer than twenty-four hours before the weekly trade deadline, I call Fogel. My pitch, which I'd rehearsed carefully, is this: While we desperately need an outfielder, and we're very interested in doing this deal with him, I have another offer from Sheehan to pick up Luis Matos. Even though we don't like this option as much, Sheehan says that if we don't act now, it's off the table.

"So the problem is that I could—"

"You don't want to lose both," Fogel says.

"Exactly."

"I'll do the deal."

I have to remember to breathe.

"You sure, Rick?"

"I'm sure."

The endorphin rush I experience is a little embarrassing. But sitting there in the front office, flanked by my scouting director and my miniature player board with its magnets, I convince myself that my emotions are not too different from those of Billy Beane or Theo Epstein or anyone else who does this for a living. Four months of legwork went into this trade and I'm enormously satisfied by the result. For the first time, I'm convinced that the sum of my own scouting has put the numbers to shame.

On the other side of the table, Nando hovers over his laptop, awaiting orders. "Send it in," I say. "Before he changes his mind."

———

Our trade with Rick Fogel is the talk of Tout Wars, and the reviews are glowing. "I really think you got the better end of the deal," writes Dean Peterson. "I wanted to compliment you on a great trade," Trace Wood says. Even Ron Shandler is impressed: "At first glance it looked like an innocuous deal, but after evaluating it more closely I realized that you did a nice job of grand theft."

The following night the trade is already playing out better than I could have hoped. While Cleveland sends Ponson to the showers after four innings, Jason Johnson, his blister problem behind him, pitches splendidly. Over the next six days José Guillen snaps out of his funk to drive in eleven runs, score eight, raise his average 52 points to .328, and hit three home runs in three consecutive games. He's named baseball's player of the week.

While it's often said that there's no such thing as clubhouse chemistry in Rotisserie baseball, the first week of May makes me believe it exists. Not long after Guillen slips on his imaginary Streetwalkers uniform, Josh Phelps has a home run called foul by the umpires, then, four pitches later, hits *another one*. Miguel Batista turns in a commanding performance, Curt Schilling drops his ERA below 3.00, and Carlos Silva picks up his fifth win. When I click on a random Boston game, I see Pokey Reese standing on the top step of the dugout, taking a curtain call.

He'd homered twice.

The high point comes on May 5, under a full moon, when the Streetwalkers Baseball Club plays like the 1927 Yankees. It's so historic, in fact, that we decide to give it a name: The Cinquo de Mayo Massacre. The final line:

6 home runs
15 RBI
12 runs
.417 BA
2 wins
1 save
1.00 WHIP
2.50 ERA

Three glorious days later, on the afternoon of Saturday, May 8, one week after the Fogel trade took effect, I check the Tout Wars standings at nineteen minutes past four o'clock, and the Streetwalkers Baseball Club has taken over second place. I paste the standings into a message and send it off to my mother, prefaced by four words: "You raised a genius."

———

Next day the phone rings. It's Nando.

"I got some bad news," he says. "José Guillen is being taken off the field on a cart."

"An ambulance?" I ask.

"No, just a golf cart kind of cart."

After collecting his third hit of the game against Tampa Bay, Guillen, the current American League RBI leader, slid into second base feet first at Angel Stadium and came up writhing.

"Did he grab something?" I ask.

"No, he just kind of rolled over on his belly and started pounding the dirt."

"Pounding the dirt?"

Nando sighs. "He was kind of doing snow angels, only facedown."

When I turn on the game, I see that the Anaheim trainers have fastened a giant air cast on Guillen's leg that runs all the way down from his knee to the top of his ankle. There is silence on the phone.

"Man," Nando finally says, "that guy has the look of dejection."

I drop the remote on the floor, and the batteries pop out and skitter under the sofa.

The early prognosis is that Guillen has a sprained right knee *and* a sprained right ankle, and there's a chance that he could have torn cartilage in both. In my box there's a message from Richard M. Fogel, with the subject line "Ouch." "I was really regretting the deal," he wrote, "until I saw the replay of the slide. Hope he comes back soon."

The next morning, just as I've concluded that my outfield is cursed, I see a story in the *Los Angeles Times*. Guillen, it says, left the clubhouse walking gingerly but smiling, confident he could avoid the disabled list and optimistic about playing this coming Tuesday night at Yankee Stadium. Doctors, the article says, found no evidence of a fracture and hadn't ordered tests to check for ligament or tendon damage.

After sitting out just one game, Guillen takes the field on Wednesday in the Bronx. In the first inning he crushes a two-run homer and by the late innings he's scored three runs, raised his average to .333, and, judging from the next message I get, pushed the fun-loving Rick Fogel out on a ledge above Wacker Drive.

"He's obviously a big faker," it said.

I'm feeling a brand of joy that's unfamiliar to me. It's both intellectual and visceral. I'm so proud of José Guillen and the rest of my players I could hug them, but I'm equally proud of my own instincts. The difficult part is feeling this way while sitting alone in my apartment with no roaring crowd, no flashbulbs, nothing to validate the moment. There's only my dog, who's staring at me blankly with a SpongeBob SquarePants doll dangling from her mouth.

Grabbing my press credential, I jump into a cab and twenty-eight dollars later, arrive at Yankee Stadium just as the fans are glumly streaming out. I find Guillen in the visitors clubhouse with a cartoonishly outsized ice pack on his sore knee, watching his home run on digital video. When he returns to his locker, he's ecstatic, electric. "I just picked you up on my Rotisserie team a week ago," I tell him.

Guillen breaks into a smile like a child of twelve and snatches my hand so hard that he jerks me sideways. He jumps in the air, so I jump in the air, too. I'm pretty sure this violates some clubhouse policy for reporters, but there we were—me and José, jumping for joy.

"YEAH, MAN!" he shouts.

I have no idea what to say next, so I tell Guillen that the guy who traded him actually took Sidney Ponson in exchange. Hearing this, Guillen throws back his head and laughs demonically, drawing funny looks from the beat writers. His laughter is infectious, though, and soon I'm laughing, too, at poor old Rick Fogel. Guillen shakes his head and puts a fingertip to one of his temples. "Dat guy," he says, "got a beeeeg old headache rye now."

Tout Wars Standings Through May 13, 2004

1. Jeff Erickson, RotoWire, 95.5
2. Streetwalkers, 87.0
3. Joe Sheehan, Baseball Prospectus, 81.5
4. Dean Peterson, STATS, Inc., 72.5
5. Steve Moyer, Baseball Info Solutions, 71.0
6. Matt Berry, Talented Mr. Roto, 67.5
7. Lawr Michaels, CREATiVESPORTS, 66.5
8. Rick Fogel, USA Stats, 64.5
9. Ron Shandler, Baseball HQ, 60.0
10. Trace Wood, The Long Gandhi, 50.0
11. Mat Olkin, *USA Today*, 42.5
12. Jason Grey, Mastersball, 21.5

¡Muy Bien!

May 15–28

Norm Kent of the Hot Sun Rotisserie League has a powerful weapon to use against his leaguemates: his drive-time radio show. For one hour in the morning in West Palm Beach, Kent ruminates on topics ranging from medical marijuana and human-rights abuses to the stupid trades and bad draft choices his opponents make. Sometimes he baits them to call from their cars. "You're driving sixty, and he's talking about what a dummy you are," says leaguemate Howard Greitzer. "I don't listen to him anymore."

· · ·

My first major road trip of the season is a weeklong swing along the East Coast that starts at Ron Shandler's house in Blue Ridge country, continues to Baltimore, where I plan to meet up with Trace Wood, and finally to Toronto, where the Blue Jays are hosting the Minnesota Twins in a series that will feature nine of my players, including Josh Phelps, Miguel Batista, and the resilient Jacque Jones.

Though I'd planned this journey weeks ago as a chance to gather intelligence and lay a little groundwork for future trades, it's starting to feel more like a tour of gloating. It's not enough just to *know* that I'm beating all of these experts at their own game, I want to witness the looks on their faces when they review the standings.

Ron Shandler, the father of Tout Wars, lives in a tidy brick house up a winding mountain road just past a donkey farm on the outskirts of Roanoke. It's a glorious Saturday morning in May, but right now the Bearded One is slouched behind a desk in his dim basement wearing shorts and sandals, his arms folded, the glow of the Tout Wars home page flooding his glasses.

"Anything surprising so far?" I ask.

"Yeah," he snorts. "There's this guy in second place who's never played before."

For the second week of May, the Streetwalkers were the best overall team in Tout Wars by a fat margin. After making strides in nearly every statistical category, we gained fifteen overall ranking points to crest at 87, just eight and a half points back from the surprise leader, Jeff Erickson. We're dominating the pitching categories as expected and holding our own on offense, where Jones, Guillen, and David Ortiz have powered us to fourth place in home runs.

If Shandler got ahold of my daily log, he'd find a handful of delighted entries that say "I'm beating Ron!" or "Ron's team sucks!" Now that he's floundering in ninth place, even some of his acolytes are starting to doubt him. "I have nothing but respect for Ron and his methods," says one post on his subscriber forum. "But I cannot see his offense sweeping anything but the floor. I will probably be proven wrong by the master, but I go on record saying that he's going down." In a strange turn of events, I find myself offering the old champion aid and comfort.

"It's early yet," I say.

Shandler's ballyhooed RIMA Plan turns out to be an acronym for "Risk Management." After years of watching injuries sink perfectly good teams, he decided on that portentous October jog to try to do something about it. Shandler created a scale of relative riskiness and graded every player based on factors like durability, playing time, age, and consistency. At the auction, he built a portfolio balanced between safe bets like Baltimore's Miguel Tejada, who hasn't missed a game in four years, and typical Shandler "skill" players like Brad Fullmer, a hitter who, by the rules of Shandlermetrics, ought to be joining baseball's elite at any moment. He even broke from his LIMA tradition to splurge on two pitchers who fared well on his danger scale, including Chicago's Esteban Loaiza. While the stats informed every step, RIMA was a bit of a departure for Shandler, a strategy governed as much by art as science.

Trouble is, it's not working. Loaiza isn't impressing, Tejada's power has vanished, Fullmer's batting .238, and outfielder Kenny Lofton of the Yankees, his sure bet for steals, is limping around with one swipe to his name. Shandler, usually loath to make any moves this early, had already traded one struggling pitcher and talked to several other Touts about picking up an extra bat.

Nonetheless, he says he's determined to stand pat. Another tenet of the RIMA Plan, he tells me, is excruciating patience. While a player's performance can wax and wane, risk is something that can be measured only at the end of a full season. If he can creep within fifteen points of the lead by July, he thinks he has a shot.

"I like my team," he says, unconvincingly.

Shandler's desk is neat but dusty, as if nothing has been moved in a while. Splayed about are four pairs of glasses in various cases: "I'm always leaving them somewhere," he explains. His monitor is guarded by a flock of figurine penguins, his favorite animal. On a stretch of bookshelves along one wall, there's a copy of every baseball reference book published in two decades, a handful of autographed balls in plastic cases, and pictures of Ron posing at various ballparks, always with the kind of joyless puss you'd expect from Queen Elizabeth.

Shandler's unconventional baseball career began in 1985 as he sat with his wife, Sue, at her brother's dinner table in Houston, stuffed with Thanksgiving turkey and, as he tells it, "bored senseless." Despite earning his MBA at night at Hofstra, Shandler had proved to be a lousy corporate climber. In seven years, he was fired by a business document company, a sporting-goods manufacturer, and a book publisher. "I'm not the kind of person who's cut out to be an employee," he concluded.

Truth be told, the business world was never his preference. If given a choice, Shandler would have followed in the footsteps of his father, a clarinet and sax player who'd been the leader of a band called Jack Sands and his Happy Revelers that worked the old Borscht Belt circuit of summer resorts in upstate New York. As a kid, Shandler was a prodigal student of classical piano and was accepted to Julliard's preparatory school, only to have his parents nix the idea. They wanted him to be an orthodontist.

After coming to terms with his unemployability, Shandler tried, for a time, to publish some of his original songs. When that didn't work, he started a business writing personalized jingles for birthdays, bar mitzvahs, and bachelor parties. He'd post flyers at catering halls and when an order came in, scratch out some lyrics, set them to keyboards, and mail out a cassette.

As the Thanksgiving table talk droned on, Shandler's thoughts drifted to his new default subject: baseball statistics. In 1985 baseball's cult of numbers was blossoming, and Shandler had been happily swept away. Innovations like Bill James's "runs created," Thomas Boswell's "total average," and Pete Palmer's "linear weights" were taking hold, putting a charge in the air. For math geeks who liked baseball, this was the Summer of Love.

What Shandler couldn't understand about all these new stats is why nobody had taken the obvious next step: using them to measure all the teams and players in the major leagues and publishing the results after the season.

Then, right there in Houston, it hit him: Hey, I should do that.

The following winter, Shandler stood up from his Commodore 64 with the text of a pamphlet called *Baseball SuperSTATS*. He put an ad in *The Sporting News* and sold one hundred copies for $9.95. While he'd been playing Rotisserie for a few years, the notion of using this data to help him play that parlor game was the farthest thing from his mind. It wasn't until he started getting letters from readers that he made the connection: People were buying his book to get an edge in their fantasy leagues.

Though he still considered himself a baseball analyst in the traditional sense, the more he purposely catered to Roto players the more copies he sold. In 1994, the first year of the *USA Today* LABR league, Shandler finally dropped all secular pretenses. He started a newsletter and added Rotisserie blurbs on every player to his book, which was now called the *Baseball Forecaster*. At the time, Shandler was living in

New Hampshire working for a specialty publishing house in Boston. It was a make-do job that he hated. So he quit.

While it was touch-and-go at first (the 1994 baseball strike didn't help), Shandler kept at it. Three years later, when he launched his first Web site, its traffic surpassed the circulation of his newsletter in nine months. Suddenly his business was growing at 20 percent per year. "That's when I knew I really had something," he says.

Flush with Rotisserie loot and freed from the bonds of geography, the Shandlers decided to move somewhere warmer than New Hampshire. So Ron opened a spreadsheet and typed in the names of every temperate city on the East Coast. He broke them down by cost of living, crime rate, mean temperature, cultural amenities, public schools, tax rates, and whatever else he could think of. He devised a weighted formula and fed the data through it until the computer spat out the nine best towns. The Shandlers visited the top five and picked a winner. Roanoke.

"Any family here?" I ask.

"No."

"Friends? Acquaintances?"

"Not a one."

Today Shandler Enterprises is a thriving business with a $100,000 editorial budget. It employs thirty writers, fewer than half of whom Shandler has actually met. He will have 7,500 online subscribers before the year is out, with accounts in thirty countries, from England to Indonesia. A full subscription costs $99 annually, which is twenty bucks more than an online subscription to *The Wall Street Journal*. Behind his desk, he's taped a chart of his Internet circulation, which is basically an arrow heading skyward at various degrees of vertiginousness. Given that he sells about eighteen thousand *Forecasters* on top of this, consultants have told him the whole enterprise could be worth three million dollars on the high end.

"It pays the mortgage," he says.

Shandler is quick to dismiss the idea that he's developed a cult following or that he holds a messianic sway over his followers. But facts are facts. One reader sent a heartfelt letter of thanks to his wife, Sue, for allowing Ron the time to bring so much joy to so many, and another sent him a case of potato knishes packed in dry ice. Some Shandlerisms have taken on the power of liturgy, and if somebody takes a swipe at the Bearded One on a baseball message board, it's not long before six people swoop in to defend him. His own site, Baseball HQ, is a distinct community with its own language and customs. At all hours, the message boards crackle with action: Somebody needs pitching help in an eighteen-team mixed 6x6 single-season league, while somebody else wants to know which of five players to activate by noon. There are lively threads with titles like "Klesko's Shoulder."

But for all his success, some of the joy has drained out of Shandler. His columns used to be lighter, funnier, with references to Groucho Marx and self-conscious jokes about "stat geeks." Nowadays, just four years shy of fifty, he seems more like an aging mafia boss, determined to take his wayward family legitimate. His columns are often passionate and pointed, and he's still plugging that word of his, "fanalytic." Gone are the days when he used to type his columns with John Coltrane or Billy Joel playing in the background. "Lately I've been writing in silence," he says.

It used to take him two weeks to write all the player blurbs for the *Forecaster*, but thanks to the deluge of information available online the research takes far longer now, even with help. Strangely, though, the more projections he does, the less faith he has in the idea that there's some golden grail of forecasting precision to be discovered. "I used to be married to the numbers," he says, "but the last few years, I've started to realize sometimes they hardly matter at all."

An hour later, while watching his daughter's softball game (Shandler sponsors the team), the Bearded One ventures into tougher subjects. He's all but given up on the Society for American Baseball Research, which still likes to pretend he doesn't exist. "These guys on their high horses!" he says, rolling his eyes. He's tired of "baseball" people asking him if he ever played the game, as if it should matter. And even now, whenever he starts to get comfortable as the undisputed leader in the Rotisserie advice business, "somebody is trying to take me down."

First it was John Benson, who, Shandler says, implicitly trashed some of his projections in 1994, prompting Ron to consult with a libel lawyer. Six years later an attorney sent Shandler a cease-and-desist letter for posting the official rules of the original Rotisserie League on the Tout Wars site without permission. (Benson had bought the licensing rights.) Once in a while, Shandler has to fight off some joker who puts up a copycat site using some (or all) of his signature metrics. And now, after all this, he's got Baseball Prospectus to deal with.

Of all the little feuds in Tout Wars, none burns hotter than the animus between Shandler and the writers of BP. When I bring up the subject, Sue Shandler, who's been standing next to us, walks off suddenly with exaggerated strides. "Uh-oh," she says.

The arrogance is nothing new, Shandler says. BP has always acted like a Sabermetric cavalry of Cossacks, hell-bent on wiping out non-believers and burning their villages, too. But so long as its writers considered themselves too "serious" for fantasy baseball, he was content to invite them to Tout Wars and watch them flounder, which they generally did. But the moment BP decided to start marketing its own projections to fantasy players, the détente barely lasted an hour.

In various formats, Prospectus writers have labeled Shandler a "pure fantasy guy" and bad-mouthed the injury analysis on his site. Nate Silver, the brains behind PECOTA, once wrote a column suggesting Shandler's projections were not nearly as effective as his, and at an appearance two days before the Tout Wars draft he said it was "ridiculous" to think Shandler's methods were more rigorous. Even Joe Sheehan, who clearly respects the Bearded One, isn't above the occasional dig. Shandler, he says, does "a good job of making it sound like he's discovered things when in actuality, he hasn't."

If there's any consolation, it's that Shandler can always fight it out in the expert leagues, where he believes he has a clear advantage. At the Tout Wars auction, Shandler gleefully sabotaged Sheehan by bidding up the pitchers he wanted. When it comes to the elite levels of Rotisserie, Shandler says, "They're really out of their league."

Back in his basement bunker as our visit winds down, I ask Shandler how it's going with the Cardinals. In late February, he'd flown to

St. Louis to meet his contact there, Jeff Luhnow, who'd given him a tour of the front office. As Shandler looked on one morning, Luhnow put in a waiver claim on Luis Martinez, a player Shandler had enthusiastically recommended, and by lunchtime Martinez was a Cardinal. Just like that, sitting there in his best khakis, Shandler had crossed the great divide.

Today, Shandler stays in touch with the team through a private message board where the Cardinals post questions about players that come available. Nine times out of ten, he says, he'll read the names and advise them to pass. But just a week earlier, when a pitcher named Will Cunnane came across the transom, Shandler urged them to pounce. Then he waited. And waited. "There was nothing but silence on the other end."

It wasn't that Shandler expected to be given the run of the place. He knew it would take time to fully change the culture of a real front office. Nevertheless, he seems pretty glum about it. The Cardinals are running things the way they always have, he says, and he's not sure if his ideas have made much of an impact. He's supposed to go back later this summer to make a more formal presentation to the team, but he's not sure it's going to happen. As he talks about this, his voice takes on a different pitch—higher, more tentative. "I think we've still got a long way to go."

It took me some time to understand what was going on here, how a guy could spend twenty years in the baseball wilderness and then, once the search party found him, be disappointed by the bumpy helicopter ride. The central irony of Shandler's career is that years ago, he chose to embrace Roto at a time when it would have been more expedient to thumb his nose. But by doing so, he actually shortened his own path to a major-league paycheck. So now he's left with a choice: rededicate himself to Rotisserie baseball and to winning Tout Wars or put the past behind him and walk bravely through the front-office door he's kicked ajar.

For now, Shandler is content to live in Roanoke, to teach one daughter the piano and ferry the other to dance recitals. He'll write his regular Friday columns and get his baseball fix from the Salem

Avalanche farm team down the road. When the girls are in college, maybe he'll sell the whole damn thing. Maybe he and Sue will move to the Bahamas. But before then, the day is coming when Shandler will have to choose which game he prefers: the one that's played on the dirt in those ballparks he rarely visits or the shadow game you can play from the silence of your own basement.

———

On Sunday, May 16, Trace Wood marches through the press entrance at Oriole Park on a crystalline afternoon, giving the guy at the reception desk a "Hi, Bill" and the elevator attendant a "Hey, Bruce." Upstairs in the press box, he pulls his laptop from a cabinet, grabs a score sheet, and takes his usual seat behind home plate.

At the moment, his Tout Wars team is languishing in tenth place, but on the phone recently Wood told me he wasn't too concerned. In fact, he expected to take over fourth in about two weeks. "I'm right where I want to be," he'd insisted. The unstated purpose of my visit, then, is to try to determine (on a scale from one to ten) just how delusional he really is.

For the last four years, Wood has worked about fifty Baltimore home games each season as a datacaster for Major League Baseball's official Web site. His job is to reduce every event on the field into a line of code. Most plays are easy enough. A groundout to second, for instance, is translated as "43/g." But if the pitcher catches a bunt pop-up and doubles a runner off first base, the resulting code would be "1/bpdp.1x1(13)."

In some ways, Trace Wood and all the other datacasters who come to ballgames are the foot soldiers of baseball's quantitative revolution. They don't just chart runs and errors but the trajectory and force of every hit and the location of every pitch in real time. The various stats companies and Web services that employ them to collect this data not only provide it to Sabermetricians, they also beam it out immediately to the scoring pages of countless Rotisserie leagues. As Wood translates ballgames on his laptop, millions of baseball fans quite literally hang on every keystroke.

By all accounts, it's a job he's exceptionally good at. During tonight's game, when Rafael Palmeiro comes to bat, the visiting Angels shift the shortstop over behind second base to account for Palmeiro's tendency to pull the ball. When Palmeiro grounds into a double play, Jim Henneman, the Orioles' official scorer, rules that the shortstop fielded the ball. But Wood, his concentration sharpened to a fine point, tells him it was actually the third baseman. Henneman orders up a replay, which confirms his mistake.

"Nice call, Trace," he says.

After dropping out of LSU where he'd studied architecture, Wood soured on a series of careers—from construction worker and art gallery manager to reference librarian at a law firm. A few years ago he retired from the office world to manage a pair of rental properties he'd inherited, take care of his newborn daughter, and devote himself to dominating the highest levels of Rotisserie. In addition to datacasting, Wood began writing articles for various Rotisserie outlets and beefing up the content on his own site, the Long Gandhi. After a strong showing in a lesser expert league in 2001, Wood received his first invitation to Tout Wars.

Between his Orioles job and the hours he spends devouring games on TV, Wood watches the equivalent of about twenty-one straight days of baseball per year, which is more than anyone else in the competition. As far as he's concerned, there's nothing frivolous about this. While the rest of the Touts gorge on numbers, Wood sticks to an increasingly quaint notion: He looks at the stats, too, but he rarely acquires anyone until he's seen him play. His motto is, "Watch the games, read the numbers, win your league."

Overall, his theory about picking players can be explained in two words: Be dull. Other than paying $26 for Boston outfielder Johnny Damon at this year's auction, he didn't draft a single bona-fide superstar. While the other Touts sparred over the big names and filled the gaps in their rosters with dollar specials, Wood focused on the forgotten middle-class, players like Matt Lawton, Matt Stairs, and Brian Jordan, all of whom have shown excellent skills in the past but who have, for whatever reason, landed in the Rotisserie remainder bins, where they sell for between $8 and $13. His roster reads like a support group for ballplayers who've been cast out, disrespected, discounted, or overlooked, which, after learning more about Trace Wood, does not appear to be a coincidence.

His story, as he described it to me, begins in 1964, when he was born to an unmarried California couple who gave him up for adoption. Wood's adoptive father, a career navy man, died of a heart attack when he was fifteen, and for a time afterward he became estranged from his mother. As a teenager, he'd excelled at the trumpet and had already begun to play professionally, before a freak collision with a sliding glass door severed a tendon in his hand.

Listening to this litany of hard knocks and tough breaks, it's clear that Wood considers them central to his character and that they allow him to play Rotisserie baseball with a rare level of bloodlessness. He doesn't feel panic, he's not prone to follow the crowd, and his principles are indelibly fixed. Although his Orioles press pass gives him access to the clubhouse, he rarely talks to players for fear of falling prey to sentiment. To the other Touts, he's got a reputation for being prickly and a bit smug. But what makes him stand out is that he doesn't seem to mind. He's not competing in Tout Wars for the camaraderie; he's in it to win. As if to drive home the point, he's tacked a poster of Albert Einstein directly above his desk at home with the caption, "Great spirits have always encountered violent opposition from mediocre minds."

By the late innings in Baltimore, Wood's seamless confidence has started to bug me. After producing a long argument about why his team is fundamentally better than mine, he predicts that he'll pass me by the end of the month. I can't remember exactly how the whole "stick of butter" theme developed, but by the final inning it's become the basis of a wager. Right there in the press box at Oriole Park, we agree that whoever finishes below the other in Tout Wars will be forced to eat an entire stick of butter, straight from the foil.

Most people would be hesitant to make this bet, or any bet, while trailing the other guy by eight places and thirty-two points in a Rotisserie league, but Wood doesn't flinch.

"You're *sure* you want to do this?" I ask.

"Sure," he says, nonchalantly. "I have no problem watching you eat a stick of butter."

Driving back to my hotel that night, I have the answer to my initial question about Trace Wood. The dude is a solid *nine* on the delusional scale.

———

Next stop, Toronto.

With the Twins in town for three games, there will be nine players of mine in the two dugouts, the highest concentration of Streetwalkers so far this season. It's my first chance to try my hand at "managing" my players.

In addition to being loaded down with provocative statistics generated by Sig, I'm also beginning my campaign to build team morale. Last month, demonstrating a hidden talent, Nando had sketched an official team logo. In it the Streetwalkers name appears in Navy script above the silhouette of a pimp in a leisure suit with a cane, a fedora, and a flowing robe with yellow fur trim superimposed on a giant moonlike baseball. I had it printed on forty heather-gray T-shirts, nine of which are now bundled in my suitcase. They look *sharp.*

Talking to ballplayers at spring training was one thing. But since the season began, I've learned that talking to *my* players is an entirely different kettle of fish. The few I'd caught up with at Yankee Stadium so far had taught me that saying, "Dude, you're on my Rotisserie team," wasn't much of an icebreaker. When I first met Anaheim pitcher Aaron Sele, whom I'd picked up as a free agent, all I could think to do was ask him for a favor.

"Can you take it easy on Ortiz and Mueller?"

"Those are your boys?" he asked.

"No, those are *your* boys."

"Sure thing," he said, laughing.

If I really wanted to have an influence on these guys, I knew I'd have to be more than a groupie. To understand them, to really get inside their heads, I'd have to come to the ballpark prepared to ask intelligent questions.

I arrive at the SkyDome in Toronto on a Tuesday afternoon just before batting practice and proceed directly to the Minnesota clubhouse, where the mood is loose and upbeat. Players slouch around on various chairs and worn leather sofas while Outkast thumps from the stereo. The Twins have been knocking the cover off the baseball and have opened up a comfortable lead in the Central Division.

I have five Twins on my Tout Wars roster, but there's only one that I'm desperate to talk to: Jacque Jones. In April my right fielder had rewarded my faith more than I could have imagined, hitting .329 with four homers, six steals, and seventeen RBI, a pace that, if he keeps it up, would put him in the company of baseball's elite. Because I'm proud of him, and because I still feel guilty for tormenting him in Florida, I've arrived here with a special token of thanks.

When I find him, Jones is tilted back in a chair at the back of the room, engrossed in a *USA Today* article about the Phillies pitching staff. Next to him, two teammates are playing an NBA video game on a hanging TV.

"Jacque, you got a second?"

He drops the paper.

"Sure, wassup?"

I remind Jones as gently as possible about the train wreck of a conversation we had back in Florida and promise that I won't be quoting from the *Baseball Forecaster*.

"Thanks," he says.

Next I tell him that I'd gone ahead and drafted him on my Tout Wars team, which is currently in second place due, in large part, to his thermonuclear April.

"I wanted to give you a couple things," I say.

First, I hand him the shirt.

"Right on," he says, holding it up. "Streetwalkers."

"You like it?"

"Yup."

Reaching into my bag, I pull out a wad of newspaper that contains the big surprise. Inside, there's a small gold cup mounted on a marble base, which I unwrap and set down on the table in front of him. Jones turns it around and reads the inscription: *Jacque Jones, Streetwalkers Baseball Club, Player of the Month, April 2004.*

"Oh, sweet!"

"It wasn't even close," I say.

"Right on."

Spotting the trophy, Twins pitcher Johan Santana pauses the video game he's playing and motions for Jones to slide it over. "Player for the Month in April," Santana says, reading the engraving with a raised eyebrow. "*¡Muy Bien!*"

Jones seems pleased. His expressive face is calm and relaxed. I ask him if he's got time for a few baseball questions, and he nods. Before I'd left, Sig had zapped over a long list of statistical queries for Jones, most of which I'd exorcised from my notes. Remembering what happened in Florida, I made sure that if he pulled this sheet out of my hands, he'd see nothing but a string of compliments.

I start off by telling Jones that one of his rarest qualities as a hitter is that he has an extreme tendency to hit ground balls but, at the same time, still manages to hit home runs in bunches.

"How do you do that?" I ask.

Jones shrugs passively. "I don't know, I can't explain it. I don't worry about ground balls, fly balls, line drives. . . ."

"Do you have two different swings?"

"No."

Moving on, I mention that Jones generally fares better the first time he faces a pitcher in a game rather than the second or third time, which seems counterintuitive.

"Any sense of why?" I ask.

"Nope."

Jones is bobbing his head to the clubhouse music. I can't tell if he's getting irritated with me or just waiting for a better question. Checking my sheet, I scroll down to the last item, something I'd added on the plane. What impressed me the most about his hot start, I say, was that he'd done it his own way. Despite all the pressure he's been under to take more pitches, Jones had managed to have one of the best months of his career while continuing to strike out three times as often as he walks. Jones lets me continue until he hears the words "walk rate," and then he stops me cold.

"All that stuff takes away from what you do on the field," he says, waving his hand dismissively. "Like I said earlier, you either like me, or you don't."

There's an awkward silence. Jones, eyes forward, no longer smiling, begins folding his Streetwalkers shirt. I stuff my list of questions back inside my shoulder bag and, in a bid to change the subject, nod to the trophy.

"So you think this will take a prominent place on your mantle?" I ask, not at all seriously.

Jones looks down at the gold cup with a surprisingly proud expression, as if he's not going to let any accomplishment be minimized, even a ten-dollar MVP trophy from some Roto nut.

"I'll find a place for it," he says.

Jones shakes my hand, gets up, and walks over to his locker, head still bobbing. As he puts the trophy on a shelf next to his shower kit and slides the shirt on a hanger, I feel like a jackass. I step outside for a few moments to berate myself in the hallway.

Back inside the clubhouse I find my first baseman, Doug Mientkiewicz, the owner of one of the most confounding surnames in the history of professional sports. He's perched on a folding chair spitting tobacco juice into a Gatorade bottle.

Mientkiewicz hails from Florida but was born in Toledo, where his father was a Lake Erie walleye-boat captain. On the field, he's sort of a throwback: He doesn't wear batting gloves, keeps his pants pulled up high on the calf, blows giant pink bubbles, and never leaves with a clean uniform. For this, he's earned the nickname "Dougie Baseball."

Most players, when I tell them they're on my Rotisserie team, respond with a nod or a smirk or something diplomatic like "cool." But after listening to my standard spiel, Mientkiewicz says something unusual.

"Sorry to hear that."

I laugh, assuming it's a joke. It's not.

"I tell everybody the same thing when they say I'm on their fantasy team," he says. "I'm like, 'Well, you're an idiot.' There are so many guys I'd take over me."

As he's apparently well aware, Mientkiewicz is a baseball misfit—not just in Rotisserie terms but in the real player market, too. He's a first baseman better known for defense than power, a guy who won a Gold Glove in 2001 but has never hit more than fifteen home runs. At the Tout Wars auction, I picked him up for $12, which was a bit below his statistical value. It's not that I'd caught the table sleeping: Most Rotisserie managers, like their counterparts in the front office, prefer to have power at the corner infield positions. "It's a shame you don't have a category for defense," Mientkiewicz says, "because I know I'd be one of the first couple guys picked."

As Dougie Baseball's make-believe manager, my only concern right now is his batting average, which has been skidding. After hovering at .311 in early May, it's dropped to .271 which, since BA is about all he's got to offer, is a genuine cause for alarm. Down in the Twins farm system there's a big Canadian first baseman named Justin Morneau who's been pounding home runs at a savage pace. If he's not careful, Mientkiewicz (and the $12 I paid for him) could wind up parked on the bench.

"I'm going through a stretch right now where I look out from the plate, and I see a big glove," he tells me. "Unless I hit it over the fence, it seems like everyone's catching it." Still, he says, he's sixty points ahead of where he was this time last year when he finished at .300, "so let's not panic."

At this I dig through my notes and pull out something I never intended to show him: a list of possible Mientkiewicz trades that I've been kicking around. In general, the idea of asking a professional athlete to help you expunge him from your fantasy roster seems like a good way to get smacked in the head. But for some reason I get the feeling Mientkiewicz is the exception.

I hand him the list.

"What do you think?" I ask, tentatively.

"If you want power, Jody Gerut's a good one, he's going to hit twenty homers," Mientkiewicz says, scanning the list. "José Cruz is going to hit, too, not for average but a lot of pop. Lawton's having a great year, too, as long as he stays healthy."

When he's finished, I hand him a jersey.

"Team T-shirts? All right!"

As I turn to go, Mientkiewicz returns to his Gatorade spittoon but not before shouting out some parting advice. "Hopefully you'll get me traded sooner rather than later!"

Across the ballpark in the Blue Jays clubhouse, the vibe is completely different. There's no music, no card games, no screwing around. Some players talk quietly, even conspiratorially, in small groups, while others are studying video. Toronto has started the year in a tailspin, and until they pull out of it there's no levity allowed.

Josh Phelps, my most controversial player, sits in a chair facing his locker. His body language is about what I'd expected: slouched, slumped, and frowning. In the middle of a 3-for-28 skid, Phelps had been benched for the last two games. Sig, rushing to his defense, insisted that Phelps is just the victim of a bad statistical sample and that if he's allowed to play long enough he'll inevitably turn it around. "No manager who understands what a standard deviation is will ever bench him consistently," he says.

I start with the question Sig made me promise I would ask.

"Do you really like math?"

"It's a subject I was good at, for the simple fact that there was always an answer," Phelps says, staring at his shoes. "Unlike in baseball, where sometimes there isn't an answer for why things happen."

By the numbers, Phelps is a bit of a basket case, or as his boss J. P. Ricciardi had put it a few minutes earlier, "an enigma." On a Sabermetric team that preaches plate discipline, he has more strikeouts than base hits and ranks near the bottom of the league in pitches per plate appearance. Stranger still, when the count was in his favor, say 2–0, Sig found, his batting average was below the league norm. But with no balls and two strikes, he was actually *better* than league average. "When the count's in my favor, I try to be aggressive," Phelps explains. "And when it's 0–2, I'm really trying to make sure it's a strike. So that might be the reason there."

Phelps clenches his fists like he's gripping a bat handle. "When it's 0–2, I'm just trying to get something in play. When I'm ahead in the count, I expand the strike zone because I want to do too much. That's something I need to work on."

I begin to suggest that maybe Phelps should just tell the pitcher to throw two strikes before he steps to the plate, but looking at him I get the feeling I might end up with cleat marks on my forehead. Instead, I hand him a shirt. "Thanks," he says, folding it up neatly. "Hopefully I'll pick it up and help you out."

That night, I watch the game from the press box. Jacque Jones rips a single and scores a run. Mientkiewicz, hitless again, strands three runners and Josh Phelps fails to hit a ball out of the infield. The Streetwalkers player of the game is Miguel Batista, who makes up for a rotten first six weeks by pitching masterfully, taking a no-hitter into the sixth, and coming away with a win.

After the game, I find Batista in the same spot I'd seen him before warm-ups, sitting alone at an empty reception desk near the clubhouse door, stroking his beard and watching something intently on his laptop.

"Breaking down video?" I ask.

"No! no!" he says. "This is one of my loves!"

He's watching *Law & Order*.

Born poor in the Dominican Republic, Batista has a limited education, but you wouldn't know it. Ten minutes into our talk he's already quoted Einstein and Aristotle and discussed the works of Edgar Allan Poe. At the moment he says he's learning to read music, studying books on how to train horses (he has eight), and watching the new *Law & Order* DVD to get ideas for his detective novel. Three years ago, with no training in the medium, he published *Sentimientos en Blanco y Negro*, a collection of poetry. "Plato said that at the touch of love, everyone becomes a poet," he says.

Best known in baseball for shutting down the Yankees in the 2001 World Series, Batista has a deep repertoire of pitches, all of which have exceptional movement. So much movement, in fact, that he's often unable to find the strike zone. Or worse, unable to avoid plunking his own teammates at spring training.

But Batista's biggest enemy isn't his throwing mechanics, it's his preoccupied brain. The unusual thing about Batista is that rather than trying to focus his mind on pitching, he encourages it to wander. On the mound, it's not unusual to see him muttering. "Sometimes I'm praying, singing, or meditating. Some days I'm thinking about a passage from a book or a quote that I read," he says. "When you find a piece of the truth, it will attack you." When his thoughts are far away from baseball, he tells me, "that's when things go well."

At this, I fold up my Batista stat sheet and wad it in my pocket. There's no sense in offering tactical advice to a guy who will purposely try to *forget it* as soon as he takes the mound.

"What episode is this?" I ask.

Batista cues it up, and we watch.

The next morning, with my business in Toronto all but concluded, I'm standing on the field in a blaze of noon sunshine, wondering why there aren't more day games. All of a sudden, there's someone standing next to me in a batting helmet.

It's Jacque Jones.

"Hey, what's going on?" he says.

"Nice day out," I venture.

"Great day."

It's clearly time for me to make amends.

"Jacque, I'm sorry for busting your balls with all this stats stuff. I'm not trying to—" Jones is smiling. He interrupts.

"You can't pay attention to the stats. If I listened to the stats I never would have made it out of high school. What were they saying then? 'He's too small, he'll never hit for power,' whatever."

"You've gotta be yourself," I say.

Jones nods in agreement.

"Why wait for a pitcher to throw his best pitch?" he continues, his eyebrows lifted. "Early in the count, they're trying to throw strikes. I don't sit and wait for a pitcher to set me up. I'm ready to hit."

Backpedaling toward the batting cage, Jones winds his bat in giant loops above his head. "A pitcher may kill me sometimes for being overaggressive," he says. "But if he makes a mistake, he'd best believe I'll be there to take care of it."

Moments later, I'm watching my right fielder dent the outfield seats with soaring baseballs, and I feel absolved. All is well, no harm done. Jacque is Jacque. I was right to believe in him. And there's nothing I can say that will screw him up.

Scallions

June

For Father's Day, Mel Frishman's young son bought him a special present: a personalized ballcap embroidered with the name of his Rotisserie team, the Frish Basemen. Problem was, the team logo, a pair of crossed bats, obscured a couple of important letters. The banner said "Frish Semen."

"I've worn that hat to every draft," he says.

· · ·

In real baseball, Memorial Day is considered the first point in the season at which to make substantial tweaks. So even as my team slipped to fourth place, I made a personal pledge to batten down my impulses for one more week.

This would not be easy. Back on May 14, just before my trip to Roanoke, Bill Mueller was held out of the Boston lineup, and in the papers the next day, Red Sox manager Terry Francona explained the situation thusly: "Billy Mueller is a little beat up right now."

A few weeks before Francona's announcement, Mueller had stepped to the plate in Toronto to face left-hander Ted Lilly. The batter's box in the SkyDome is nothing more than a little dirt piled over a concrete floor, and players say it tends to be "sticky." Mueller went to pivot during a swing, and, he later told me, part of his foot didn't pivot. "I heard a click in my right knee," he said. Mueller had kept the problem quiet, of course, playing through the swelling and discomfort without so much as a grimace, though not especially well.

For five days after hearing this news I was the picture of restraint—or, more appropriately, denial. After sitting out for one series, Mueller seemed to validate my passivity by returning to the lineup to tag the Devil Rays for three hits. But two games later he was scratched again and diagnosed with mild patella tendonitis.

If I'd been ruthlessly objective about Mueller, I might have caught some early clues about his physical condition. In Florida I'd watched him remove a brace from that very same knee while talking about "staying healthy," and a few days after the draft, when I sent a copy of my roster to Steve Phillips, the former GM of the New York Mets, he told me, "I like Mueller, but last year was the first year he stayed healthy in a long time. I will keep my fingers crossed for you."

To cover the bag for Mueller, the Red Sox called up Kevin Youkilis, a minor leaguer best known as one of Billy Beane's favorite prospects. No sooner had he unpacked his Pawtucket duffel bag than he became the first Boston player in seventeen years to homer in his debut. Since Youkilis hadn't been claimed in the Tout Wars reserve draft, he was a free agent and thus available for FAAB.

So far, the mystery of FAAB has proven to be exactly that. Bubba Crosby started off hot but fizzled. Dicky Gonzalez, a pitcher I'd seen in Puerto Rico, stunk so badly in the majors after I acquired him that Tampa Bay eventually sold his contract to the Yakult Swallows of the Japanese league. We've already blown more of our FAAB budget than all but one team.

As ever, the Streetwalkers front office is sharply divided on the subject of whether to bid on Kevin Youkilis. After watching the guy play baseball, Nando's convinced he may be good enough to stick around, even when Mueller heals. But even though Billy Beane loves the guy, Sig still thinks we should avoid him like a pothole. His philosophy is that most minor-league call-ups have almost zero value, so in the name of embracing risk, we're better off spending our money on starting pitchers with major-league jobs.

Other than tossing my assistants into a Jell-O pit and letting them settle it themselves, I can think of only one person to appeal to:

Boston GM Theo Epstein. When I caught up with him during spring training, Epstein had mentioned, offhandedly, that if Youkilis was ever called up to the majors, he was a good candidate for a .360 on-base percentage and a .380 slugging percentage, numbers that would give him a value demonstrably higher than zero. My only remaining concern is that the ominous media reports on Mueller's knee might be overblown and that after a soak in the whirlpool, Mueller will return to the lineup and knock Youkilis back to the minors.

To find out, I send an e-mail.

In his reply, Epstein tells me that Mueller will have a second opinion on Monday, and while this is hardly classified information, it effectively settles the argument. From what I know about Bill Mueller, he wouldn't go for a second opinion if the first opinion was "Dude, you're fine." When Friday comes, I bid $16 on Youkilis, which is a healthy $4 more than the next-highest bidder, Jason Grey.

But in a week's time, I have no regrets. Mueller's second opinion says he should undergo arthroscopic knee surgery and miss the next six weeks. And on the same day Mueller is having this operation, Kevin Youkilis knocks in three runs and reaches base for the tenth straight game. He'll score fifteen runs in his first thirteen starts and be named AL rookie of the month.

Sig is eerily quiet.

"We got lucky" is all he says.

———

Thanks to his instincts on Youkilis and his earlier brilliance in helping me pull off the Cinquo de Mayo Massacre, I decide to promote Ferdinando "Bonecrusher" Di Fino to general manager of the Streetwalkers Baseball Club, reserving for myself the title Owner and President of Baseball Operations, or, as Sig likes to call me, Sambrenner.

Nando's new job is to study the player pool from morning to night and harass the other Touts with horrendously lopsided trade offers. I like this arrangement because it frees me up to spend more time harassing real baseball executives.

As Memorial Day approaches, our first priority is to shore up our outfield, which, despite the addition of José Guillen, remains alarmingly feeble. Dmitri Young is on the mend, thanks to a metal plate and seven screws attached to his fibula, but there's no telling when he'll be back in action. From the beginning, the REMA Plan dictated that sometime in the middle of the season we'd start trading from our pitching surplus to pick up more offense. And now that we're leading the Tout Wars pitching race with 53 points out of a possible 60 in the five categories, we have a big enough cushion to think about swapping one of our middling arms for an outfielder. After studying our pitching roster as actuarially as possible, Nando and I settle on the same expendable name. Brad Radke.

The decision has nothing to do with merit and everything to do with the other half of that old Wall Street axiom, *sell high*. After a slow start, the robotic Radke has been ripping through opponents as if the Twins upgraded his software. "I just feel like my pitches are a little sharper," he told me in Toronto. Even then I already had an inkling that he might have to go, so while Radke was busy lacing up his shoes after the game, I swallowed hard and told him. "Don't take offense," I said, "but I may have to trade you."

Radke said nothing at first, so I started to blabber. "It's not that I don't like you, it's just that my pitching is lights-out and other guys in my league have—"

"Hey, whatever it takes to make your team better," he said.

"So it's okay by you?"

"Oh, shit, yeah. Deal me out, trade me, I don't care." Springing to his feet cheerfully, Radke 6.0 flashed the briefest of smiles.

"I won't take it personally," he assured.

As Nando begins blasting out Radke trade offers to the other Touts, I'm fully aware that some of them won't see him as quite the Rotisserie jackpot that I do. But after a few responses, the indifference is worse than I thought. Some yawn, others laugh. When I ask Trace Wood if he'd take Radke for Matt Lawton, his response is characteristically curt: "I hate Radke."

The only serious offer comes from Joe Sheehan, which is really just that old horseshit backup offer, plus interest. He's willing to send us Baltimore center fielder Luis Matos, but only in exchange for Radke and a payment of $6 from our dwindling FAAB budget. (FAAB money is a common sweetener in Rotisserie trades.)

Luis Matos had arrived in Baltimore last year smacking home runs, stealing bases, and hitting better than .300, but this season he's been an undisciplined mess at the plate. I'd seen Matos play a couple games in Puerto Rico, where he batted behind Alex Rios in the Caguas lineup. He'd walked, stolen a base, and hit a *"doble!"* as the announcer described it, but the praise had been sparing. "Great in the outfield," was all Mako Oliveras said about him.

In the front office, it's Kabuki theater. Nando loves Matos because he's a physical specimen who can score for us in five categories. He notes that Sheehan paid $17 for him at the auction, which was considerably more than Radke's $11 price tag. Sig, on the other hand, runs the deal through Zoladex and determines that it's barely even. Add the fact that Matos is far more likely to lose his job than Radke, and he thinks the deal is mediocre. Playing my prescribed role, I tap out a message to yet another overindulgent baseball executive: in this case, Baltimore co-GM Jim Beattie.

"For this to be a good deal," I write, "I'm operating under the impression that Matos is just taking a while to make some adjustments, that his role in CF is secure and that he's sure to heat up eventually. Is that all safe to say?"

From: Beattie, Jim
Subject: Matos
Sam, Luis is secure in his job and has started swinging the bat better. As for how he will continue to play, or if he will "heat up" . . . well . . . I guess that is the fun of the Rotisserie league!
Jim

As I pick up the phone to call Joe Sheehan, I'm surprisingly tense. The only roadblock to the deal is finding a way to talk Sheehan down from the $6 FAAB he's asked for, but I have a feeling Sheehan is a tougher negotiator than Rick Fogel and that if I'm not careful I may end up trading him Radke for two cocktail napkins and a swizzle stick. So in a cloying voice I hardly recognize as my own, I ask him to knock the cash payment down to $3 FAAB.

At this, there's a long, startled pause—which tells me that I've clearly been suckered by a bluff. Sheehan never thought he'd get an extra dollar out of me, let alone three. "I'm not going to let three bucks stand in the way of a deal," he purrs. *Shit.*

When this deal is posted on the Tout Wars home page, the reviews are a little different than last time. Jason Grey calls it "highway robbery by Sheehan" and one real American League executive describes it to me, privately, as *horrible.* "I really think you're underselling Radke," he says.

The reviews on the field aren't much better. As Matos plods along unspectacularly, Radke pitches fourteen innings of liquid nitrogen over two starts, striking out nine and lowering his ERA by 57 points. Then, in a matter of days, Streetwalkers benchwarmer B. J. Surhoff wins a starting job, the Blue Jays call up Alex Rios earlier than expected, and Dmitri Young returns to the lineup in Detroit. After throwing Brad Radke under the bus to cure a shortage of outfielders, I suddenly have too many.

One of the sensible old axioms of Rotisserie baseball is that it's never a good idea to act rashly on the heels of a mistake, lest you make a second one and compound your losses. Knowing this, I decide to do what any rookie would do in this predicament: Make another trade as soon as possible.

My first call is to Dean Peterson, the quiet computer engineer. While nobody paid him much attention at the draft, Peterson had cornered the market on youthful promise, picking up a stable of emerging phenoms like Bobby Crosby, a rookie shortstop from Oakland (no relation to Bubba), whom the scouts describe as an "outrageous" talent. He'd be a nice replacement for my current shortstop, Rey Sánchez, whose stats in twenty-five games were outrageous, too, but in the opposite sense:

Average: .227
Runs: 3
RBI: 1
Home runs: 0
Steals: 0

Predictably, the only player of mine who Peterson covets is Alex Rios, who, for reasons both practical and sentimental, I had no intention of trading. But just as I'm about to hang up and move on, Peterson says something I never thought I'd hear once, let alone twice. "It's too bad you traded Ponson." I wait a few seconds for the inevitable "just kidding," but it never comes.

Peterson's interest in the big Aruban isn't totally preposterous. To finance his powerful offense, he'd chosen to forsake pitchers with low WHIPs and ERAs in favor of cheap, durable starters who collect a good number of wins and strikeouts just because they pitch a lot. To him, Ponson is a decent volume buy.

As I hang up the phone, a dangerous idea pops into my head. If I can convince Rick Fogel to trade Ponson *back* to me in exchange for one of my spare outfielders, I could call Peterson a few minutes later and offer him Ponson in return for Bobby Crosby. "A three-way trade!" Nando exclaims after I run it past him. "That's why you're the boss!"

Rick Fogel is, to say the least, surprised to hear from me. Almost every player I'd traded him in our earlier blockbuster was now struggling, injured, or parked on his bench, and his team has since dropped to eighth place. "Looks like it's turning into a lost year for USA Stats," he'd moped in an e-mail. Still, I had a feeling Fogel might like to hear what I was about to ask him—whether he'd consider trading me Ponson for one of my extra outfielders, like B. J. Surhoff.

"Seriously?" he asks.

"Seriously."

Fogel gives me carte blanche to send that deal to Commissioner Liebowitz whenever I feel like it.

My next move, of course, is to call Peterson and propose swapping Ponson for Bobby Crosby. Under normal circumstances, there's no way I'd have the gall to try something this silly, especially in an "expert" league. But a couple of weeks into the season, while passing through Chicago on unrelated business, I'd spent a breezy Saturday afternoon with Peterson and left town with one very distinct impression: This guy can be *pushed*.

At forty-three, Peterson lives in a condo in the suburb of Palatine, where the decor might best be described as twelve-year-old chic. The couch is decorated with NFL throw pillows. There's a Nerf hoop near the door, a Nerf hoop in the dining nook, and an inflatable plastic armchair in the living room. Bobbleheads and Beanie Babies, some wrested from the bottoms of cereal boxes, cover every surface, from the headboard of his bed to the rear dash of his Toyota. He's got complete sets of baseball cards from every year since 1971, an extensive collection of Christmas music, and a handy bottle of Instant Fart Spray. Peterson's only roommate is Hot Cocoa the guinea pig, who lives in a cage on the floor. On a wall in the guest bedroom, there's a framed certificate from *The News-Dispatch* of Michigan City, Indiana, which reads: Outstanding Newspaper Carrier Award. "I won it twice," he said. "I got to have breakfast with the governor."

Peterson plays in five Rotisserie leagues in addition to Tout Wars, two Strat-O-Matic leagues, a league that uses bygone players, two baseball survivor pools, and a "sim" league where he manages an imaginary franchise full of make-believe players with names like "Bud Weiser." All summer, from his desk in Palatine, he tracks the stats of more than three thousand ballplayers, some of whom don't really exist. "The past six weeks have been a blur," he said. I'd wondered why Peterson was so enamored of rookies and other young upstarts, but after taking the tour it made perfect sense. He considers himself one of them. "I'm a kid at heart," he said.

I catch Peterson on a Friday morning in his office at STATS, Inc. For all that baseball dominates his life and fills his days at work, he's one of my only opponents who has nothing to tout. He doesn't make public projections or write books or engage in punditry. To him, Rotisserie is mainly a hobby and should therefore be pleasant and non-confrontational. In an attempt to speak his language, I raise my voice an octave, trying to make our Ponson adventure sound like a trip to Six Flags. "What if I can get Ponson?" I ask.

"Could you do that?"

"I think so!"

For a minute it seems as if Peterson will do the deal on the spot. But before agreeing to hand over Bobby Crosby, he says he'd like to run some numbers, which in my limited experience sounds perfectly reasonable. The transaction deadline is still a few hours away, so I wait. And wait. Half an hour before the deadline, Peterson calls back with a counterproposal. We would send him Ponson, a backup catcher, and $5 FAAB for three players currently sitting on his bench, none of whom is named Crosby.

"That's interesting," I say, switching into salesman mode, "but let's talk about the other deal for a second." With Nando feeding me lines written on index cards, I tell Peterson that Ponson's career ERA in June is 3.67 (which is true) and that some scouts think Bobby Crosby is overmatched by major-league pitching (which is not). "If you help me out with this deal now," I say, "I'd be a lot more inclined to trade you Zanbe—" Nando, realizing his cue card is upside down, flips it over. "I mean Javier Vazquez."

Peterson hems and haws. He stops to think. I get the feeling he's trying desperately to avoid any sharp words.

"I just don't know," he says.

"Come on, Dean!" I say, not at all politely.

More awkward silence.

"Maybe we should wait a week," he mews.

"So you'll do it then?" I ask.

Peterson thinks for a few beats.

"Probably."

Beaten, I hang up the phone.

Now what?

With the deadline bearing down, it's time to make a tough decision. Fresh from scribbling out all that praise for Ponson, Nando seems to believe it. He tells me we should trade Surhoff for Ponson anyhow, because if Surhoff were to lose his starting job Fogel would never trade us Ponson, which means we'd never get Crosby. Besides, he tells me, he's totally convinced that Ponson is going to come through with a good outing this week.

"Why's that?" I ask.

"I had a premonition."

With eight minutes to the deadline, I am, for the first time, desperate to talk to Sig Mejdal. I try him at home, at his NASA office, and on his cellphone, leaving a series of increasingly disconsolate messages. All the while, Nando (the clairvoyant) is giving me his "Come on, roll the dice!" look and trying to persuade me that Ponson could turn out to be the prodigal son. In the end, with two minutes to spare before the weekly deadline, I decide to invest in blind enthusiasm. We send in a message announcing our second deal with Rick Fogel.

Surhoff for Ponson.

Five minutes later, the phone rings. It's Sig.

"No way would I do this!"

In the days that follow, my decision spiral becomes a vortex. Ponson gets pounded for five runs against the Diamondbacks, while Bobby Crosby homers twice. The Streetwalkers fall to fifth place, with none other than Dean Peterson taking over fourth. "Wait a second," my wife says, looking at my roster in the front office one evening. "How did you get Ponson back?"

Now Nando is eerily quiet.

A week later, in one last gasp, I send Peterson an adjusted offer, Crosby for Ponson and $10 FAAB. This is followed by four voice mails and an agonizing hour spent staring at the telephone. "I'm so sorry!" Peterson writes, shortly after letting the deadline pass. "I just got back to my desk. I've had visitors here the past two days and I've been very busy. So I guess at a minimum we have another week to mull over what works best for both of us." Translation: Enjoy Ponson, you *dumbass*. Dean Peterson, the pushover, has just played me like the rookie I am.

On the evening of June 3 a new, heretofore unspoken five-letter word popped up in the pages of my Tout Wars diary.

"Slump."

When my ballclub posted a .091 batting average a few days earlier, I'd actually laughed. Hey, *it happens,* I told myself. Two days later, it was a .212 and the following night a .115, and all of a sudden, the Streetwalkers have fallen to sixth place.

The nights begin running together. A .194 is followed by a .207, and by the seventh of June David Ortiz, Josh Phelps, and Jacque Jones are a combined 11 for their last *105.* Jones had fallen into such a funk that he's yanked from the lineup for what Twins manager Ron Gardenhire calls a "mental health day." Since the day I presented him that MVP trophy, Jones has hit a buck fifty-six.

Every time I flip on the TV, something transcendentally awful happens. *Click!* Alex Rios grounds out to the pitcher. *Click!* Ponson gives up two doubles in a row. *Click!* Kevin Youkilis goes down on three pitches. After somehow throwing my back out, I wind up at St. Vincent's Hospital in the middle of the night, pleading for Vicodin. "Have you been under a lot of stress?" the doctor asks.

On June 10, we drop to seventh place, one spot behind the surging Trace Wood. "Butter boy!" Wood says over the phone. "How do you want that butter? In a restaurant? Can I bring some biscuits?"

Sleep eludes me. The ibuprofen I'm now taking for my back pain gives me a hellacious case of heartburn and leaves me mewling around the house in a black, foul mood. When I decided to play Rotisserie, I figured there would be moments of frustration but never like this. I haven't cared this much about sports—or been this despondent about a setback—since the fourth grade, when Michigan blew the 1979 Rose Bowl. (I locked myself in the bathroom.)

In the bleary hours of the morning, I begin searching the Internet for slump cures. Shoeless Joe Jackson collected hairpins. Wade Boggs ate chicken before every game, and Richie Ashburn used to take his bat to bed with him. The best of the lot is a quote from Babe Ruth, who said, "Scallions are the greatest cure for a batting slump ever invented." I sprinkle scallions liberally on my chicken salad.

We hit .207.

Boycotting the news doesn't help. When I finally do peek at the wires, Aaron Sele has landed on the disabled list and Mariano Rivera has been shut down with tightness in his back. Schilling has an MRI on his ankle, Guillen has an MRI on his knee, and Reese has an MRI on his thumb. Turn off the lights and half my team would glow in the dark. A few days later, when my wife opens a refrigerator drawer and happens upon my stash, she informs me that imported scallions have been known to carry hepatitis A.

Excellent!

For his part, Nando has decided to ride out the slump by partying. Whenever I call, he's drinking grappa with Bosco or tequila shots at Asia de Cuba or shouting into the phone from some club where he's supposed to meet a pack of Hawaiian Tropic models. The worse the slump gets, the more his relentless optimism grates on my patience. When Ponson strikes out two hitters in the first inning of a routine start, Nando sends a text message: "There could be magic in the Maryland air tonight!"

Sig is even less useful. A few days before the skid began, he'd jetted off to Europe for a month's vacation, on an itinerary that includes Venice, Barcelona, and Biarritz, where he plans to do a week of drinking with a tetherless clog of adventuresome Brits he's befriended. All he left me is a Yahoo! address, a cellphone number for some Italian guy named "Andrea," and this bit of advice: "Trust the paradigm, stay linear, and don't think too much."

As it turns out, Sig Mejdal is something of a bon vivant. Just before the winter meetings, he'd taken a sabbatical to climb Mount Chimborazo in Ecuador. And while I was slogging around Florida, he decamped to Panama for two weeks of surfing. Even when he's home, his life seems a whirl of parties, dates, golf lessons, recreational hockey, and San Francisco Giants games, where he's a regular consumer of something called the "Big Beer."

It took me a while to figure out how a scientist of Sig's caliber could spend so much time *not* working, but now I get it. Once you give yourself over to the scientific method and work voraciously to collect the best data, there's really not much left to do. On my refrigerator, there's a photo Sig sent me from spring training. In it, I'm crouched in my seat, trying to hold the radar gun steady while scribbling in a notebook on my knee. "Sam collects some qualitative information," the caption says. "Sig watches the game."

On June 15, the slump reaches its nadir. *Half* my players are out of the lineup, and if not for a lousy pair of singles we'd have been 0-for-25. In three weeks, our batting average has dropped by 20 points, and the Streetwalkers have become perfectly bipolar: first place in overall pitching and dead last in offense. Early the next morning, over a plate of scrambled eggs and hepatitis, it dawns on me: This team, in its current form, will never win Tout Wars.

It's time to reload.

———

Since his promotion, Nando has been working the other Touts like a subprime lender. When he grows tired of waiting for a response to some harebrained trade idea, he just fires off another one. Jason Grey grows so tired of saying no that he rejects one offer with a poem. After fielding a dozen messages about Josh Phelps, Jeff Erickson asked me if Nando works on commission.

But on June 16, his persistence pays off. Joe Sheehan of Baseball Prospectus answers one of Nando's trade queries with a counteroffer that even Nando would have been too embarrassed to propose. He'll take Orlando Hudson and Bronson Arroyo in exchange for White Sox outfielder Magglio Ordóñez.

Though he's not the biggest name in baseball, the Venezuelan Ordóñez is a Rotisserie demigod who hits for average and power, drives in runs, steals an occasional base, and has done so consistently for years. Sheehan paid $35 for him at the auction, up there with the likes of Vladimir Guerrero and Manny Ramirez, while Arroyo and Hudson, the guys he wants in return, cost $15 *combined*. Even though

Sheehan desperately needs pitching, the proposal is so lopsided that I start to get suspicious. Maybe Sheehan, using his own baseball contacts, knows something I don't. Ordóñez had undergone knee surgery earlier in the season and wasn't due back from the disabled list for a couple of weeks, which makes me wonder if there's been some setback in his rehabilitation. But after making a few calls, I'm confident that there's nothing fishy going on. Sheehan is having his own rookie panic.

That same afternoon, with no further debate, Nando sends in the paperwork on the Ordóñez deal, and once it's been approved and logged I get a message from Sheehan. "I can hear the laughter now," he writes. Looking at my roster and picturing Ordóñez patrolling the outfield, the sting of the slump abates. In fact, I'm getting the distinct feeling we could actually win.

Hopped up on adrenaline, Nando and I head over to Pete's Tavern for a quick toast, which escalates into a series of toasts, a round of cheeseburgers, and some unchaperoned thinking. Nando begins scribbling numbers on a napkin. Earlier in the day he'd calculated that if our hitters could just revert to the league average, we'd be back in third place in the blink of an eye. And now he determines that if we traded one of our three REMA Kings (Schilling, Rivera, or Vazquez) for one of the ten best hitters in the American League, we could pick up seven points, which could put us in the lead.

"The lead?" I ask, sipping my third martini.

"The lead."

The following day, with absolutely no input from Sig, Nando and I trade Curt Schilling, Kevin Youkilis, and Sandy Alomar, a backup catcher we'd picked up in FAAB, for Yankee catcher Jorge Posada, Minnesota third baseman Corey Koskie, and Chicago setup man Damaso Marte. I don't mean to convey the impression that we acted hastily. There were scouting reports consulted, phone calls made to various baseball potentates, and a compulsory e-mail sent to Sig's Yahoo! account, which he'd promised to keep an eye on from Internet cafés. Before he left for Europe, Sig had worked up a spreadsheet we could use to track player values as the season wore on, which we'd taken to calling Inflatable Sig. Before pulling the trigger, we'd dutifully typed all the numbers into the program, which had scored the deal at 21 value points coming in and only 17 going out. Not exactly grand larceny but clearly some form of actionable misdemeanor.

Back at Pete's Tavern that night, Nando and I belly up to the bar to celebrate all over again. After weathering two hideous trades and a decision spiral and falling into a slump, we'd righted the ship and reloaded, all while staying on point and (more or less) on paradigm. "To Magglio," I say, raising a glass.

"To Joe Sheehan," he corrects.

On the night of June 29, I boot up the Tout Wars standings, and there it is. Three home runs. The following night we hit four, and by July 2 we are back in fifth place as if the whole slump had been a midsummer's dream. Bill Mueller, recovered from knee surgery, returns to the Boston lineup. He has two hits.

Nando sends a note.

"July may be our month!"

Tout Wars Standings Through July 2, 2004

1. Dean Peterson, STATS, Inc., 90.5
2. Lawr Michaels, CREATiVESPORTS, 88.0
3. Jeff Erickson, RotoWire, 86.0
4. Trace Wood, The Long Gandhi, 74.5
5. Streetwalkers, 69.0
6. Joe Sheehan, Baseball Prospectus, 65.5
7. Rick Fogel, USA Stats, 64.5
8. Matt Berry, Talented Mr. Roto, 63.0
9. Steve Moyer, Baseball Info Solutions, 62.5
10. Ron Shandler, Baseball HQ, 55.0
11. Mat Olkin, *USA Today*, 32.0
12. Jason Grey, Mastersball, 29.5

Baseball Men

During a stint as the official scorer for the Baltimore Orioles, Bill Stetka had an unusual problem. A group of his Rotisserie leaguemates had taken seats directly above the press box at Memorial Stadium. Every time Stetka made a ruling that favored a player who happened to be on his Rotisserie team, the entire press box could hear the cries of protest. "STETKA!"

"They sat there," he says, "just to torture me."

. . .

One month into the season the news had come down in a cryptic message from Jason Grey: Mat Olkin had resigned from Tout Wars, and Gene McCaffrey of Wise Guy Baseball, the 2001 National League champion, had agreed to take over his team.

No reason was given.

Of all the Touts, Olkin had been the most elusive. He didn't show up in New York until the morning of the auction and later vanished from the postmortem before I'd found the bottom of my first pint. His *USA Today* team was floundering, thanks to poor starts by pitchers Barry Zito and Derek Lowe, but that didn't seem like any reason to throw in the towel. So back in May, during my East Coast road swing, I met Olkin for lunch at a Greek restaurant near his house in Centreville, Virginia, to get the lowdown.

Thirty-three years old, babyfaced, and a bit plodding, Olkin will never be mistaken for a popinjay. He rolled up to my hotel in an old aqua Ford Taurus and stepped into the brilliant sunshine wearing khakis with no belt, brown shoes with tube socks, and a flannel shirt. He doesn't own a cellphone, he says, because "I'm not important enough."

The first thing you notice about Olkin is the beatific look. When asked a question about baseball, he allows a lot of time to pass, staring off in the distance with a placid expression that borders on rapture. Thinking is Olkin's favorite pastime, in general, and thinking about baseball is next to godliness.

Though I've read his columns in *Sports Weekly*, all I really know about Olkin is that he'd talked to the New York Mets a few months back about a possible job as a statistician, and rumors of his candidacy had popped up in an unlikely place—the gossip pages of the *New York Post*. In the end, the Mets hadn't hired him, and he'd taken the news pretty hard.

Olkin tells me he grew up in Norwich, Connecticut, where his father was an elementary-school teacher and his mother a yoga instructor. He never played baseball as a kid, due in large part to being undersized and having plantar fasciitis, which required him to wear orthotics. At eighteen he was diagnosed with diabetes, and before forking into his Greek salad, he injects insulin into his side so casually that I barely notice. "No big deal," he says.

Olkin first learned about baseball from his father, an agonized Red Sox fan, but it wasn't until 1984, when his mother bought him a copy of *The Bill James Abstract*, that he started to breathe its oxygen exclusively. "That," he says, "was the end of my interest in other things."

Two years later, Olkin dashed off a letter to Bill James written in pencil on a sheet of notebook paper, detailing the similarities between two acquisitions the Milwaukee Brewers had made, one for Gorman Thomas and the other for Rob Deer. Some months later, the phone rang. It was Bill James himself, speaking in his authoritative basso, calling to ask permission to publish the letter. The day the 1987 *Abstract* came out, Olkin raced to the bookstore at the Norwich Mall, and there it was, his name posted on page 266, followed by (gulp) a pointed rebuttal of his argument. Nevertheless! For the price of a postage stamp, he'd stepped inside the baseball looking glass and returned with a sacred talisman. "It's still on my bookshelf," he says.

By the time he got to college, Olkin's knowledge of baseball was so encyclopedic it began seeping out in unlikely ways. To help pay his tuition at the University of Connecticut, he applied for a job as a cashier at Big Y Foods. During the interview, the supermarket manager presented him with a laminated list of 150 produce codes. To have any future in the grocery checkout field, the manager said, he'd have to be able to memorize all of them. Olkin took one look at the list and smiled. "I think I can handle it."

The code for cabbage was 264, which, Olkin knew, was the exact number of hitters Luis Tiant struck out in 1968. From that day forward, he says, "cabbage was Luis Tiant." Lettuce was George Brett, lemons were Pedro Garcia, and watermelon, code 388, became the embodiment of Rod Carew's 1977 batting average. Olkin was the best cashier Big Y Foods had ever seen.

As an undergraduate, Olkin sent letters to every GM in the major leagues, asking them for advice on breaking into the front office. A few responses sounded the same note: A law degree wouldn't hurt. So after college, Olkin took out a loan and enrolled in Pace Law School in White Plains, New York, where he was the only student who had no interest whatsoever in the law.

After graduation, Olkin moved to Boston, where he became the most overqualified office gofer and Xerox man ever to work at Fleet Bank. When he wasn't temping, he followed in the footsteps of Bill James and Ron Shandler by writing his own annual book of analysis called the *Baseball Examiner*, which he distributed for free. During baseball season, Olkin trained his firepower on a national contest called Bill James Fantasy Baseball—an open competition with thousands of players that was hosted by STATS, Inc. Olkin had been fanatical about his Rotisserie leagues in the past, but this was an entirely different sort of devotion. The grand prize was a chance to watch a spring-training game with James himself. And in 1995, after finishing three times in the top four, he won.

The following March, Olkin flew to Florida to meet his boyhood idol, and after three hours of conversation had demonstrated that he knew James nearly as well as James knew himself. "I would finish sentences for him," Olkin remembers. While James was no stranger to adulation, something about Mat Olkin stood out. So much so that when Olkin applied for a job at STATS, Inc., later that same year, James remembers, "We hired him the same day."

After three underpaid years at STATS, Olkin moved back east to take a job as a copy editor for *USA Today's Baseball Weekly*, where he began writing an occasional column called Mat at Bat. It was then that Olkin's Rotisserie career took flight. He began competing in LABR and was one of the handpicked experts Ron Shandler invited to Tout Wars. In 1999 he ran away with the AL title, setting records for RBI, home runs, and margin of victory.

By the time of his seventh Tout Wars draft at the Wyndham in March, Olkin had settled into a monastic rhythm of work. In addition to his regular job, he'd written the ninth *Examiner*, covered six teams for the STATS scouting notebook, and contributed material to Baseball Prospectus. By April he'd worked himself to the brink of collapse and, as usual, barely earned enough to make the minimum payments on his credit cards. "There's a clause where it says that if you get to seventy, your student loans will be forgiven," he says. "I think that's my out."

Our salads finished now, I ask Olkin about his Tout Wars defection. There's another long pause, then a story.

Years ago, just out of high school, Olkin contacted Craig Wright, an author and baseball analyst who'd become a sort of insider's Bill James, working as a Sabermetric consultant for more than a dozen major-league teams. "I want to do what you do," Olkin said. In time, Wright began giving him work tracking player news in *Baseball America* and the two became friends.

After the 2003 season, Bill Bavasi took over as GM of the Seattle Mariners and was determined to supercharge the team's statistical operation. He was looking for a numbers guy, somebody who "thinks out of the box," he told reporters. Bavasi's first move was to call Craig Wright and try to coax him aboard. Wright had long since hung up his calculator, so he politely declined. But he left Bavasi with the name of a guy he knew, this kid from Virginia. It was the beginning of the end of Mat Olkin's Rotisserie career.

———

One of the first invitations John Hunt sent for the inaugural LABR draft in 1994 landed in the mailbox of a New York baseball analyst named Mike Gimbel.

Gimbel was a college dropout who made his living certifying water pressure and procuring treatment chemicals for the city's Bureau of Water Supply. When he wasn't moonlighting as a union activist or tending to his collection of pet reptiles, he had taught himself how to write computer programs that would spit out heretofore hidden truths about ballplayers. Each year, he published his calculations in a book called *Mike Gimbel's Baseball Player & Team Ratings*.

In short order Gimbel would establish himself as Rotisserie's leading eccentric. One year at the LABR draft in Florida, he burst into the room late and out of breath, his hair alarmingly matted, clutching a giant briefcase and wearing a rumpled gray suit with no tie—an outfit he'd inhabit all weekend despite the tropical temperatures. Having neglected to eat, he unwrapped a comically overstuffed sandwich and began blurting out bids with hunks of meat and dressing clinging to his beard. He was a character, Olkin remembers, "as if somebody had drawn him."

But back in the summer of 1991, Gimbel read an article that said Dan Duquette was about to take over as general manager of the Montreal Expos. The moment he noticed the name, Gimbel knew he'd seen it before: Duquette, it turned out, had ordered the last two copies of his book. After calling Duquette to introduce himself, Gimbel met him at the team hotel for a brief interview, and a few weeks later, Duquette quietly hired him as a part-time statistical consultant for $10,000 a year. He became the first elite Rotisserie player to work for a major-league team.

True to his nature, Gimbel was unafraid to make counterintuitive suggestions, and as more of the players he touted blossomed in Montreal (Pedro Martinez being the most prominent), Duquette began to rely on his counsel. Before the 1994 season, Duquette sent Gimbel a note on Expos letterhead thanking him for his service, which Gimbel promptly published on the back cover of his book. When Duquette took a job with the Boston Red Sox, he brought Gimbel along and by 1997 trusted him enough to let him address the coaching staff at spring training.

Emboldened by his growing authority, Gimbel gave a freewheeling interview to *The Boston Globe*, in which he all but took credit for scores of Duquette's personnel moves and talked openly about the team's desire to trade shortstop John Valentin—something Duquette had publicly denied.

The resulting article was anything but positive. The *Globe* described Gimbel as a "Queens Community College dropout" and a "Rotisserie League fanatic" and unearthed details of a 1994 raid on his Brooklyn loft where health officials confiscated an iguana, five turtles, and six exotic South American caimans. When asked to comment, Duquette dug a deeper hole by praising Gimbel as a "math wizard" and "a very interesting guy." In exchange for his loyalty, Duquette was labeled a "Rotisserie GM."

The story struck a nerve with baseball writers, and for days afterward Duquette was pilloried. Former Red Sox slugger Jose Canseco likened his use of Gimbel to "calling the Psychic Hotline." One particularly inelegant column in the *Boston Herald* called Gimbel a "psycho," an "egomaniacal blowhard," and a "nut." The damage was done. Two weeks later, the *Globe*'s Will McDonough ran a small column item stating that Gimbel had a one-year contract for less than $25,000 and that when it expired "he goes along with it from the Red Sox payroll." Though nobody bothered to examine Gimbel's track record, which was pretty darn good, he had been publicly denounced as a Roto geek and had therefore become a liability. Gimbel, all but exiled from baseball, hasn't surfaced since.

Before this episode, most baseball people thought of Rotisserie as a benign nuisance. They loved to answer dumb questions from reporters by saying, "This is not Rotisserie baseball." Bobby Bonilla once famously derided Davey Johnson, his former manager, by saying he "wouldn't even have him manage my Rotisserie team." But the parlor game was still harmless enough that Tom Grieve, then the GM of the Texas Rangers, played it in the 1980s while simultaneously running a real ballclub. The only people who seemed to get worked up about the game were writers like syndicated columnist Mike Lupica, who denounced Roto players as "nerds" who would rather "calibrate" than "celebrate" baseball.

The Gimbel affair changed everything. Suddenly Rotisserie could be hazardous to your professional health, and the game developed a whiff of toxicity that still lingers in front offices. During my travels at spring training, one American League GM happily broke down some of his players in fantasy terms, then pleaded with me not to make him sound "too much like a Rotisserie guy." Even the younger, more quantitatively minded generation of executives views the hobby warily. Cleveland GM Mark Shapiro has a regular procedure when he receives résumés from people who describe their Rotisserie exploits. "They go right to him," he says, pointing to his assistant, Chris Antonetti. "A lot of them say, 'I finished first in my Roto league four years in a row,'" Antonetti says with a snort. "That's not exactly the skill set we're looking for."

Some of this is just posturing, of course. It's the nature of any exclusive fraternity to reject those who seem to want to join a little too fervently. But there is one persistent knock on Rotisserie players that contains a kernel of truth. For all that they know about ballplayers, they have no grasp on the reality of running a baseball *business*. What they don't understand, Toronto's J. P. Ricciardi says, "is that there's actually *money* involved in Major League Baseball. Guys aren't willing to play for nothing. You actually have to have a personality to deal with these players. You don't just say, 'Okay, you come play for us.' It's a people game, too."

———

On an icy morning in December four years after the Gimbel fiasco, a short, goateed Harvard graduate named Keith Law pushed through the revolving doors of the Sheraton Boston, the site of baseball's 2001 winter meetings.

For a baseball aspirant, Law's résumé was anything but typical. He spoke five languages, including a little Mandarin. He was a gourmet cook who read P. G. Wodehouse, played the guitar, and had an MBA from Carnegie Mellon. He was, as Billy Beane calls him, "the kind of guy who could write his ticket to Wall Street."

For the last six years, Law had been a columnist for Baseball Prospectus, and while he wasn't going to advertise it, especially at the winter meetings, he'd also become one of the nation's top Rotisserie players. He'd already won LABR and was a founding member of Tout Wars, where he had finished fourth the year before.

Law had come to the Sheraton to meet J. P. Ricciardi, who'd just been installed as the new GM of the Blue Jays. Law and Ricciardi had some mutual friends, so a few days after Ricciardi took office, Law had called to wish him luck. When Ricciardi picked up the phone, he was deep in thought about how to dump the team's overpaid mistakes and restructure it with players whose talents were more in tune with the new statistical principles he'd absorbed while working in Oakland for Billy Beane. The two men began a conversation about players that stretched out for two weeks, with Law serving as an informal sounding board. "Keith, do you like Eric Hinske?" Ricciardi asked one day. Law said yes. "So do I," Ricciardi replied, and Eric Hinske became a Blue Jay.

The winter meetings in Boston, then, were to be Keith Law's major-league tryout. If he made good recommendations without insulting the scouts or pulling an iguana out of his pocket, the Blue Jays might actually give him a job.

Law met with Ricciardi and his superiors and was told to keep his phone charged in case he was needed. "There's a proposal on the table," Ricciardi said, ringing him from a private meeting, "and I need to know—who's an extra guy we could get from the Dodgers?"

It was a simple question that, when you break it down, was anything but. There are thirty major-league teams, each with forty players on the official roster and another one hundred assorted farmhands and signees on the payroll. It's often hard for a GM to keep track of all

his own players, let alone those on other clubs. About the only baseball civilian who could answer such a question under that kind of pressure was a guy who played in expert Rotisserie leagues. Law ran through the Dodgers farm system in his head, picturing each player and conjuring his numbers. "How about Chad Ricketts, the pitcher?" he finally said. "Good arm, and he's Canadian, too."

"Thanks, Keith."

Ricketts, too, became a Blue Jay, and at about the same instant so did Keith Law. In the days that followed, Ricciardi hired Law as a consultant to baseball operations and began rehearsing his lines to the press. "Yeah, yeah, Tout Wars," he says now, rolling his eyes at the memory. "I knew all about his Rotisserie background." While he wasn't thrilled about it, Ricciardi says, he'd learned in his years in baseball, especially under the tutelage of Beane, not to pigeonhole people. So when the time came to discuss the matter with the beat writers, he decided to address the inevitable comparison head-on.

"This guy," he told them, "is not Mike Gimbel."

Still, it would be up to Keith Law to prove him right, to learn how to work within the parameters of the old baseball fraternity, a place where scouts still held sway, where "makeup, toughness, and character" often superseded the quantifiable, and where a Harvard kid in a rep tie had better be able to tell a good pussy joke.

For all that Law had mastered baseball, he was utterly ignorant of its private culture, having no idea what went on behind the scenes in a big-league ballpark. "I thought the locker room and the clubhouse were two different things," he says. Just a few months into his employment, in June 2002, Law got his first test. After a miserable start to the season, Ricciardi fired manager Buck Martinez, and the Blue Jays clubhouse took on the solemnity of a funeral parlor. As Law passed through the room, one of Martinez's coaches, still sizzling from the shock of the announcement, lowered his shoulder and nearly knocked the consultant for baseball operations on his Harvard ass.

"No question it was deliberate," Law says.

It was a literal collision that mimicked a larger, more symbolic one:

the competing interests of people who grew up playing baseball on the diamond and those who grew up playing baseball in their minds. Stunned and angry, Law sized up the coach, who was, as baseball men generally are, big enough to mash him like a warm potato. So after lingering a few seconds to avoid looking like a chickenshit, he took the elevator back upstairs to the executive suite. "The best thing to do was keep my mouth shut," he says.

As a replacement for Buck Martinez, Ricciardi tapped Carlos Tosca, who became one of a tiny group of big-league managers who'd never played professional baseball. At 5'7", Tosca might weigh 175 pounds, but only in leaded boots. The coach with the sharp shoulder promptly quit.

Law still works for the Blue Jays, who have promoted him to the role of special assistant to the general manager. Other than taking an occasional potshot from local writers, who like to call him "Rain Man," he's settled in comfortably. He watches games with the boss, evaluates players and tactics, and recently took a scouting trip to Taiwan. He still visits the clubhouse, but rarely. In 2003 the revamped Blue Jays won a surprising eighty-six games.

As for Rotisserie, Law decided to quit Tout Wars, figuring that his supreme access to information would give him an unfair edge. But during his first season on the other side, he decided to continue playing in a friendly league he'd founded in high school, where the player pool is limited to the National League. During the season, one of the outfielders Law had drafted on his fantasy team became a serious acquisition target in Toronto, thanks in large part to Law's relentless enthusiasm. Professionally, he was thrilled. But under the rules of his Rotisserie league, if this outfielder was traded to the American League in real life he would immediately vanish from Law's fantasy roster.

"If I didn't pursue this guy for the Blue Jays because he's on my Rotisserie team, I'm an asshole," Law remembers thinking. "But if I do, and I lose him from my fantasy team, I'm an idiot."

He hasn't played Rotisserie since.

———

For all they might prefer to keep it quiet, current and former fantasy players have made inroads at every level of baseball. It begins with Red Sox owner John Henry and continues through upper management with John Higgins, the CFO of the Devil Rays, and Jeff Luhnow of the Cardinals. Cleveland media-relations director Bart Swain plays in a league, as does Blue Jays scout Kimball Crossley. Former pitcher Jim Deshaies, now a broadcaster for the Houston Astros, runs a league from the press box. Every spring Billy Beane says he inevitably gets a call from baseball agent Arn Tellem, who, he says, always wants to "hound" him for Rotisserie advice. And at the winter meetings in New Orleans, baseball agent Scott Boras told me that he doesn't just tolerate the office Rotisserie league, he's made it *mandatory* for all members of the salary-arbitration staff. The only person who's not allowed to play is Boras. "They think I'll figure out the rules and come up with some loophole," he says.

Though Boston GM Theo Epstein didn't take to Rotisserie, he does fiddle around with some of the same player-projection systems we're using in Tout Wars. And no baseball luminary can avoid the game entirely. Devil Rays owner Vince Naimoli takes "research" calls from his Rotisserie-playing daughter, Cubs GM Jim Hendry talks Roto with his neighbors, and Yankee hitting coach Don Mattingly told me he gets regular calls from one particularly obsessive Roto nut, his good friend Meat Loaf.

Ironically, ballplayers are about the only people who aren't allowed to take part. Sandy Alderson, baseball's executive vice president of operations, says there's no specific rule prohibiting players from joining a Rotisserie league, but if there were any amount of money involved it would clearly be viewed as a conflict. "You could construct a situation where a player's fantasy-league interest could interfere with his competitive responsibilities," Alderson explains. Or, as Anaheim pitcher Scot Shields puts it, "If you have Miguel Tejada on your fantasy team, you'd be giving up home runs just to win." To wit, the small handful of ballplayers and coaches who play Rotisserie like to keep their involvement quiet. One major-league coach drafts his team under the name Mr. X to conceal his identity.

But between the clubhouse popularity of fantasy football and the general pervasiveness of Rotisserie, something remarkable has happened. No matter how many millions of dollars they make and how many games they win, modern ballplayers can't escape their Rotisserie alter egos. Some have even come to view their baseball careers on two parallel tracks: team player, fantasy player. Seattle outfielder Randy Winn, sitting barefoot in a chair in the clubhouse before a spring-training game in Arizona, told me he fields fantasy teams in football and basketball and that his brother is in a Rotisserie league. The season before, Winn's first in Seattle's commodious Safeco Field, some of his statistical totals had declined a tiny bit. But when I asked him about this, he said, "Yeah, my numbers were off. They were off in *fantasy,* I should say." At this, I decided to ask him the inevitable follow-up question: If Randy Winn could play Rotisserie baseball, would he draft Randy Winn?

"Hmmm," he said, his eyebrows knitted. "I *guess* I'd want myself on my team." Winn stared off thoughtfully to the middle distances. "I don't know. I'd have to look at the categories."

———

At the time of this year's auction, there were *five* current or former Tout Wars participants who held some position of influence inside baseball. They ranged from Keith Law and Ron Shandler to Tony Blengino, who quit Tout Wars in 2003 to take a job as a scout for the Milwaukee Brewers. Now there are six.

On a quiet night in June about a month after our lunch, Mat Olkin padded down to his basement in sweatpants and tuned the satellite dish to the Seattle game. He put his feet on the coffee table, and his cat, Tom, hunkered down next to him. Ever since the Mariners hired him as a player personnel consultant, he'd been spending about ten hours per week researching possible call-ups or studying new ways to use the bullpen. Some days earlier, he'd worked out a possible change in the batting order, zapped it off in an e-mail to the front office, and forgotten about it. But when the Mariners lineup flashed on the screen, he bolted forward. *There it was.*

The last time I spoke to Olkin, he told me his Rotisserie days were officially over. He'd decided to fold the *Baseball Examiner* and stay out of the newspapers. Apparently, the shadow cast by Mike Gimbel was as long as ever. "I'm scared shitless to say anything that might give the impression I was taking credit," he admitted.

Shortly after Olkin went underground, the Mariners made a trade with the Chicago White Sox. One of the players they acquired was minor-league outfielder Jeremy Reed. One of the players they sent to Chicago was pitcher Freddy Garcia. When I checked the Tout Wars rosters, my hunch proved correct. Whether or not he had anything to do with this transaction, Mat Olkin had, for all intents and purposes, traded two of the players on his Tout Wars team.

In real life.

"Thadda Be Great"

July

Colorado attorney Lee Christian was fed up with the forgetfulness of his leaguemates. The draft was long enough without Doug Drabek being nominated five times. So he came up with a novel deterrent: alcohol. Botch a name and do a beer funnel. Nominate a player who's already taken and do a shot of a mystery liquor that tastes like tar. One owner, already well lubricated, staved off yet another belt by throwing out a name he knew was still available. "He drafted my mother," Christian says, "and we allowed it."

· · ·

At the season's halfway point, just before the All-Star break, the big surprise in Tout Wars is the collection of Rotisserie muscle knotted at the bottom of the standings.

The first of the bunch is Ron Shandler, whose team is in ninth place and a daunting 31 points off the lead. So far, his "Risk Management" Plan is not living up to its moniker. Between injuries to key players and subpar performances from otherwise safe bets, he's lost about $32 in expected value. Worse, Shandler blew nearly his entire FAAB budget on outfielder Raúl Mondesi, a National League immigrant who managed to play only eight games for the Angels before tearing his right quadriceps. While he hasn't conceded the title yet, the Bearded One is starting to sound a bit manic. "Finally out of tenth place!" he writes.

One notch below him is the contrarian Steve Moyer and his Hollywood Squares team. With its average age of thirty-three, the first concern about Moyer's squad was what would happen when the Geritol wore off, which it did in May, just after Moyer had managed to briefly take the lead. Within a couple of weeks, Kevin Brown got hurt, Rafael Palmeiro stopped hitting home runs, and the creaky Juan Gonzalez doddered back to the disabled list. For the life of me, I can't figure Moyer out. Not only does he have Bill James on speed dial, it's his *job* to tell major-league ballclubs things they didn't know. And yet here he is, third from the bottom in Tout Wars.

Eleventh place belongs to the defending champion, Jason Grey, whose season is starting to look like an absurdist play. Two weeks after he traded Scott Hatteberg to make room for Minnesota call-up Justin Morneau, Hatteberg went on a hitting rampage while the rookie was shipped back to the minors. In April, he flew to Cleveland to see what was the matter with his favorite pitcher, Jeremy Affeldt, but never got an audience. The game was rained out. Already, 32 percent of Grey's team, by auction value, has landed on the disabled list with maladies ranging from a pulled hamstring to migraine headaches. "Jason thought he had it all figured out," Steve Moyer crows, "and now look where he is." When he finally returns a phone call, the usually verbose champion has only this to say: "I don't think the three-peat is going to happen."

The cellar belongs to the team drafted by Mat Olkin and now shepherded by Gene McCaffrey. This team's offense consists of exactly two productive players, a fact that has driven McCaffrey, among the blunter characters in the expert fantasy world, to most decidedly *not* look on the bright side of things. "I hate my team and would like to trade them all," he writes.

At the shiny end of the standings, Tout Wars is shaping up to be a five-team race. The leader by a single point is Lawr Michaels, who's managing his team while struggling to maintain an air of detachment.

"How does it feel?" I asked when he took the lead.

"It doesn't," he replied.

While others jumped in early at the auction to make impulsive purchases, Michaels had stuck to his principles, hanging back until prices softened in the fifth round, where he picked up two ace pitchers, and again in the thirteenth, where he grabbed Carlos Guillen, Ronnie Belliard, and Jody Gerut. After the draft, Sig had added a feature to Zoladex called the Black Box, which weighs a ballplayer's current totals in each category against the overall league totals to pinpoint exactly how much he's produced in Rotisserie dollars. According to the Black Box, those three players Michaels bought in round thirteen had so far delivered a lascivious $37 profit. By most accounts the only thing standing between Michaels and a second championship is Michaels. "Lawr is not intoxicated," Shandler assures me, "but he often trades like he is."

Second place belongs to the quiet Dean Peterson, whose Clearasil draft plan has worked marvelously. His kids have been dominating the offensive categories, and Anaheim's Chone Figgins, who cost Peterson $2, has topped all other sleepers in the American League on the Black Box by delivering a $27 profit. In addition to sticking me with Ponson, who's now lost *nine* games in a row, Peterson has managed to stabilize his pitching staff while hanging on to 80 percent of his FAAB budget. "Dean's never won anything before," Moyer gripes, "and now he's going to look like a big genius."

In third place, to the horror of my HMO, is the cantankerous Trace Wood, my partner in the great butter wager. In addition to a dazzling performance by pitcher Johan Santana and a surge from Matt Lawton (the fourth most-valuable hitter in the AL according to the box), the cast-offs on his team are producing solid numbers, too. Wood has used his time advantage to make 157 lineup changes so far, the most in Tout and about double the league average. And by picking up some tremendous free agents, he's been able to compensate for his biggest shortcoming: I don't think Wood has the bullshit skills one needs to broker a lopsided trade.

One notch below him is the conservative Jeff Erickson, who, for a

time, seemed to have extrasensory powers. At the auction, he paid $9
for four questionable arms, including Kenny Rogers and Jake West-
brook, who have, so far, turned an unfathomable $66 profit on the
Black Box. But after building up an embarrassing lead on the rest of
the field, he's now starting to burn up on reentry. Two of his marquee
players, Carlos Delgado and Roy Halladay, went down in the same
week, and he's dropped to fourth.

The last contending team is, thankfully, mine. With the slump a
distant memory now, the Streetwalkers have a hammerlock on fifth,
and are seventeen points from the lead, a gap that is, by all accounts,
surmountable. With Magglio Ordóñez nearly back in the White Sox
lineup, Nando and I are walking around the front office with a hint of
a swagger. When Sig returned from Europe to see the name Ordóñez
scrawled on our roster, he nearly suffered a disruption of oxygen to
the brain. "That's not supposed to happen in an expert league," he
said.

But on July 9, Sig sends over a new spreadsheet that kills the mood.
After performing a simulation of the rest of the season based on each
team's performance so far, he discovered that if every team continues
at its present level of production we would likely finish *seventh*. In the
two hours between leaving my first frantic phone message and the
moment Sig finally calls back to explain his methodology, I've bought
a pack of Merits and laid waste to five of them.

All along we've been planning to trade our next REMA ace, Javier
Vazquez, for a top hitter who should be able to shore up our offense,
and after the upcoming All-Star break, we're planning to revisit that.
But to catch the pack ahead of us, Sig estimates, we'll have to
scrounge up 46 extra runs in the second half of the season, raise our
batting average by 10 points, and pick up 20 more stolen bases. These
numbers suggest that we should reshuffle our offense right away,
swapping one of our power hitters for a basestealer with a high average who scores lots of runs.

To that end, Nando puts together a list of our players who are expendable under this new calculus, ranked by their midseason values
on the Black Box:

Player	Salary	Earnings	Profit/Loss
José Guillen	$15	$23	$ 8
David Ortiz	21	28	7
Jacque Jones	22	22	0
Josh Phelps	15	4	(11)
Dmitri Young	17	3	(14)
Magglio Ordóñez	35	12	(23)

Ordóñez and Young, still recovering from injuries, are clearly more valuable to hang on to than to trade. Phelps, now riding the bench in Toronto, won't attract much interest. Jones has the potential to steal bases, which makes him indispensable (not that I'd trade him anyhow), and moving Guillen would leave us with another vacancy in the outfield. The only option we can't immediately rule out is trading David Ortiz, which is all but unthinkable. Just as I'd suspected at spring training, Big Papi is having a breakout season. He leads the American League in RBI and ranks third in home runs. He hit .365 in June, and recently clubbed nine homers in fourteen games. You'd have to be a blockhead to even consider the idea.

Or would you?

———

On the afternoon of July 12, on the eve of the All-Star Game, I'm standing in an upstairs ballroom at the Four Seasons in downtown Houston surrounded by a mass of cameras, sound booms, microphones, and tape recorders, the likes of which I haven't seen since the last time I covered the Super Bowl.

The occasion is the annual "meet the players" media session, and the American League stars are in the room now, sitting at tables behind big placards with their names on them. At the beginning of the season, when I booked my flight to Houston, I thought of this as a reconnaissance trip—a chance to figure out which superstar hitters to target when we're ready to start trading our REMA aces. But Sig's gloomy midseason review has turned my trip to the midsummer classic into something else: a referendum on the future of David Americo Ortiz.

Every year, without fail, some budding star who's never been to the All-Star Game separates himself from the pack as a *personality*. This year, it's Big Papi's turn. Surrounded by a huge contingent of media, he's decked out in a shiny gray three-piece suit, with a diamond loop in one ear and a giant pair of jeweled sunglasses with a gold Chanel logo.

"What does the insignia mean?" asks one reporter.

Ortiz flashes a goofy smile.

"*Beeeg* and rich," he says.

To his teammates, this emergence is no surprise. Over the years they've come to adore Ortiz for his utter lack of guile. When they're not swindling him in card games or smearing his underpants with peanut butter while he's in the shower, they're puzzling over his random clubhouse pronouncements, like "Nobody look at my nipples!"

Even after the media session, Ortiz continues to steal the show. That night at the home run derby, he hits a mammoth shot that bounces off the ballpark's retractable roof. All in all, he's making himself awfully hard to trade.

An hour before Tuesday's All-Star Game, I take my seat in the auxiliary press area, which is located in the deepest, farthest reaches of center field. From there, home plate looks so distant that I have to fish through my bag to find my glasses. Powering up my laptop, I find a message from Nando: He's got the first nibble on Ortiz. Joe Sheehan, our new favorite dance partner, said he'd consider swapping him for another All-Star, Texas second baseman Alfonso Soriano.

Of all the players who fit our profile, Soriano is one of the best. He scores runs, steals bases, and hits for average. He'd also clouted 17 homers, which wasn't too far behind Ortiz's 23. Best of all, Soriano, a middle infielder, would finally (finally!) allow us to release Rey Sánchez. In the first inning of the game, as if auditioning for the role, Soriano golfs a Roger Clemens pitch over the left-field wall.

Nando sends a text message.

"Soriano looks goooood."

By the sixth inning, I'm paying scant attention to the game, which has become an American League rout. Instead I'm gazing at the Tout Wars scoring page and growing more convinced that Soriano is the missing piece of a championship team.

KWAK!

With one runner on, Ortiz had lumbered to the plate to face Carl Pavano and worked the count even at 2–2. Then Pavano threw a slider that came up 86 on the radar gun, and now the entire ballpark is standing to admire the result. Looking up, I see a white dot rise through the air and just sort of hang there, framed against the black sky, not moving laterally or vertically, only growing larger. And larger.

This ball is headed *right at me.*

In the climactic scene of the movie *The Natural*, Roy Hobbs comes to bat with one last chance to put the New York Knights in the World Series. Up in the press box, his archenemy, sportswriter Max Mercy, has already made his prediction, sketching out a disparaging cartoon of Hobbs that depicts him whiffing at a baseball with a pair of goat horns protruding from his head. Just then, Hobbs hits a towering foul ball that shatters the press-box window right in front of Mercy, showering glass on him and his skeptical cartoon. Then, of course, Hobbs hits the triumphant home run.

As the ball begins to descend, I clap down the lid of my laptop and stand up to defend myself. I can't dismiss the idea that Ortiz, like Roy Hobbs, is sending me a message in the form of a hardball aimed at my dental work.

Big Papi's home run comes to rest 423 feet from home plate, where it's caught by a fellow sportswriter two rows directly in front of me. On the replay, as the camera traces the ball's flight, I see a blurry image of myself, palms outstretched, bracing for a concussion.

I knew that trading Ortiz wouldn't be easy, but now I'm starting to think the decision could be the defining moment of my season. In one ear I hear the old scouts telling me that I've just seen the answer with my own eyes. In the other I can hear the incessant tapping of Sig's mechanical pencil. "Be actuarial!"

After the game, my thoughts in a knot, I find Ortiz in the American

League clubhouse, leaning on a sofa with his uniform untucked, mobbed again by reporters. I wait until he's alone at his locker loading his equipment into a Red Sox duffel bag. After reminding him about Tout Wars, I skip right to the hard part.

"I may have to trade you for Soriano," I say.

Ortiz looks at me quizzically, then shrugs.

"He's a *goot* player."

"So you think that's a fair trade?"

Ortiz starts to laugh. He thinks this is funny. "Depenze on wha you need," he says.

"Well, I'm okay with home runs, but I need some stolen bases."

"Well, den, dare you go."

"So you think it's a good deal?"

"Thadda be great."

"So I should do it . . . ."

Ortiz smiles mischievously.

"Thass up to you."

"You're not planning on stealing a bunch of bases all of a sudden, are you?"

"Hey, you *never know.*"

Not three minutes later, Alfonso Soriano marches through the clubhouse door carrying the Tiffany crystal trophy awarded to the All-Star Game's most-valuable player. He sets the trophy down gently on a folding chair, and the reporters descend. Now that Papi has given the trade his tacit approval, I turn my attention to Soriano and my one burning question: Why has he stolen only nine bases so far this season?

Edging to the front of the pack, I ask him.

"I always want to steal a base," Soriano says, "but the pitchers don't give me a chance. I have to take what they give to me." Soriano has worked diligently on his English, but it's not always perfectly clear, so I decide to ask him again, more directly.

"Do you have a red light?"

"No, no, no," he says. "I have the green light. I'm just not getting a lot of good jumps. The pitchers, they hold me on."

The assembled reporters, anxious for a compulsory quote from the MVP, have started to grumble, but I don't care. I have a *Rotisserie* team to manage. I ask Soriano if he thinks he'll run more. "Depends," he says. "If I have a good jump, I want to take some steals, but it's up to the pitchers."

"But you'd *like* to steal more," I say, prompting a chorus of groans from behind.

"Yes, yes," he says, nodding vigorously.

As I wander out through the ballpark tunnel, bound for my hotel room, I have asked all the questions I could think of and heard satisfactory answers. But this time, rather than illuminating the truth, they've left me twice as confused.

———

Two days later, I'm sitting in a thirty-dollar box seat behind the third-base dugout at Network Associates Coliseum in Oakland, where the Athletics are preparing to host the White Sox.

My trip to Houston was only the first leg of a three-city western swing that will allow me to visit three ballparks, eight of my players, and four of my Tout Wars opponents. Tonight's plan is to watch a ballgame while flanked by Sig, my executive vice president for statistics and unceasing torment, who's driven up from Silicon Valley in his blue Honda, and Andrea Mallis, my director of baseball astrology, who's just arrived from Berkeley via mass transit. The topic to be discussed is, of course, whether to trade David Ortiz for Alfonso Soriano.

Andrea Mallis is a bright and bubbly woman in her forties with long dark curly hair and hazel eyes. When I meet her at the ticket windows, she's wearing black shoes, a black skirt, black tights, and a black shirt embroidered with the zodiac wheel. She's carrying a backpack that's brimming with newspapers, notes, astrological reports, two yogurts, and a sandwich—along with a pair of plastic bags to handle the overflow. As we took our seats, she handed me a yellow bookmark with all the upcoming dates when Mercury is retrograde. "Goddess knows when you might need it," she explained.

Mallis grew up in Queens, where she followed the Mets through the 1970s. She knew she'd be a baseball fan for life on the day she saw a group of nuns at Shea Stadium holding a sign that said "Ya Gotta Believe." While attending Berkeley, she discovered astrology and eventually decided to combine her two loves. She's since become such a ballpark regular that the A's flagship radio station, KFRC, has given her a regular segment called "The Astrology Minute," which is introduced by the theme music from *The Twilight Zone*. By sitting with the player's families during ballgames and attending team functions, she's been able to get precise birth times for some players.

Early on Mallis explained to me that she doesn't make exact predictions—there are too many variables involved to determine, for instance, how many strikeouts Rich Harden will register tonight. "I can predict energy," she says, "but not necessarily events." In her view, astrology isn't a substitute for scouting or statistical analysis. "It's really about being more holistic and getting information from many different oracles."

Sig is doing everything in his power to be polite. When I told him about the evening, he'd written back: "Going to a ballgame with an astrologer? What has happened to me?" Already there's been one close call: Outside the ticket window, Sig asked Mallis how long she'd been doing astrology. "In the past, many lifetimes," she said. "But in this lifetime only since 1989."

"Geez," he said, turning to me. "And I thought *I* padded my résumé."

"Be nice!" I whispered.

As dissimilar as their methods may be, Andrea Mallis and Sig Mejdal have the same ultimate goal: to work as a consultant to a major-league ballclub. "I'm so unique, people don't realize they need me yet," Mallis says.

"Me, too," adds Sig, dryly.

When I decided to consult an astrologer for Rotisserie advice, I'll admit my expectations were low. I'd incorporated Mallis's forecasts into Hunchmaster, but during the Tout Wars auction I couldn't bring myself to make any draft picks solely on the basis of something she told me. But now, more than halfway through the season, I wish I'd paid more attention. Her track record isn't just good, it's *spooky*.

Mallis said pitcher C.C. Sabathia would hit a rough patch in late June. He walked off the mound with a tweaked shoulder on the twenty-sixth. She told me Seattle closer Eddie Guardado would struggle early in the season with a low energy cycle. He blew three saves. She prophesied that Jarrod Washburn would have two good months before Neptune crossed him up. He won seven games in April and May and only one in June. She'd warned me to stay away from Barry Zito (Neptune again), whose ERA is currently 4.62.

As the game begins, Mallis rummages through her backpack and pulls out a black folder containing the charts she's prepared on Ortiz and Soriano and spreads them out carefully on her lap like sacred texts. Each sheaf of paper has a zodiac wheel overlaid with so many numbers, points, and coordinates that they look like flight plans for the Mars lander. There are two types of astrologers, Mallis told me: those who just pull things from thin air and those who keep up with the latest software.

She's one of the latter.

Mallis starts with a caveat. Ortiz and Soriano are both from the Dominican Republic, where municipal record keeping is notoriously inexact. If the birth dates on file for them are not accurate, this could change the results considerably.

"Understood," I say.

"Ortiz," she begins, "is a monster. I'm hard-pressed to bet against Scorpios—they're so determined and intense and thoughtful—and he's got Saturn in harmonious aspect to his Sun, which is his vitality. His Mercury, which is his movement on the field, is more stable. I'm thinking a strong second half."

"So no trade?" I ask.

Mallis tilts her head and sighs. "I just hate to part with Ortiz, unless there's a really compelling reason to trade him. I don't know. Do you need a second baseman?"

"And steals," I say.

"Yeah, Ortiz isn't going to steal any bases."

Mallis pauses for a half minute, staring at the chart. "You really want Soriano, but you don't want to give up Ortiz. . . . What do you think, Sig?"

Sig has been sitting stiffly in his chair, watching the game and trying to think benificent thoughts. Still staring forward, he clears his throat and answers Mallis slowly and evenly. "I like it because we're in fifth place, half the season is already gone, and we should welcome some chance and uncertainty. If we get twenty extra steals from Soriano, we're hopping over quite a few people."

"But Ortiz is such a monster!" Mallis repeats even more emphatically.

Sig turns stiffly, his expression controlled. "Ortiz's first half has been wonderful, as good as you could expect," he says. "But there's not much more for him to do. If there's anybody whose stock is high, it's his. So yeah, I hate to lose the monster and his totals, but we're not trading him for a fringe player, we're getting another monster who I think has more upside." He stops for a second. "How are Soriano's stars, have we looked at that?"

(Now *this* is synergy.)

"Capricorn," Mallis says, holding his chart up to her nose, looking for signs of Mars and activity in the sixth and tenth houses. "There's no real red light saying he's not going to be good," she says, dropping the chart to her lap. "He does have this wiry energy about him. But he sort of makes me nervous."

By the late innings, Sig has done a commendable job stifling his scientific gall and giving Mallis her say. Other than asking her a few loaded questions ("What if somebody is born by induced labor?"), he'd been courteous, cordial, and even chatty. He gave Mallis his exact time of birth so she could run his chart.

After the game, we give our team astrologer a lift back to Berkeley, where we drop her at a modest apartment complex in the center of the student ghetto. Once we've waved good-bye, Sig and I exchange a silent glance. On some level, I'm hoping he may have turned a corner tonight, that talking to Mallis made him think that maybe there is some part of baseball that's influenced by celestial forces. Of course, if I was to tell him the truth, that I'm pretty impressed with her work, I know he'll spend the entire ride home pounding me like doughnut batter.

But back at the hotel bar, I can no longer restrain my curiosity. "So," I say, "do you believe any of it?"

"No."

"Not even a little bit?"

Sig takes off his glasses and rubs his face, something he does when he hears a question he can't believe he really has to answer. "Let's see. Do I believe that the exact moment David Ortiz came out of the womb has something to do with how well he hits a spherical ball with a cylindrical bat?"

He pauses for effect.

"No, I don't."

Sig's opinion of the Ortiz trade hasn't changed since he first ran the numbers through Zoladex. According to the Black Box, the deal slightly favors Sheehan. But if Soriano starts stealing bases again, the balance would tilt in our favor by as much as 30 percent. So in the name of embracing risk, he's all for it.

Intellectually, I get this. Ortiz may be able to guide us to a respectable finish, but Soriano could help us win. As good as some of my hunches have been, and for all that my inner scout tells me not to do this, I know that I have to start listening to Sig. As the season wears on, Tout Wars becomes less like poker and more like chess, where the math undergirds everything.

But sitting on a barstool at my budget hotel there's one thing I still can't dismiss: that titanic home run Ortiz hit my way in Houston. Is it possible, I ask Sig, that I'm overlooking the clearest and most inscrutable omen of the season? By trading Ortiz after seeing this, doesn't that cast me in the role of Max Mercy? Doesn't that make me just another shriveled press-box cynic?

Sig smiles indulgently. In the movie *The Natural*, he says, Roy

Hobbs hits a heroic home run at the end. But in Bernard Malamud's book, he reminds me, the *real* Roy Hobbs goes down swinging.

"He fails," Sig says, "so maybe Ortiz will, too."

———

Now that I've made up my mind to trade Ortiz, there's another small matter to contend with. Joe Sheehan, perhaps smarting from the Ordóñez trade, has decided to flavor his offer with a teaspoon of castor oil. He doesn't just want Ortiz, he wants $15 FAAB, too. Still scrapping for pitchers, Sheehan is now determined to stockpile more FAAB than anyone else in the event that Arizona's Randy Johnson gets traded to the Yankees, as rumor suggests—and an extra $15 would put him over the top.

While I'd scoffed at the idea at first, it had since become clear that Soriano was the best player we could get for Ortiz, which made Sheehan's premium seem less obnoxious. Having already squandered so much FAAB, there was something strangely alluring about the idea of cashing out.

"How much FAAB do we have left?" I'd asked Nando back in Houston.

There was a halting pause on the line.

"Thirteen," he'd mumbled.

We were two bucks short.

From that moment, Nando had been working the phones, trying to turn some bag of bones on our bench into two crummy FAAB dollars. He'd shopped worthless backup outfielders, pimped promising minor-league pitchers, and even tried to sell Doug Mientkiewicz for $30 FAAB. But the morning after the A's game I awaken in my hotel room to find a text message on my cellphone. It's from Nando, and it says "no dice."

It's now Friday, and I'm stuck in Oakland with exactly six hours left until the weekly transaction deadline. I'm basically out of options, save one.

Winding my rental car through the hills of El Cerrito, I pull up in front of a purple-and-teal ranch on the high side of the street. There's a burnt-orange BMW in the driveway and a view of Mt. Tamalpais from the living room. This is where the Zen master lives.

From the time he opened his first pack of baseball cards in 1960 to the moment he joined his first Rotisserie league, Lawr Michaels had a hunch that his brain was extraordinarily well equipped to absorb and process baseball information. But even after years of cleaning up in local leagues with teams like Lawr of Averages and Lawrence's Arabians, it took a call to John Benson's 900 number to set him down the road to Tout Wars. Benson was so impressed with Michaels that he offered him a job editing player summaries for his annual. Soon Michaels branched out, writing columns for a slew of publications and Web sites before launching CREATiVESPORTS, which he likes to call *"The New Yorker* of fantasy sites."

After cooking us a breakfast of eggs and home fries, Lawr Michaels directs me to his mocha-and-periwinkle living room, where I explain my dilemma and lay out a proposal. For $2 FAAB, I will sell him Michael Ryan, an injured Minnesota benchwarmer on my reserve list that he doesn't especially need.

With his team in first place, there's no rationale whatsoever for Michaels to do this. But after a couple hours, he hasn't said no. Truthfully, he's had a hard time staying on any one topic for more than forty seconds. As the trade clock ticks, he plays me some recordings of his band, Midlife Crisis, and some videos of himself jamming on the guitar at various local bars. In the meantime, we discuss everything from *Cyrano de Bergerac* to the intricacies of writing HTML. The problem, I realize, is that Lawr Michaels is *baked.*

From the moment I walked in, I noticed that the Michaels household smelled of marijuana smoke, and after a time Lawr had cleared up the mystery by tripping into the living room with a freshly rolled joint dangling from his lips. "This shit is four hundred dollars an ounce!" he exclaimed. There must have been a bewildered look on my face, because a few minutes later he dug up a prescription jar and waved it in front of me.

"Don't worry, it's legal."

As a child of ten, Michaels was diagnosed with Crohn's disease. He was sick for most of his teenage years and didn't start growing until he was in high school. He's had seven surgeries and has been told on several occasions that he's not supposed to be alive. After doctors removed eleven feet of gangrenous intestine, they told him he'd never be able to eat solid food. For the pain, they put him on a cocktail of steroids and narcotics, but these only made him miserable and killed his appetite. The first time he tried pot, he ate three slices of pizza and never looked back. He's smoked nearly every day for thirty-eight years.

In the middle of our visit, Lawr's wife, Cathy Hedgecock, rises from a nap and trundles to the dining room wearing a velvet jacket and a silk scarf. She's a sunny soul who shares his taste in literature, with a soft spot for P. G. Wodehouse. "Sometimes I'll hear her giggling about Bertie and Jeeves," Michaels says. Two years ago, Hedgecock joined a Rotisserie league at Michaels's urging and was instantly sucked in. She drafted her first team with an eye to picking up players with unique names like Gookie Dawkins and Augie Ojeda. "She thought that would be very Wodehousean," Lawr says. When he talks about Cathy, Lawr's voice rises to a sweet tone. "I say that we have probably the best relationship of any couple we've ever known," he continues. "We just really like each other. We never fight, we never argue, we've never called each other a name, we've never yelled at each other. Ever. Honestly."

Nine months ago, after a long remission, the cancer Hedgecock had battled in the past returned to her body and quickly spread to her brain. Convinced she wouldn't live through that September, doctors placed her in hospice care. But here it is July, and she's still kicking. In the house today she walks stiffly, taking pains to smile, talking only sparingly. Some days she'll knit or paint a mandala. Other days she walks the dog around the block or practices tai chi in the backyard while her husband watches baseball. They rent movies: Hitchcock's *North by Northwest* or *Rebecca* and anything by Kurosawa. "Cath is kinda fuzzy," Lawr says, "but hanging in there."

Now and then in an unguarded moment, the Zen master weakens under the weight of this. It took enormous courage for Michaels to come to the Tout Wars draft. He showed up only because Cathy insisted. After he'd spent an afternoon wandering through Central Park, I asked him if he'd ever consider moving to New York. "You never know," he said, softly. "Chances are I'm going to be alone in a short while."

If the heartbreak has given Michaels anything to be thankful for, other than an appreciation for the value of a day, it was the confidence to be himself. Exhausted by the trials of the long winter, he showed up at the draft ready to take his Zen philosophy to the final stage of evolution. For years he'd been cheating a bit, coming to the table with a mental list of players he wanted or the faint outlines of a draft strategy. This year there was nothing—no plan, no fear.

It was his best draft yet.

"I don't scare very easily," he says. "Twice in my life I've been told that I would not live through the night. Several times I wasn't sure if my wife would live. I can play serious fantasy baseball and not give a shit. I'll find something more concrete to get upset about."

I'm guessing it's about twenty minutes before the trade deadline, but I'm not sure. For some reason I'm having trouble gauging time. But when our conversation loops back to Tout Wars and my $2 FAAB proposal, the future of my Ortiz trade, if not my entire season, rests squarely on the shoulders of a man in a black turtleneck.

Maybe Lawr Michaels is just selfless at heart. Maybe he's just stoned to the bejesus. But in the toughest Rotisserie league in the country, with his team holding the lead by a hair, he gazes upon the the anxious rookie before him and decides to cut him a break.

"How much do you want for Ryan?" he asks.

"Two bucks," I say.

"Fine, let's send it in."

———

Two days later, I've flown to Los Angeles for the final leg of my western tour. I'm sitting in the right-field bleachers at Anaheim Stadium under a blazing sun watching the Angels play Boston with Hollywood Matt Berry.

When we made plans to attend this game, I assumed it would give me a chance to check in with my large contingent of Red Sox. But now that I've traded most of them, I'd be perfectly content to see everyone but Bill Mueller undone by sprained ankles, slumps, or maybe rubella.

This afternoon's game is especially unnerving. Last night, during his debut as a member of the Baseball Prospectus team, David Ortiz clubbed a home run. So far this afternoon he tripled in the first and hit a screaming meemie in the fourth that should have been a double. Matt Berry is hammering me on the trade with Sheehan, which he can't believe I really made. The only thing that quiets him is the sight of Ortiz coming to bat in the sixth and clobbering a ball into right field that flies over our heads. This time, it's a three-run homer.

"Didn't you own Ortiz at one point?" Berry asks, as Big Papi ambles around the bases.

When he hits an RBI single the following inning, Berry says, "You do realize he's a double away from the cycle?"

"Yes, I do, *thanks.*"

Watching this display, I am, for the first time in my Rotisserie career, feeling an attack of moral outrage. If David Ortiz knew he was about to go on a murderous baseball-mashing rampage, he should have had the decency to warn me during our conversation in Houston. Instead, he just smiled and shrugged and let me waltz down the path to oblivion. So when the game ends, I march down to the clubhouse to find Big Papi and give him a piece of my mind.

When I approach him, he's standing next to his locker wearing a black Cowboy Up T-shirt the size of a car cover. He sees me. I throw up my palms.

"Papi. You're *killing* me!"

"Wha?" he says with a coy smile.

"I've got major trade remorse."

"Why, hoo you trade me for?"

"Soriano!"

"Heh, heh, heh." Ortiz is chuckling. The moment he sees the anguished look on my face, he begins to laugh even harder, his giant shoulders heaving like hydraulic pumps.

"Dude, you shodona leezen to me, becoze I'm abow to get *hot*. Theens are abow to get *UGLY*."

"But Papi, you've gotta cool off sometime . . ."

Ortiz has stopped smiling. He puffs up his chest, plants a finger between his pectorals, and booms out one final piece of advice.

"YOO BETTA GET ME BACK!"

Tout Wars Standings Through July 21, 2004

1. Lawr Michaels, CREATiVESPORTS, 86.0
2. Dean Peterson, STATS, Inc., 85.0
3. Trace Wood, The Long Gandhi, 83.5
4. Jeff Erickson, RotoWire, 77.5
5. Matt Berry, Talented Mr. Roto, 66.0
6. Streetwalkers, 64.0
6. Rick Fogel, USA Stats, 64.0
8. Joe Sheehan, Baseball Prospectus, 61.5
9. Ron Shandler, Baseball HQ, 58.5
10. Steve Moyer, Baseball Info Solutions, 51.5
11. Jason Grey, Mastersball, 42.5
12. Gene McCaffrey, Wise Guy Baseball, 39.5

The Provocateur

August

As New York governor Mario Cuomo's Rotisserie partner, Marty Stead-man knew the golden rule: There must be one Italian American on every team. After years of losing his shirt on Righettis, Francos, and Colangelos, Steadman picked up a Latin player with a passably Italian surname, hop-ing the governor would be fooled. He was not.

"He made me trade," Steadman says, "for an Italian."

. . .

On the final night of my western circuit, I'm heading back to Ana-heim to watch a ballgame with three of my fellow Touts. The pretext is innocent enough—just a few guys in the same Roto league getting together to see the Angels play the Indians while drinking beer and making fun of one another. But for me, this evening is ripe with evil opportunity.

With August looming and my team parked in sixth, I'm about to employ a new set of tactics. Other than hiring Christine Price to prance around at the draft and telling a few white lies during trade talks, I've been a Boy Scout. If I want to win Tout Wars, I need to de-velop a killer instinct. Tonight's plan, then, is to goad these guys into making a dumb trade that will help me beat all of them.

At the far end of our row is Jeff Erickson, the Tout with a flair for caution. Driving to the game in his meticulously clean Camry, he rarely exceeded the speed limit and apologized for making innocuous lane changes. "My crazy driving," he called it. At the ballpark, he eats his chili dog with a fork. "Otherwise it gets all soupy," he explains.

After earning a law degree at Loyola, Erickson joined some college buddies to start a free Rotisserie information site called Rotonews, and after John Hunt plugged it in a 1997 *Baseball Weekly* column, the site began pulling two million page-views per day. Within two years, it was one of the top seven sports sites on the Web, and Erickson and his partners sold the company to Broadband Sports, an Internet-era highflier that promptly failed, leaving them with gobs of worthless stock. Rather than calling it quits, they moved across the street and changed the name to RotoWire. Today they have about ten thousand subscribers per year paying as much as seventy dollars. Headquarters is a cramped office in Culver City with seven desks, a foosball table, and two televisions constantly tuned to sports.

The company has writers spread out across North America, and it's Erickson's job to oversee them. Their primary business is pounding out short updates that help Rotisserie players manage their rosters—from blockbuster trade rumors to the status of Junior Spivey's left-shoulder subluxation. Since RotoWire caters to all fantasy sports, Erickson is already preparing for the fantasy-football season, and, as such, Tout Wars sometimes takes a backseat. Even though his team is a wounded shambles, he's gone three weeks without making a FAAB move. If anyone should be itching to make a trade from the ballpark tonight, it's him.

On my left, sporting a new pair of white Reeboks and a fresh buzz cut, is Joe "the Volcano" Sheehan, who may be the only able-minded adult in Los Angeles without a driver's license. When he can't bum a ride, he takes the bus. And when there's no bus, he hoofs it. Airplanes are just as problematic: his flight to New York in March was a white-knuckle ride. But for all his phobias in the world of transportation, Sheehan is as sure-footed as they come in playing games of the mind. His shelves at home are lined with Strat-O-Matic trophies, and last December he won his first poker tournament.

In the early days of Baseball Prospectus, Sheehan worked two extra jobs to make the rent. And even now, with BP earning steady revenue from its annual book and subscription Web site, he's not exactly rolling in cash. He lives in a modest house in an LA suburb with his wife, Sophia, and his cat, Mattingly. He works in an airless office in the back, writing four columns a week with only an oscillating fan to cool the magma.

While his work is seldom ignored inside baseball, some executives are decidedly *not* fans, as I would learn over the course of the season. When I showed the Tout Wars standings to White Sox GM Ken Williams, he said, "It's good to see Baseball Prospectus down there at the bottom." Another recent Volcano target put it more succinctly: "Joe Sheehan can kiss my ass."

For my trade scheme to work tonight, I'm counting on Sheehan to be his usual blunt, outspoken, and competitive self and to direct these energies toward adding the starting pitcher he desperately needs. Since his team doesn't have a prayer of beating mine, I'm happy to watch him hoodwink someone else.

The last arrival is Matt Berry, who's dressed to the nines in jeans and a T-shirt. Taking his seat, he hauls out his weather-beaten Black-Berry, which rattles and blinks so furiously that it rarely spends two minutes in his pocket. Between working on three screenplays, managing his personal Web site, writing columns for Rotoworld, keeping a blog, doing three live chats a week, appearing on radio shows, and working on various entrepreneurial schemes, Berry has *ten* Rotisserie teams—including one he's running for his Hollywood agent. "We're in third place, and he loves me for it," he says.

While he started playing Rotisserie twenty years ago at age fourteen, Berry doesn't do projections, write books, visit clubhouses, churn out data, or really do anything that a guy off the street couldn't do. "It's all about confidence," he says. "I'm a fantasy expert because I call myself one." Most people with his attention deficit would be terrified to draft a team in Tout, but not Berry. "Once you've gone broke in Hollywood," he says, "everything else is a piece of cake." Not that he's broke right now, mind you. By the standards of Rotisserie pundits, Berry lives lavishly in a stylish contemporary in the hills of Sherman Oaks with his wife, Rachel, a development executive for Aaron

Spelling. They have no kids. He drives a gold Lexus. But with his Hollywood career demanding less of his time, Berry has bodily hurled himself into the Rotisserie business, where his biggest paycheck to date is the roughly one hundred dollars a month he's paid for his Talented Mr. Roto columns on Rotoworld. In a few weeks, he'll be unveiling his newest moneymaking scheme: RotoPass, which offers purchasers access to six fantasy sites, including Shandler's and Erickson's, for $150 a year. If fantasy sports is a billion-dollar industry, he writes in a pitch letter, "why aren't we billionaires?"

In Tout Wars, Berry is pulling off one of the season's more miraculous performances. Despite losing $96 worth of players to injury or general ineptitude, he's hanging on with help from curiosities like Chicago closer Shingo Takatsu and former punch line Rod Barajas, who hit twelve homers in the first half. Berry has just passed me to take over fifth place, and now that some of his big guns are starting to fire, he's primed to leave me in his wake.

Unless, of course, I can sabotage him.

The whole point of tonight's exercise is to screw Matt Berry. Not just to stymie his team, but to pay him back for turning the room against me at the auction when I nominated Sidney Ponson. After months of plotting, I've finally found a way to return the favor.

In his blogs and chats and general ramblings, Berry has made it clear that he's fed up with Angels pitcher Bartolo Colón, who was horrible in the first half. "Bartolo Colón is big fat and shitty," he likes to say. His loathing has become so reflexive, he doesn't seem to care that the last time out Colón held the Red Sox to one run in six innings, or that Colón's underlying stats suggest he's not too different from the pitcher he's always been. I have a hunch it's only a matter of time before Colón pulls himself together and gives Berry a shot at first place. It's time to separate the two of them.

In the sixth inning, when the mood is loose, I fire my opening salvo. "You know what would be really cool?" I say in a bubbly tone. "We should make a trade right here from the ballpark!" Heads bob, glances are exchanged. The first voice is Sheehan's soprano. "If I get something, I need Colón," he says, as if reading my mind. Berry leans over to engage him. "Who do you have?" he asks, and we're off.

For the next twenty minutes, to the supreme confusion of the fans seated around us, my three opponents shuffle through the names of at least two dozen players, looking for an amenable trade combination. Sheehan, playing his part impeccably, tells Berry he needs more FAAB to secure a possible bid for Randy Johnson (this is not true) and proceeds to talk Berry into offering him Bartolo Colón plus $5—a carbon copy of the juke he pulled on me with Brad Radke.

I'm delighted, of course.

Finally they settle on a complex trade involving four players that would accomplish my goal. Berry would send Colón and $5 FAAB to Sheehan while picking up the notoriously fragile Detroit outfielder Rondell White, who's been limping on a sore foot.

"Make the deal!" I say.

Matt Berry is no longer smiling. In some corner of his overtaxed brain, he must realize that by giving in to personal pique and trading Colón, he's basically locking in his losses and conceding the title. But Berry is in a tight spot. The only way he can save himself is by scotching the deal and the friendly buzz. For a guy who prides himself on being the life of the party, that's not a happy prospect. He asks for a toss-in pitcher. He gets one.

"We made a deal!" I blurt.

Berry, suddenly quiet, succumbs.

He sends in the deal announcement on his BlackBerry.

The post-trade bonhomie lasts all of three minutes. "This is validating to me," Sheehan crows. "I am a fantasy savant!" At this, Berry's face takes on a white pallor. He asks Sheehan what he *really* thinks of the deal they just made.

"I think I won the trade," Sheehan says.

After the game (the Indians won 8–5), Matt Berry drives home, logs on to the Tout Wars Web site, discovers that Sheehan already has more than enough FAAB to get Randy Johnson, and fires off a message to the three of us. In the spirit of "full disclosure or fair play," he says, he'd like to amend the trade to get his $5 back. In a separate message sent to me, Berry is seething. He calls Sheehan's move an act of "questionable ethics."

"He's being a wank," Sheehan says the next day, biting into an enchilada at a tiny Mexican restaurant near his house in Rosemead. Of course he knew he didn't need any more FAAB to get Johnson, he says, "I was just trying to squeeze, which I think you've got to do in the trade market." After polishing off his refried beans, Sheehan puts it more bluntly: "Last night I bent Matt Berry over a table."

In the end, Berry gets his $5 FAAB back, but only in exchange for a backup outfielder. And in a matter of days, it's a hollow concession. Colón not only improves, he wins his third game in a row while striking out six and holding Texas to one run in seven innings.

"FUCK BARTOLO COLON!" Berry writes to the three of us. "And while I'm at it, fuck you Sheehan! There. Now I feel better."

Mission accomplished.

———

I return to my steamy apartment in New York to find that somebody forgot to feed my players while I was gone.

Since the All-Star break, Bill Mueller, Jorge Posada, and Corey Koskie have a collective .160 batting average. Luis Matos, his average hovering among the worst in the majors, bangs into an outfield wall and comes up hobbling. Magglio Ordóñez is scratched from the lineup with lingering knee soreness, and José Guillen, already nursing a stiff back, is benched for a game for unspecified *disciplinary* reasons. On July 22, Rick Fogel's USA Stats team overtakes us. Then, thanks to Bartolo Colón, who's more dominant than I'd ever imagined, Joe Sheehan knocks the Streetwalkers down to eighth.

Even Nando is depressed.

"I can't believe this team is so bad," he says.

The next day I get a message from Sig, which I'm actually eager to open. In times of trouble, the good doctor Mejdal can always be counted on to brush off a bad stretch with some comforting bromides about the role of chance and the peculiarities of statistical deviation. But this time the subject says, "Oh, shit," and the message field contains a headline plucked from the wires: "Ordóñez Back on DL, Could Spend Eight Weeks on Crutches."

In idle moments, I'd wondered how I might react to a disaster of this magnitude. I'd imagined taking a seven-iron to my laptop or running around the city throwing eggs at smiling tourists. But now that it's really happened, there's no way I could summon the energy. I drop my head to my keyboard and leave it there as random characters fill the screen.

A few days earlier in Oakland, when the White Sox were in town, I made a point to ask Ordóñez how his knee was feeling. He told me he'd been thankful for the All-Star break, which gave him a chance to "start healing." This seemed like an odd thing to say after sitting out forty games, but after watching him belt a home run that night, his first for the Streetwalkers, I'd erased it from my mind. Now the prognosis is bone-marrow edema.

A few weeks from now, while sitting in a dugout with White Sox GM Ken Williams, I'll ask him what it was like to lose Ordóñez for real. "Did you smash anything?"

"No," Williams will say, calmly sipping black coffee from a Styrofoam cup. "I tend to internalize. It's just slowly eating away at the lining of my stomach."

"I can't imagine being a GM," I'll offer.

At this, Williams will give me a sideways glance that says, You Don't Know The Half of It.

They say that before death, one feels a tranquil sensation or sees a celestial glow. That evening, my Ordóñez-less Rotisserie team puts up its best numbers since Cinquo de Mayo: four homers, sixteen RBI, ten runs, two wins, six strikeouts, one save, and a subterranean ERA. It's enough to vault us back into fifth and give me a short reprieve from the inevitable gloom. Over the next two days, of course, we hit .222 and .120, and I'm back to eating scallions in my bathrobe. I spend the weekend engaged in some intensely mindless housecleaning.

———

As I emerge from the mother of all funks, my kitchen spotless, I can see the flaws in my approach with a new clarity.

Every time the baseball gods have taken a whack at my roster, I've ignored the fact that Rotisserie is a game of increments and tried to repair the damage with a grandiose move. The trouble is that when one of these moves backfires, it's possible to wake up and discover that Sidney Ponson is back on your team. As eager as I am to replace Ordóñez, there's no sense in acting rashly.

My other failure is a lack of imagination. To this point I've used my privileged access to baseball mostly to gather intelligence about players. There's nothing wrong with this, I've just been doing a hair too much of it. If all I do is take notes, I'm not living up to my pledge to play this game *differently*.

I decide it's time to stop worrying about trades and injuries and start trying to help the players on my team to perform better. Not by hanging around and offering them pointers but by pleading on their behalf to the people they work for. In other words, I'm about to become a clubhouse provocateur.

The idea came to me earlier this month, quite by accident, when I showed up at Yankee Stadium to check on Jason Johnson, the Tigers pitcher I'd picked up in the Fogel massacre. While Johnson had been pitching well, I was thinking about trading him. Last season in Baltimore, his velocity dropped and his ERA spiked in the last two months, and I was worried about a repeat performance.

In Johnson's case, there was a ready explanation: He's a type-1 diabetic who has to wear an insulin pump on the mound. While nobody comes out and says it, least of all Johnson, most baseball insiders assume the condition affects his stamina.

Sifting through his record, Sig noticed that when Johnson works a lot of innings, his performance does, indeed, fall off more steeply than the average pitcher's. But last season, right before Johnson fell apart, Nando noticed that he'd thrown a grueling 124 pitches in one outing and 125 just ten days later. These were Johnson's biggest workloads of the year, nearly back-to-back. Hearing this, I started to wonder if his manager had simply pushed him too hard.

In the visitor's clubhouse, I tracked down Tigers pitching coach Bob Cluck, who may be the youngest fifty-nine-year-old I've ever met. At the moment he was wearing a pair of trippy, round John Lennon–style sunglasses and snapping gum. When I showed him my spreadsheet on Johnson's pitch counts, his eyebrows danced. "Come here," he said, pulling my arm.

Seconds later we were in the office of Tigers manager Alan Trammell.

"Sam, you know Tram," Cluck said.

I nodded like I was Trammell's best pal, rather than a guy who used to have his baseball card taped to my locker in junior high.

Cluck held the sheet under Trammell's nose. "Here's Johnson in August last year," he said, pointing with two fingers. "At this point his ERA was 3.77. Then he had a couple 120s, and in September look at his ERA."

Trammell's eyes widened.

"Takes a toll," he said.

As the two of them studied the paper, I asked Cluck if he'd ever consider letting Johnson throw 125 pitches again.

"Not on a regular basis."

"Once in a while, maybe?" I tested.

"If we did, I'd make sure to cut him off early the next time."

That night, Johnson took the mound and ripped through the Yankee lineup. By the eighth inning, he'd only yielded one run, and the Tigers hadn't bothered to get anyone loose in the bullpen. When Johnson's pitch count hit 97, I started to wonder if Cluck would keep his earlier promise, or let Johnson's tally ride up into the hundreds. But after he'd given up another base hit, Cluck's face appeared on the press box TV monitor. He was fumbling for the bullpen phone with such alacrity he nearly knocked off his shades. Four pitches later, Johnson was finished for the day.

I left the ballpark that night thinking that if I could do this much for one of my players without even meaning to, imagine what I could accomplish with a little scheming!

———

For my first intentional feat of lobbying, I turn my attention to Minnesota first baseman Doug Mientkiewicz.

On July 26, five days before the real major-league trading deadline, there are rumors that the Twins are shopping Dougie Baseball. Given the way he's played so far and the fact that Justin Morneau, the prospect right behind him, has been pillaging the minor leagues, this is no surprise. So far Mientkiewicz has dealt with these rumors just as one might have expected—by talking about them with embarrassing candor. "I feel like a ship with no harbor," he told reporters. After a few days of this public moping, terms like "clubhouse cancer" and "martyr complex" are popping up in posts on the TwinsGeek chatroom. "It would behoove him to just shut up," says one.

Sad as I am to see one of my players shipped out, it also presents an opportunity. Reports say the two teams most interested in Mientkiewicz are the Red Sox, who would probably use him as an occasional defensive substitute, and the Pittsburgh Pirates, who would play him every day. In Rotisserie terms, I'd much rather see Mientkiewicz go to Pittsburgh, where he'll be a mainstay in the lineup.

At noon Sig and I begin to pore over the numbers, looking for some compelling and heretofore undiscovered reason why the Pirates should acquire our $12 first baseman, and after wading through all the lukewarm arguments, we strike pay dirt. Sig notices that the Pirates home infield is a difficult surface to play on. In fact, in the last two seasons there were 42 percent more infield errors committed at Pirates home games than Pirates road games, which is the biggest deviation in baseball. Nonetheless, I notice that the Pirates' starting pitchers have a strong tendency to give up more ground balls than fly balls, and the bullpen is even more extreme. So not only do the Pirates have a bad infield surface, they've built a pitching staff that actually exacerbates the problem. If there's any team that needs a Gold Glove first baseman, it's this one.

Hanging up with Sig, I dial a number with a 412 area code.

"Dave Littlefield," a voice says.

I'd talked to Littlefield, the general manager of the Pirates, in New Orleans about Tout Wars and my Rotisserie team, and thankfully he remembers the conversation. Right off, I tell him that I'm calling to nakedly lobby on behalf of one of "my" players, Doug Mientkiewicz, whom I'd like to see in his dugout.

"Okay," he says.

When I ask about the trade talks, Littlefield says he's done all the due diligence on Mientkiewicz, looking at scouting reports, medical factors, and personal attributes. The trouble is money, or as he puts it, "the financial piece." This is Littlefield's way of saying that the shoestring Pirates aren't thrilled about paying the $3.75 million Mientkiewicz is slated to earn in 2005.

"Well, here's something you might find interesting," I say. When I'm done explaining the team's unique infield problem and the clear and obvious merits of adding a solid defender, Littlefield hasn't hung up. In fact, he seems intrigued.

"You bring up some good points about ground ball–to–fly ball ratios on the staff," he says. "And I didn't know that figure about more errors at the ballpark. That's significant." There's a pause on the line. "Interesting stuff," he says.

The next day, our gambit seems to be working. Reports say a deal between the Pirates and Twins "appears close," and that night in Minnesota Mientkiewicz is pulled from the lineup, prompting speculation that a trade is imminent.

Then, bupkes.

In the days that follow there is conflicting news. Some say the Pirates are in the running; others say they're out. One report says the Twins are having trouble finding any serious trading partner for Mientkiewicz (I can relate.) "I find it hard to believe nobody wants me," he tells reporters.

On Saturday, July 31, the major-league trade deadline passes quietly. At the Metrodome in Minnesota, Mientkiewicz, having heard nothing, dons his uniform for batting practice, assuming he's still a Twin. But right before game time, he's summoned to the manager's office, where he's told that he's been swept up in a seven-player deal between four teams that has delivered him, just as I feared, to the Red Sox. The Pirates, unable to find the dollars, had passed.

If there's any consolation for the news, it's that the sting of my first defeat as a lobbyist is nothing compared to the ordeal that Mientkiewicz is about to go through.

In the clubhouse, he peels off his home uniform for the last time after nine years in the Twins organization. He'd already said his good-byes and packed his gear into two duffels, fully expecting to be loading them on a plane that night. But there would be no trip to the airport. The Red Sox aren't just Dougie Baseball's new team, they're tonight's *opponent.*

So with a couple of clubhouse kids carrying his bags, Mientkiewicz leads a sad little procession through the swinging doors of the laundry room, where the machines clack and hum, through a second pair of doors, and into the visitors' clubhouse. "Toughest twelve-foot walk I've ever had to make," he calls it. On the Red Sox lineup card, he sees that he's starting at first base and batting sixth. By the time the Boston equipment managers finish steaming all twelve letters of his last name on the back of a Red Sox jersey, the game has already started.

"At least they spelled it right," he says.

When Mientkiewicz comes to the Metrodome plate for the first time in a gray road uniform, the Twins pitcher, Brad Radke, steps off the mound and tips his cap. The hometown fans give Dougie Baseball a standing ovation. Then he grounds out to Justin Morneau, the kid who just stole his job.

In the seventh inning Mientkiewicz singles to center and finds himself standing on first base next to Morneau. Since spring training, the two had grown accustomed to the awkwardness, but this was different. As Mientkiewicz would tell me later, the conversation went something like this:

"You know," Morneau said, talking from the side of his mouth, "if you would have done that sooner, maybe you'd still be over here."

Mientkiewicz shot him a look. "If you would have caught some ground balls at spring training, maybe I'd have been gone at the *beginning* of the season."

Six days later, undaunted by the Mientkiewicz defeat, I'm standing along the dugout rail before a night game at Yankee Stadium with my next lobbying target: Toronto manager Carlos Tosca. I've come here to stump for Josh Phelps.

Ever since he was pulled from the Blue Jays' everyday lineup, Phelps has become the bête noire of my Roto team. Every week Nando and I agonize over whether to keep him in our starting lineup or drop him to the reserve. Each time we keep him, he's colder than a Swanson dinner. But in the weeks we've benched him, he's hit over .300 with five homers. Even Sig is frustrated.

"This is a cruel joke," he says.

Ever since he went to the mattresses to keep Phelps off the trading block, Sig has been monitoring his numbers, looking for some small measure of redemption for his initial ardor. But now he's actually got something. In the month of July, Phelps had posted a 1.206 OPS (on-base percentage plus slugging percentage), which wasn't just high, it was one of the best in the majors. When the Blue Jays have played Phelps, he's been one of baseball's most valuable hitters.

"What more do you need to start the guy?" Sig wonders.

Reading this number on my stat sheet, Tosca grows quiet.

"Is that right?" he finally asks.

"Only Barry Bonds was better," I say.

"I'll be darned."

"Knowing this," I say, "do you think you'll play him more?"

Tosca hands the paper back to me. "I was going to play him Wednesday, but he had a sore neck," he begins. While there are certain right-handers he won't use Phelps against, Tosca tells me, there's a good chance he'll be in the lineup for all three games in the upcoming series with Cleveland. "I would like to give him a little more playing time, period."

Pulling out my cellphone, trying to look nonchalant, I dial the front office to tell Nando that Carlos Tosca was putty in my hands, and to most definitely put Phelps in our starting lineup for the following week. As he's doing this, Phelps himself brushes past me on his way back to the clubhouse. I'd love to tell him I've just lobbied on his behalf, but he seems preoccupied.

Twenty minutes later, riding home on the subway, I'm feeling a sense of accomplishment, tempered by queasiness. While I've just helped to change the course of baseball ever so slightly, my motives are anything but noble. I don't care if the Blue Jays lose the rest of their games, so long as Josh Phelps gets his plate appearances. There's something unsavory about trying to bend the game to my own selfish interests, no matter how badly I want to win Tout Wars.

Back at home, I flip on my computer to check the box scores, and that's when I see the story, which was posted on the wires about ten minutes earlier. Josh Phelps has been traded to the Cleveland Indians for a minor leaguer.

This is not a hoax.

The same time Carlos Tosca was making promises to me about Phelps, his boss, J. P. Ricciardi, was standing thirty feet away on his cellphone, making arrangements to ship him to Ohio. When Phelps had brushed past me, he was headed to the clubhouse to hear the news. So while I was sitting on a 4 train having an internal dialogue about ethics, Phelps was giving a final tearful interview to the beat writers and then, after eight years in the Blue Jays system, packing his glove and heading outside to hail a Town Car.

Never mind that I'll never see any substantial return on my $15 investment in Phelps, who's even less likely to start in Cleveland. What I really want to know is whether Tosca was lying to me or if he really had no idea Phelps was about to be dumped. I was damn sure going to find out the next time I saw him, but I never got the chance. Two days later, Ricciardi fired him.

This experience taught me two things. First, that my whole "lobbying" plan left something to be desired. Baseball is a complex organism that won't be budged by some Roto dork with a press badge and a stat sheet. If the Blue Jays think Josh Phelps belongs on the bench, I need to accept that and move on.

The second thing is that no matter what the circumstances, you should never leave Yankee Stadium early. *Never.*

———

With six weeks left in Tout Wars, my attitude toward my players can best be summed up in two words: *Screw them.*

The moment Magglio Ordóñez limped off my roster, I knew it was time to let go of the idea that I could divine the truth about ballplayers by my hunches alone. Tout Wars has become the Sig Mejdal show now, a clinical exercise in which all names are to be replaced by values and no decision is to be made without a mathematical rationale. When my wife tells me I need to take occasional breaks to avoid burnout, I find myself saying something I've never said before.

"Show me the data!"

With the Tout Wars trade deadline closing in at the end of August, I decide to get a head start. Javier Vazquez, our second REMA king, is the first to go. We trade him to Gene McCaffrey, this time for All-Star Texas shortstop Michael Young, who's hitting .327 this season and who told me in Houston that he wants to steal more bases.

Next we unload Minnesota pitcher Carlos Silva, one of our team's brighter surprises, for Tampa Bay shortstop B. J. Upton, a recent call-up from the minors whom Big Daddy Williams describes as "the real deal." This spring, Williams told me, he saw Upton belt a home run that traveled 480 feet. "Pretty good for a shortstop," he said. On the heels of this deal, with only a halfhearted objection from Sig, I trade Josh Phelps to Jeff Erickson for another role player, Texas outfielder David Dellucci. This does little for our title hopes other than giving the Streetwalkers its first full blooded *paesan*.

"Finally!" Nando says.

Just as we'd hoped, the Tout Wars standings have begun to bunch up, and our offense is showing some vital signs. After bottoming out in ninth place, we make a steady climb back to sixth, just 14 points from the lead, before falling back. The tension is getting unbearable. Sig calls to say he's been having night sweats about Magglio Ordóñez. Nando has been hitting the bars again, where he's taken to calling me and handing the phone to random drunks, most of them female. "Here," he tells them, "cheer my buddy up." My saintly wife, her nerves nearly shot, issues a household moratorium on the word "GODDAMMIT!" which leaves me stewing in silence.

Late in the afternoon on deadline day, we set our sights on making one last blockbuster deal with Rick Fogel, the only Tout we've thus far been able to manhandle. Fogel answers his cellphone in a moment of perfect vulnerability. He's on a commuter train with no access to the stats. Wasting no time, I offer to trade him Miguel Batista, our poet laureate, for Tigers fireballer Jeremy Bonderman.

At a glance, it's a sure thing. Batista is a $14 pitcher with a proven track record, and Bonderman is a $2 scrub whose ERA was higher than 6.00 less than two weeks earlier. Naturally, he jumps at the idea. "If you think it will help both of us, then let's do it!" he says. What I didn't mention is that this would really only help me. Just as my team is starting to lose points in strikeouts, Batista has decided to indulge his aversion to them, averaging less than two per nine innings. Bonderman, on the other hand, has found religion, fanning fourteen batters in a single start eight days ago.

If Joe Sheehan was in this situation, he would squish Rick Fogel right now like a wad of bubble gum. But I'm feeling uneasy. I know that if Fogel goes home and looks at the numbers, there's no way he'll make this trade. And if he makes this trade and then goes home and looks at the numbers, he'll never speak to me again.

I pause on the line, searching my conscience. Then I crumble. "Why don't you check the numbers and call me back," I say, "just to be sure."

An hour later, Fogel calls, his tone clipped.

"I'm gonna pass."

So much for the killer instinct.

Just under the wire, we do manage to make our eleventh and final trade of the season, which would best be described as "pass the trash." Jason Grey gets Aaron Sele, who may be headed for the Anaheim bullpen, in exchange for a Kansas City rookie catcher named John Buck and two marginal pitchers we don't really need. At midnight on September 1, when the deadline passes, I'm down the street by myself, soaking up a martini and twirling the glass obsessively on a bar napkin.

In the last five months, I have vanished from polite society. I've stopped calling friends and lost touch with colleagues. I have skipped four weddings and forgotten to send my brother a birthday card. I have spent sixty days on the road without taking a vacation, much less a day off, and leaned on my wife to manage our household affairs. If I tallied up every last bill, I've spent close to $46,000.

This investment of time and money might still prove to be worth something. Sidney Ponson has managed to win six of his last nine. Alfonso Soriano has stolen three bases in two days. Mariano Rivera continues to be supremely good, and Alex Rios is flirting with a .300 batting average. In other news, White Sox pitcher Damaso Marte has been wearing his Streetwalkers T-shirt during warm-ups, and the only reason he doesn't wear it under his uniform during games, he says, is because "the sleeves are too short."

Nonetheless, the thunderheads continue to gather. Luis Matos is officially out for the season with a stress fracture in his right shin, and Jacque Jones is on pace to have the lowest batting average of his career. Some of my trades have made me look like Il Pagliaccio with a brain injury, and all my lobbying has amounted to nothing: Jason Johnson's ERA doubled in August, Doug Mientkiewicz is a bench player, and Josh Phelps is no longer on my team. I've got five huge holes in my lineup and no way to fill them. As I twirl my martini glass, I'm trying hard to banish the thought, but let's be honest.

I'm not going to win.

At the bottom of my second drink, I allow myself to feel the haunt of disappointment. You can't invest this much of your mind and body in a failed crusade without beating back a few tears.

In the early hours of the first day of September, I take a meandering route down the side streets and under the leafy canopies of the West Village. The streets are silent save for the tinny rattle of tired air-conditioners in high-up windows. I may have conceded the title, but I still need some goal to pursue, an achievement that would allow me to look back on this process with some genuine point of pride. Second? Third? Then it comes to me.

In Tout Wars this season there are two competitors who've never played before, which means that the one who finishes highest can rightfully lay claim to another title, rookie of the year. As I push open the glass door of my apartment building, I have a new goal for September. I'm going to beat Joe Sheehan. Whatever it takes.

Tout Wars Standings Through August 31, 2004

1. Trace Wood, The Long Gandhi, 82
2. Lawr Michaels, CREATiVESPORTS, 80
3. Dean Peterson, STATS, Inc., 77
4. Matt Berry, Talented Mr. Roto, 70
5. Rick Fogel, USA Stats, 69
6. Ron Shandler, Baseball HQ, 68
7. Joe Sheehan, Baseball Prospectus, 64
8. Jeff Erickson, RotoWire, 63.5
9. Streetwalkers, 62
10. Jason Grey, Mastersball, 52
11. Gene McCaffrey, Wise Guy Baseball, 51
12. Steve Moyer, Baseball Info Solutions, 41.5

Rookie of the Year

September

On a commuter train to New York one fall morning, Ernie DiFranchi noticed in the paper that Magglio Ordóñez, the star of his Rotisserie team, had injured his wrist. So when he arrived at work, DiFranchi cut short his regular cigarette break to go upstairs and remove Ordóñez from his lineup. Had he lingered for a few more minutes, rather than leaving to make the roster move, DiFranchi would have been trapped in an elevator inside the World Trade Center. It was September 11, 2001.

"Magglio," he says, "is always my first pick now."

• • •

On the first day of September the city is eerily tense. The Republican National Convention has invaded Manhattan, accompanied by wandering packs of anarchists on bicycles. The only sound is the *thack thack thack* of a police helicopter.

Against this ominous backdrop, the Streetwalkers sneak past Joe Sheehan by night's end only to watch him bounce back the following day with fourteen strikeouts, and a .427 BA. With barely five weeks to go, the race is *on,* whether he realizes it or not.

While anything can happen in Tout Wars, the list of likely champions is down to three. The leading contender—I never thought I would be writing this sentence—is Trace Wood. Since our butter bet in May, the Prickly One has surged ten spots to the top of the standings, where he's reigned for a month with a lead of as many as eight points. Steve Moyer has pegged him as the likely winner, Ron Shandler says "It's Trace's game to lose," and Lawr Michaels calls his team "scary."

When it's all over, I'll study every move Wood made to figure out how he did this, but for now I see two reasons: One is Minnesota pitcher Johan Santana, who's turned in what is arguably the most dominant performance by a pitcher in four years, allowing fewer than one base runner per inning since May. The other is Wood's uncanny ability to plug holes: Every time one of his players implodes, he's subbed in another forgotten soul who puts up serviceable numbers.

What's most surprising about Wood's ascent is that he's done it without making any brilliant trades. In fact, he's alienated half the league with lowball offers delivered without a hint of contrition. He once proposed sending me a bunch of potatoes from his bench in exchange for Mariano Rivera—a deal so lopsided I didn't even bother to counter. Instead, I sent back a note asking him what he was drinking. "I was formulating a trade offer and hit 'send' by mistake," he responded. "I wasn't finished putting names into the equation."

As Lawr Michaels clings to second place, he's exercising his own unique brand of team management. In idle hours, he's trained himself to *think* about his players but not to *worry* about them, because, he says, "I think they can feel that energy." If all goes well, the Zen master is convinced he can pick up the ten pitching points he'll need to clinch the title. If he pulls it off, he tells me, he'd be the first Rotisserie expert to win a national championship without any semblance of an auction strategy. That, he says, "would put Zen drafting into legendary, mystical status."

To the other Touts, of course, the question isn't whether Michaels will sabotage his chances but when. Even as he continues to plump his lead in the power categories, he still hasn't repaired his pitching staff, which consists of a handpicked bunch of lemons from the free-agent pool. Most of the Touts would have ditched these guys weeks ago, but for some reason Michaels won't part with them.

If I had to make a wager, I'd say the Tout Wars trophy (if there was one) would end up in Chicago in the possession of Dean Peterson.

And I'm not the only one who thinks so. Jeff Erickson is already calling him "the eventual champion."

At first, I thought Peterson's fixation with young players was just an outgrowth of his Peter Pan complex—the Nerf hoops, the Beanie Babies, the chocolate crepes for breakfast. But now I recognize that he'd been the only one to see a subtle inefficiency in the player market: a glut of promising youngsters with starting jobs who, thanks to the absence of major-league stats, would likely sell for less than they ought to in a room where stats mean everything.

Peterson used his shyness as a tactical advantage at the auction, taking a seat in the corner and throwing out occasional smoke-screen bids. By hoarding closers and shortstops, he gave himself a surplus at two thin positions. So while Nando and I were forced to chase after talent like sailors on shore leave, Peterson sat back and let the deal offers come to him.

His only weakness is his patchwork pitching staff, which has given him fits all season. At one point he went nearly two weeks without picking up a win. The last time we spoke he said, "I just need anyone that looks like he has an arm."

For the Streetwalkers, September is an emasculating month. With no trades to broker and no FAAB dramas, I have nothing to do but watch my ballplayers and gnaw my fingernails like everybody else in fantasyland. On my regular trips to see players at Yankee Stadium, I'm reduced to the crudest motivational tactic I can think of.

Cheerleading.

On September 3 I arrive in the Bronx to see Sidney Ponson, the current major-league leader in hits allowed. Some weeks earlier, in the depths of his skid, *The Washington Post* reported that Orioles owner Peter Angelos was looking into the feasibility of voiding Ponson's contract because he'd failed to stay in top physical condition. But in recent weeks Ponson had dropped ten pounds and started to find his groove, winning six of his last nine starts. When I last saw him in May, I'd told him that I'd traded him, so I'm hoping he'll be buoyed by the news of his reacquisition.

"Mechanics problems," he says when I ask him what went wrong.

"I would try to throw it off the plate, and it was coming on the plate." Standing on the field during warm-ups, Ponson demonstrates how he'd been twisting his torso too early. "I wasn't staying closed," he explains.

"Keep it up!" I offer, handing him a shirt.

In the Orioles dugout ten minutes later, I'm talking to Jim Palmer, the legendary Baltimore pitcher turned broadcaster. He confirms that Ponson was having mechanical difficulties, but his explanation is a bit simpler: "If you have a weight problem, you're not in sync." While Palmer elaborates on the problems of rotund pitchers, Sidney Ponson walks up behind him. It takes a few seconds for Palmer to register the look of panic on my face, but when he wheels around Ponson is glowering at him. Palmer, trying to play it off, points to me.

"He has you on his Rotisserie team."

"Ya! He traded me!" Ponson says, stomping off.

So much for team spirit.

Back in the Bronx six days later, I step inside the office of Lou Piniella, the manager of the visiting Devil Rays, who's at his desk eating steak and manicotti in an undershirt. He motions for me to sit.

Sweet Lou is one of the world's greatest baseball guys, an Aqua Velva prince if I've ever met one. But his short attention span is killing my Rotisserie team. No sooner do the Devil Rays grant one of my players a job than the guy gets benched, shipped back to triple-A Durham, or, in one case, sold to the Japanese league.

Piniella's never met a lineup card he liked.

My goal today is to rustle my pom-poms on behalf of B. J. Upton, the twenty-year-old shortstop prodigy I picked up in a trade from Dean Peterson. Even though Upton is hitting .286 with two homers in thirteen games and even though the Devil Rays are out of the postseason race, Piniella keeps benching the poor kid. The knock on Upton is that his defense needs work, which it does, and Piniella has decided not to play him at shortstop until he grows into the job. But what I can't understand is why he's taken his bat out of the lineup, too.

"Why not DH?" I ask.

Piniella scrapes up one last mouthful of ricotta, chewing over his answer. "My problem," he says, swallowing, "is you feel kind of stupid as a manager putting a twenty-year-old kid at DH."

"Stupid?" I ask.

"Sort of," he says.

In broad terms, Piniella has just told me that my shortstop wasn't collecting hits, runs, and RBI for me—or even for *him*—because his manager is too embarrassed to write a rookie's name in a place on the lineup card that's usually reserved for grizzled veterans. On the way out the door, I feel like setting my hair on fire.

But the next night, when I flip on the Devil Rays game, B. J. Upton is the starting DH. I have no idea if our little talk had any influence on his decision, but I don't really care. Upton will play in eleven of the team's following thirteen games.

Like I said, Lou's the *greatest*.

On September 17, the Red Sox rumble into the Bronx for another episode of baseball's epic rivalry. The series has attracted such a caterwauling horde of media that the only seat I can find before the game is a folding chair in the basement media room hard up to the men's lavatory. I've come here tonight to see Bill Mueller, who's tweaked his knee again—this time sliding to catch a foul ball in Seattle. Inside my bag, I'm carrying a gift that should raise his spirits.

As I wait for Mueller to emerge from the trainer's room, I see a familiar face, Doug Mientkiewicz. He's slumped over, looking a little green, sitting inside a circle of fluid containers he's arranged around his chair like pillars at Stonehenge. It's been seven weeks since he was traded to Boston, where, as expected, he's been used mostly as a defensive replacement in the late innings of close games. Today he's battling the flu.

If anybody could use some cheering up. . . .

"Hey, Doug. What's up?"

"Have you traded me yet?"

"No."

"Well, then, that's your own fault."

Mientkiewicz takes a sip of some blue concoction in a clear plastic bottle. "You're not winning," he continues. "I *guarantee* you you're not winning. You're not even good, are you?"

I shake my head.

"Look," he says, holding out a palm, "give *me* your money. Don't just give it to anybody!"

This is the first time I've seen my first baseman since his trade from the Twins, so when he's done berating me I ask him how he's feeling about it. "I understand that they're rebuilding," he says. "I understand they want to go younger. I'm not old, I'm not young, I'm in that limbo region where . . ." his voice trails off. "You know, they wanted somebody else, that's fine."

I'm trying to think of some words of encouragement, but Dougie Baseball has had a season that's too bizarre for words. After hitting .361 in the first nine games, he sprained his foot. After hitting his first two homers, he wrenched his back so badly he could barely put on his pants in the clubhouse. No sooner had he broken a June slump with homers on consecutive nights than he fouled a ball off his instep. Another streak ended when he got nailed by a line drive at batting practice, and his hot start in Boston was doused when he popped his shoulder sliding into second. As soon as he recovered from that, he says, "Boom, I get sick."

I ask Mientkiewicz if there's any explanation for this profound run of sorry luck. He pauses, glancing around the room like he's wondering if he should say what he's about to say.

"Well, there is *one* thing."

Back in May during a road trip in Seattle, he says, "I walked under a ladder and I haven't hit .300 since."

"Is there any . . . cure for that?" I ask.

"Every time I see a ladder, I try and walk under it to double it, you know, to reverse it."

At this, I see Mueller return to his locker, which gives me a perfect excuse to escape before Mientkiewicz is able to describe any encounters with black cats, gris-gris dolls, or the grassy knoll. "One more thing," Mientkiewicz says, waving a finger as I stand up to leave. "Don't *ever* predict my numbers before the season again. Please."

Bill Mueller is wearing spandex shorts, and his bum knee is slathered in some sort of transparent jelly. In July, he had single-handedly flayed the Yankees with a dramatic home run off (gulp) Mariano Rivera. Early this month, finally healthy, he'd raised his average to .293 not long before hurting his knee again. He's not in tonight's starting lineup, and it must be killing him.

"I've got something for you," I say, sheepishly. "A little taste of home."

It took a week's worth of phone calls to track it down, but Nando finally found it at a ShopRite in suburban New Jersey. Reaching into my bag, I pull out a six-pack of Schaefer beer, the brand Mueller had reminisced about back in Florida.

"No way!" Mueller squawks, taking the cans and cradling them like a newborn. "It's what my grandpa used to drink, like all the time!"

"Two-ninety-nine for a six," I say.

"It's going up! It used to be a buck-fifty."

Mueller starts looking around the clubhouse for an attendant. "I'm going to get the boys to put this on ice." Smiling, he limps over to a table and waves the six under the nose of teammate Mark Bellhorn. "Anytime you want one of these," he says, "a good *American* beer."

Bellhorn squints at the labels, then looks at Mueller as if he's insane.

My work is done.

Out in the Boston dugout before the game, seeing as I'd rostered eight of his players, I present Boston GM Theo Epstein with a team shirt. He tosses it over his shoulder nonchalantly.

"So how are you doing?" he asks.

"I'm getting drilled," I say, running through the list of the injured, benched, and cursed on my team.

"You have time to get back into it?"

"Not really."

I show him a list of my trades.

"You got Ponson *back*?"

I nod. He lets it go.

"You traded Ortiz?"

"For Soriano. . . ."

"Did you talk to Ortiz about that?"

I nod again. He smiles.

Since the point is now moot, I tell Epstein about my attempt to derail his Mientkiewicz deal. "Nothing personal," I say. Soon I'm running through a litany of reasons why I never should have drafted Mientkiewicz, from the presence of Morneau to his chronic lack of power. Epstein listens to me with a tranquil expression. He's clearly heard it all before. "He'll be fine," he finally says. "He's a better real player than he is a Rotisserie player."

———

As the game begins, the weather deteriorates. In the third inning, the skies open, the tarps come out, and play is suspended for more than an hour. My wife calls, wanting to know if I'm coming home. She's well aware of my vow to never again leave Yankee Stadium early, but I repeat it anyhow.

"Umm, okay . . . ," she says.

By the ninth inning it's already past midnight, and I'm about to give up hope. The Yankees are up 2–1, and Mariano Rivera is about to take the mound. Even though my Tout Wars team could use the save, I'm unabashedly pulling for the Red Sox. If they win, Bill Mueller and I can crack a cold Schaefer after the game. If they lose, no way.

To get a jump on the crowd, I pack my bag and head to the main concourse to watch the last outs from a hot-dog counter near the exit. Rivera walks Trot Nixon to lead off the inning, and two batters later there's a collective gasp from the stands: Rivera has just plunked Kevin Millar, putting two runners on with one out.

My phone rings. It's my wife again.

"Rivera's about to blow it," she says.

"Yeah, can I call you right back?"

There's a pause.

"I need to talk to you," she says.

"Right now?"

"I'm *pregnant!*"

In the universe that all husbands inhabit, this statement is an un-ambiguous signal that it's time to drop whatever the hell you're doing and go home.

"I'll be right there," I say.

"You're leaving the game?"

"YES, right now!"

The hot-dog lady is eavesdropping. I give her a look.

On a concourse TV I see the next batter, Boston's Orlando Cabrera, crack a single to right. Now the game is tied.

"Uh-oh," my wife says.

In the middle of one of the most nakedly joyous moments of my life, I can't shake the thought that my third baseman has a six-pack on ice in the clubhouse with our names on it.

"Wow," I say, "I can't believe—"

"Stay."

"No way, I—"

"Stay. Just come right home afterwards."

"Buh—"

"I don't want you to mope if Boston wins."

Man, I love my wife.

Thirty minutes later, thoroughly frazzled, I'm standing in the Red Sox clubhouse. Johnny Damon had singled in a run to give Boston the lead, and the Yankees had gone down in order in the bottom of the ninth. On the floor at Mueller's locker, there's a blue cooler stocked with Schaefer on ice.

The logistics are a bit of a problem. Since the game was postponed by two rain delays, the first team bus back to the hotel is about to leave. Worse, there's a throng of TV cameras clustered around catcher Jason Varitek at the next locker. The last thing Mueller wants is to show up on *SportsCenter* having an adult beverage with a reporter inside Yankee Stadium. Already dressed in street clothes, he opens the cooler, grabs a couple cans, disappears for a minute, and returns with two full paper cups.

"Cheers," he says.

We bump cups and sip the Schaefer.

It tastes like horse piss.

I force myself to finish my traveler on the way home in a hired Town Car. By the time I see my pregnant wife, I've got a bellyful of cheap, acrid Midwestern brewski, and my throat is kind of raw. I'm not sure this night did anything for Mueller's morale, but I know it did a lot for mine.

Did I mention that I love my wife?

———

Three days later, I'm in Chicago.

The visiting Twins have just clinched the division title, and down in the clubhouse, the celebration is on. The Twins have changed into their commemorative T-shirts and started spraying Bud Light and Korbel Extra Dry in twisting streams, living the dream of generations of little boys. Brad Radke is beaming. Torii Hunter is wearing goggles, and Corey Koskie, my other third baseman, is walking around with no pants on. Twins manager Ron Gardenhire, smoking a Cohiba, credits the win to his lucky tights. "It's bingo bango in these," he says, pinching the spandex.

At the height of the maelstrom, I realize I haven't seen Jacque Jones. After a minute of searching, I spot him at the far edge of the mob, standing by himself with a halfhearted smile. He's got a limp hold on a bottle of champagne, but he's not wearing a drop of it.

I walk over, we grip hands.

"ARE YOU HAPPY?" I shout over the commotion.

"Yeah," he says.

His voice is barely above a whisper.

"REALLY?"

"Yeah. Feels good."

Since we last met in Toronto, Jones's promising season had taken a disappointing turn. Though he's been healthy all year and his 22 homers and 74 RBI are better than his totals from 2003, his average has skidded to .256. "It just hasn't worked out on the average side the way I wanted it to," he'd told me before tonight's game. "I hit more balls hard this year than I ever have. I just have nothing to show for it." Jones flashed a weary look, as if he hadn't been sleeping. "I know the numbers I'm capable of putting up, and this season has been humbling."

"It must drive you crazy," I said.

Jones nodded laconically. "I've tried to *keep* from going crazy."

Five hours later, as his teammates continue to douse one another, Jones excuses himself and slips quietly through the mob. He sets his bottle on the floor, ducks under the plastic sheet covering his locker, finds a toothbrush, and heads off to the showers alone.

My hair is plastered to my forehead in sticky clumps. The red "Media" sticker on my chest has bled through my white shirt, leaving a pink blotch. There's champagne in my pants pockets and a glob of unidentified orange goop on my shoulder that smells like baby food. When I clamber out to the tunnel, people laugh.

I should be laughing, too, but I'm not. I'm wondering what's the matter with Jacque Jones.

———

With two weeks to go the Tout Wars front-runner is still Trace Wood, whose airtight pitching staff has given him a five-point cushion. Next to Johan Santana, he's added some new FAAB miracles—a pair of overachievers named Bush and Howry. He's already broken the AL strikeout record and dislodged me from the top of the pitching leaderboard with a staff that cost nearly half as much. My skepticism has turned to admiration.

Lawr Michaels spent the early part of the month in a gruesome slump, led by the bizarre unraveling of his ace pitcher, Oakland's Mark Mulder. "I cannot get a bloody win," he wrote on the eleventh. As his team sank briefly to third, he became a neurotic mess, checking the standings "about once every eighteen seconds," he said. Finally, on September 17, the Zen master had picked up a pair of wins and climbed back to second.

"It ain't over yet," he told me.

Dean Peterson, caught in a pitching meltdown, has fallen to third. He'll need five quick wins to have a shot, but he's currently suffocating under a pile of lousy arms from the FAAB market. He seems to lack Trace Wood's gift for spotting uncut diamonds.

Meanwhile, Peterson is also partly responsible for the banner headline of the moment in Tout Wars: Ron Shandler, once left for dead, has vaulted into fourth place.

Just eight days earlier, Shandler's team had been stuck in *seventh,* just ahead of mine and one spot behind Joe Sheehan's. Not only has his patience with his RIMA players started to pay off, but he's used what FAAB he's collected to pick up some nice surprises, like Baltimore pitcher Bruce Chen. Shandler's finest move, however, was a four-player trade he made in August with Peterson. In exchange for Texas closer Francisco Cordero and pitcher Esteban Loaiza, he picked up Ted Lilly and Anaheim shortstop Orlando Cabrera, who he later flipped to Trace Wood for Johnny Damon. It was, on both ends, an outrageous blowout.

I know there's no way Shandler can keep this miracle alive much longer, but it's still nice to see the old master back in the hunt for a respectable finish. I can't imagine the depths of depression if *he* lost to the rookie from Baseball Prospectus.

The story of my season is starting to sound like a plot summary for *Il Trovatore*. Lots of sudden twists, mistaken identities, plenty of gore, and a nice helping of joy turned to sorrow. One day I see that Jason Johnson had a mild diabetic reaction. On another, B. J. Upton spends a fourth consecutive game on the bench with a case of the rookie yips. I'm in eighth place.

My joust with Joe Sheehan is beyond frustrating. If my players hit .300 one night, his team hits .374. If we score eleven runs, he gets twelve. Even though Randy Johnson never did come over to the American League, I managed to help Sheehan land all the pitching he needed. By September 20, Bartolo Colón had exceeded even my wildest predictions, giving Sheehan ten wins and single-handedly doubling his lead over the Streetwalkers.

Just when I thought my trade balance with Sheehan couldn't get any more lopsided, it did. At the precise moment Alfonso Soriano finally starts stealing bases at the felonious level we'd hoped for, he dives into third and mangles a hamstring. What follows is a carnival of medical contradictions: One day there's a lousy prognosis, the next day a promising one. Finally, after an MRI, the verdict blurps over the wires. Soriano has likely torn a tendon.

He, too, is finished for the year.

"Do you realize that EVERY guy you traded me is now out for the season?" I wrote Sheehan after reading the news. "You can take the pins out of the straw doll."

His reply is not the least bit contrite.

"Removing pins . . . Now."

There comes a point in every baseball season when logic, reason, and patience wear out, and the only way for a manager to get through to his players is to break something. On my desk, I see the Troy Glaus Russian nesting doll the Angels were handing out at the stadium the night I helped Sheehan coax Berry into trading Bartolo Colón to Baseball Prospectus.

The doll buys it.

That night, the Streetwalkers, nearly devoid of star power now, respond to my tantrum by launching a rally. Jacque Jones homers twice in three days. Michael Young hits a grand slam one night and collects four hits a couple days later. Alex Rios steals two bases in one game, Mueller returns to tag Baltimore for four hits, and Jason Johnson chips in eight strikeouts. I get nine more punch-outs from a pair of free agents who sound like delegates to the United Nations: Cha Seung Baek and Francisco Cruceta. Sheehan's team stalls and all of a sudden I'm only six points back.

Then four.

Then three.

Heading into the final week, all that's separating me from rookie honors is one homer, ten RBI, three runs, and two saves.

In other words, *one decent night.*

————

On September 25, eight days before the end of the baseball season, José Guillen is plunked by a pitch in the eighth inning of a tie game against Oakland. He's okay, no harm done. But as Guillen trots to first, Angels manager Mike Scioscia makes a fateful and not particularly enlightened move: He pulls him for a pinch runner.

Some ballplayers can handle being extricated from a close game in the heat of a pennant race. Others, like José Guillen, cannot. In the dugout, Guillen blows his stack—hurling his glove against the wall and tossing his batting helmet. Anybody who knows Guillen is not surprised. After being taken out of the lineup one day while playing for Cincinnati, he'd responded by ramming a few bats through the clubhouse wall.

But before the next game, Angels GM Bill Stoneman makes an announcement that's so inexplicable, I'm convinced it's a prank. In the wake of his outburst, he says, Guillen has been suspended from the team, without pay, for the remainder of the season. And if the Angels make the play-offs, he'll be suspended for those games, too. In the middle of their own late-season dogfight (to say nothing of *mine*) the Angels have just banished one of their best hitters for the heinous crime of wanting, very badly, to play baseball.

I knew José Guillen wasn't very popular in the clubhouse. Already this season he'd irked the front office by publicly blasting his own pitching staff for not retaliating when he was hit by a pitch (though they had) and by telling reporters he'd skipped a mandatory team meeting (though he hadn't). In interviews Scioscia and Stoneman hinted there had been worse transgressions off camera.

But even so, Guillen has played through a pulled hamstring, a swollen knee, a sprained ankle, and a bizarre circulation problem that caused his wrists to swell. All season long, whenever the Streetwalkers went dark, Guillen was always the first guy to show up with a candelabra. "He must sense that we're batting .100," Nando once wrote, "and decide to go nuts."

The next two days I barely sleep. The stagecoach pace of the last nine months is catching up to me. I've got bags under my eyes, my back hurts, my eyesight is shot, and I haven't had a haircut since June. Without Guillen, it will take a miracle to beat Sheehan. I have every reason to crawl under my comforter and spend the next five days groaning in bed.

But I can't, and I won't.

To this point I've lugged my stupid wheelie bag 21,850 miles since

December in pursuit of a Tout Wars championship or, at least, some title I can engrave on a trophy. I've pestered hundreds of ballplayers and imposed on a dozen GMs. As long as there's a sliver of hope, I've got to do everything in my power to save this team. Even if it means buying two plane tickets for California, departing *tomorrow.*

On the morning of Friday, September 30, Nando and I glide into downtown San Francisco and park our rental car outside the Renaissance Parc 55 hotel. Sig, who's driven up for the day, is waiting for us in the lobby. After Guillen's suspension, the players union filed a formal grievance, and the Angels agreed to meet with Guillen and an arbitrator before one of their games in Oakland. The meeting, I'd learned, was scheduled to take place on Friday morning at the team hotel: The Renaissance Parc 55.

We're not here to crash the meeting. That would only get us arrested. Instead, we're going to try to save our Rotisserie team by exercising one of our fundamental Constitutional rights. We're going to stage a protest.

In the nineteen hours since we landed in San Francisco, Nando and I have visited Kinkos, Staples, and The Home Depot. We've bought poster board, markers, stencils, duct tape, and wooden stakes, and made picket signs that say "Free José," "Reinstate José," "Fantasy Owners Are People, Too," and Nando's favorite: "Sciame on Scioscia."

Calling ourselves the National Association of Fantasy Baseball Owners, we printed four hundred leaflets on fluorescent green paper. At the top, there's a smiling photo of Guillen, followed by our manifesto:

Last Sunday, the Anaheim Angels SUSPENDED José Guillen, without pay, for the remainder of the season. His "CRIME" was publicly expressing his displeasure after manager Mike Scioscia removed him from a game the night before. Rather than having his enthusiasm and passion for baseball RE-WARDED, the bumbling Angels tossed him out on the street. This RASH move was made without any consideration for the impact it may have on the FIVE MILLION people WORLDWIDE who play fantasy baseball, including thousands of our armed forces serving in war zones. Many of us who drafted

José, or acquired him in trades, take great pride in his ALL-STAR caliber sea-
son, in which he's hit .294 with 27 home runs, 104 RBI, 5 steals, and 88 runs
scored. We believe that José Guillen has been unjustly STOLEN from us, and
we DEMAND that Angels management reverse this RECKLESS course and
restore José to the lineup.

In the best case, I'm hoping we'll be joined by hundreds of ag-
grieved Guillen owners in a Rotisserie version of the Boston Tea
Party, and that when the Angels get wind of this they'll send for
Guillen with a horsedrawn carriage full of rose petals. Worst case, we
spend a night in jail.

In front of the hotel at nine o'clock on the nose, I give the order.
"Signs up!"

Right off the bat, the response is wildly encouraging. Cars honk.
People make their way over to grab leaflets. A woman passes us on
the sidewalk with a raised fist. "Solidarity!" she says. I had no idea José
Guillen had so many fans!

Our next visitor is Kent Knoblauch, director of security at the Renaissance. He is not amused. That morning, he tells us, ten San Francisco hotels locked out 2,600 workers in a contract dispute—some of
whom are beating drums and blowing whistles outside a Hilton
down the block. In other words, we've chosen an extraordinarily in-
sensitive moment to picket outside a hotel. By law, Knoblauch explains, we must not cross the line onto hotel property. We must keep
moving at all times. If we block or bother any hotel guests, he says,
quite seriously, we will be prosecuted.

"I'd prefer it if you'd just leave."

"Sorry," I say, "but you're stuck with us."

For two hours, we make a slow procession along the sidewalk,
signs aloft, tracing a deliberate circle from the lobby doors to the
valet. Knoblauch sends some workers out with hoes and they begin
scraping gum off the sidewalk, sometimes blocking our path. I feel
like Che Guevara (minus the social conscience).

I meet a group of Londoners who play fantasy soccer. I ask them to join us. They laugh. A woman takes a picture of us with her camera phone. A group of Lufthansa flight attendants ignores us. While Nando's leafleting seems prejudiced toward young brunettes, Sig is energetically handing them out to dozens of people, from a tiny Vietnamese woman who speaks almost no English to a pair of passing beat cops. By hour two, he's getting philosophical. "My parents came to this country so I could have the freedom and opportunity to. . . . Well, maybe not to do specifically *this,* but this in general."

He may be kidding, I can't tell.

Near noon I glance inside the lobby windows and see two men standing and pointing. It's Mike Scioscia and Bill Stoneman, the duo responsible for destroying my Rotisserie team. We stop to face them, to give them a taste of dissent. Stoneman, the crusty GM who blew me off in New Orleans is . . . *laughing.* Scioscia smiles and flashes a thumbs-up.

Sig drops his sign, points two thumbs at himself, and hunches his shoulders, as if to say, What about my needs?

This makes them laugh harder.

Minutes later Scioscia rambles outside with some of his coaches. He signs a few autographs and then makes his way over. "That's the first time I've ever seen my name on a picket," he says, smiling all the more. "What's this all about?"

"Mike," I say, handing him a leaflet, "we're going to lose without José."

"You got him on your team?"

"Yeah."

"He had a hell of a year for you, man."

"But the year's not over."

"Can't you trade him?"

"It's too late."

Scioscia lowers his chin to read the leaflet. He starts chuckling. "That's beautiful man, that is beautiful."

This RASH move was made without any consideration for . . .

"Oh, that wasn't a rash move though, you guys," he says. "This was a long time coming." At this, a cab pulls up, and his coaches pile in. I have time for one more question.

"Mike, when you made this decision, did you ever bother to think about what it would do to fantasy players?"

"Fantasy players. . . . What, are you *kidding* me? I think about the fans."

As Scioscia stands at the door of the groaning taxi, he slips the flier in his jacket pocket and waves to us. "Very clever, guys."

Then he's gone.

It's now clear that the big arbitration meeting, if it happened at all, is over. But there's no sight of Guillen. We decide to keep marching a little longer in case the arbitrator happens by.

Not five minutes later Angels first baseman Darin Erstad and closer Troy Percival emerge from the hotel heading toward a white stretch limo. I walk up behind Erstad and ask him if he'd like a flier.

He glances at my picket sign.

"Uh, *nooooo.*"

As Troy Percival walks around to the limo's street-side door, Sig plants himself close by and thrusts out a leaflet.

"Would you like to join our cause?" he asks.

Percival sweeps past him without a word. Then he pauses at the door, his stubbly face drawn tightly into a sneer. "Suck my dick," he says. "I don't give a shit about your fantasy team."

He yanks open the limo door and pauses for one more thought. "The guy's an asshole."

Slam. The limo roars off. The three of us are left standing there, frozen, our picket signs drooping to the sidewalk. Nando breaks the silence.

"Did he just tell us to . . ."

"Yeah, he did."

One hour later, after being intimidated, ridiculed, and insulted, in roughly that order, we pack up our pickets and drive across the bridge to the Oakland Coliseum, the site of tonight's Angels game. Our goal is to make one last stand. To try to turn this little protest into a spontaneous movement. "Free José!" I say, handing a flier to a long-haired guy in an Angels cap.

"*Shoot* José," he says.

Next, a tan guy in a UPS uniform waltzes over to say he plays Rotisserie, too, and delivers some unsolicited advice: "That's what you get for picking an asshole."

Before long, a white SUV rolls by our post and stops. I recognize the driver. It's Billy Beane. He gives me a disgusted look and drives away. Now I'm embarrassed.

The four ballpark security guards who escort us off the premises are about as friendly as the Taliban. Our protest, like our Rotisserie season, is clearly finished.

But just as I'm thinking that fantasy-baseball owners will never be able to form a unifying force to protect their interests, one of the guards, Jennifer Weinstein, leans over to tell me something sotto voce. "I know what you're going through," she says. "I had Guillen on my team, too."

THE POSTSEASON

Just Desserts

October

The year Daniel Katz won the Water Street Rotisserie League, he forgot to read the fine print. At the annual postseason banquet at a Maryland steak-house, his leaguemates started ordering lobsters. Then more lobsters. Then twenty-dollar cigars. And finally a snifter of Louis XIV cognac. Unbe-knownst to Katz, the league constitution requires the winner to pay for anything above the dinner's original budget. The final tab was $3,500.

"It's funny," Katz says. "In retrospect."

. . .

It's a Friday morning in late October, and Ron Shandler stands before a crowded hotel ballroom near Phoenix, dressed in his best approxi-mation of resort casual: baggy khakis and a powder-blue shirt that's two sizes too big.

He's working his way through a slide show, which he's using mostly to make jokes at his own expense. On a list of ten reasons to attend this gathering, number nine is: "Unlimited heckling at the idiot who told you to draft Brad Fullmer."

Matt Berry, seated in the audience, raises his hand.

"Shouldn't that say *three years in a row?*"

The room breaks up.

Shandler is celebrating his tenth year as the host of this event, a postseason symposium called First Pitch Arizona, which, to the Ro-tisserie elite, is sort of like Davos, Renaissance Weekend, and Mardi

Gras condensed into three days. Here Shandler acolytes pay $299 to rub shoulders with the experts in an environment where nobody thinks you're a dork for knowing that the Myrtle Beach Pelicans play in an extreme pitcher's park.

Nine of my fellow Touts are here, serving on panels, promoting their services, or taking part in Shandler's private-label auction. Though I'm not altogether surprised, it's still a bit jarring to see a group of attorneys, civil engineers, and high-school principals listening intently to Joe Sheehan (and taking notes!).

Since I last saw him in May, there's a palpable lightness to Shandler. He's not smiling per se—that would be too vaudevillian for the Bearded One. He just seems comfortable in his skin, unburdened. In a September surge for the Tout Wars record books, Shandler made up more than fourteen points in three weeks. On the final day of the season, he picked up three wins from a collection of pitchers who cost eight bucks. He finished second.

It wasn't the championship he'd envisioned a year earlier when he jotted down the principles of the RIMA Plan, but in a way it's his crowning achievement in Rotisserie. At a time when even some of his disciples were questioning his relevance, the old lion found another way to roar. Chronicling his climb in my journal, I'd run out of superlatives. My last entry was "Ron Shandler is God."

"I like the sound of that," he says.

In other Shandler news, the Cardinals made it all the way to the World Series, and even though the Red Sox muscled them aside in four games, it hardly mattered. On the cover of the 2005 *Baseball Forecaster*, he'll add the promotional banner of his dreams: "Advisers to the St. Louis Cardinals, National League Champions."

After several months of feeding the team information without much feedback, Shandler was, indeed, summoned to the Gateway City over the summer for two days of meetings. Afterward he posted a pair of fascinatingly candid columns about the visit. He revealed the team's motives for player moves, discussed the "parochial" infrastructure of most ballclubs, and painted Cardinals manager Tony

LaRussa as a bit of a stick-in-the-mud. They were monuments of incaution.

Shandler's not sure if he'll continue his role with the Cardinals or if he'll be invited back next year, but if the relationship ends I'm pretty sure he'll get over it. He'd climbed the baseball mountaintop, had a look around, and learned something about himself: When push comes to shove, he'd rather win Tout Wars than a World Series.

At the close of his remarks, Shandler makes his first and only mention of the Cardinals. "In case you were wondering what happened at the World Series. . . ." Pausing, he pulls a floppy ballcap from the pocket of his khakis and scrunches it on his head.

The logo is a Boston "B."

Everybody laughs.

"So there you have it," he says.

Sitting to my right is Lawr Michaels, who has just turned fifty-two. He's wearing Converse sneakers with ripped jeans, and his long, frizzy mullet hangs over the back of a Dodgers jersey. As successful as he's been in Tout Wars, he's still working hard to uphold his flaky facade. After a group dinner at the Pink Pony in Scottsdale the night before, he bade a group of us farewell at the hotel elevator with the following: "Okay, I'm going to smoke some drugs."

This season, more than any other, has worn Michaels out. Toward the end he was working ten hour days at SBC while datacasting Oakland games at night for MLB.com, writing his regular columns, and managing his Tout team. A serious kidney infection—nothing unusual—laid him up for a few days. And on the penultimate Friday of the season, with his pitchers fading and his team hitting .189, he finished coordinating three hospice appointments for Cathy and realized he'd forgot to send in his FAAB bids.

"I always say, If I didn't have a family and all that shit to distract me, I could play fantasy so much better," he told me over the phone a couple weeks ago. "I can say that, and Cathy just sort of giggles. She's giggling now."

I hear Cathy's voice in the background.

"What did she say?" I asked.

"She said *maybe*."

There's no question that Lawr Michaels could have won. Although his pitching staff faded down the stretch, his trades were decent, his injuries manageable. What really sank the CREATiVESPORTS team was its owner's unshakable loyalty to a cadre of cheap pitchers whom he refused to dump, no matter how miserably they played. These were Lawr's *guys,* and he never abandoned them. If you think about it, there's nothing surprising about this. Given all the tragedy in his life, Michaels has learned to embrace chaos and tolerate messiness with unending faith and optimism. As much as this quality makes him a brave and formidable man, it proved to be his undoing in Tout Wars. He finished sixth.

Hollywood Matt Berry has turned up at First Pitch Arizona wearing a polo shirt with the logo of his new business venture, RotoPass. He's tweaked his BlackBerry to receive a message every time somebody subscribes, and as soon as one arrives he blurts out the RotoPass motto: "Six great sites for one low price!" Late in the season, he was let go from his columnist job at Rotoworld. (He thinks it had something to do with his constant promotion of his own enterprises.) In any event, he made up for this by landing his own fantasy-sports radio show on the ESPN affiliate that broadcasts Angels games.

Over the long season I learned that Berry's method of evaluating players has a lot in common with the way he pitches scripts to movie studios. He doesn't crunch his own numbers or study hours of video or use any rigid methodology. He just wades quickly through all the relevant points, picks the one that seems the most salable, and runs with it. It's actually not a bad way to play Rotisserie. In baseball, as in other walks of life, first impressions are often correct.

But the Hollywood approach has its downside, as Berry learned when he traded Bartolo Colón. By downplaying science, Berry has made himself especially vulnerable to his own prejudices, and to him, Colón was the worst sort of Tinseltown cliché. The hot new star arrives on the scene with a fat contract, his face on billboards. He lures you in and then, through his own sloth and incompetence, screws you.

Berry's been around Hollywood long enough to know how this fable is supposed to end: The fat loser gets kicked to the curb, *roll credits*. With Colón, all Berry did was finish the script. He came in fifth.

One of the selling points of "Shandlerpalooza" is the chance to see the Arizona Fall League, an obscure instructional showcase where major-league teams send top prospects for off-season polishing. Most baseball fans couldn't imagine buying a ticket for this, but to Rotisserie junkies it's Christmas in October. At the ballpark in Scottsdale tonight, the First Pitch attendees are packed behind home plate with pencils and clipboards, looking for the next great sleeper.

The hyperkinetic Jason Grey is here, holding court in his customary Mastersball shirt. For several years he's literally written the book on the Fall League, churning out a guide that covers three hundred of its players. Major-league scouts buy copies, and it's now visible in the hands of about a dozen conferees. Tonight he's hoping to have a look at a Minnesota pitching prospect named Jesse Crain. "Is that who I think it is?" he says, as Crain jogs to the mound.

"Cool."

In the end, Grey turned out to be an easy mark. The other Touts hammered him at the auction, forcing him to pay an extra $23 for six of his handpicked hitters and to basically abandon the strategy he'd used to win twice. Worse, the players he'd been touting were often the players he bought, even if he had to pay a premium to get them. Together, according to Sig's Black Box, three of Grey's shoe-leather specials—Jeremy Affeldt, Jay Gibbons, and Scott Schoeneweis—earned just $3 on his $35 investment. Finding himself with nothing to sell, Grey's considerable talent for hustling deals was all but useless. He made only two trades all season and finished eleventh. "Sometimes you can outsmart yourself," he conceded.

A few rows behind home plate, Steve Moyer is watching the game in a Cleveland jersey and a Diamondbacks jacket. Professionally, it's been a fabulous year for Moyer. The Red Sox, World Series champions as of yesterday, are his company's biggest client. "The Red Sox win is huge for us," he says. Nonetheless, he's feeling a little melancholy tonight: Before the season, he told me he didn't care where he finished in Tout Wars if he didn't win—but this year's result has changed his view. "I'm so embarrassed," he says.

Moyer's problem is that he's been a nonconformist from the cradle. Growing up, all the other kids in the Lehigh Valley loved the Phillies, so he adopted the Cardinals. When his dad coached his church softball team, Moyer followed him around the dugout, offering managerial suggestions gleaned from Bill James. Even today he makes his living helping major-league ballclubs think in unconventional terms.

But now that everybody in the Rotisserie world is using advanced Sabermetrics to evaluate players, he'd rather scoop up the leftovers. And even as Tout Wars gets tougher to win, he's convinced himself that skill is less of a factor. "Half the time," he says, "good luck beats all anyhow." For the first time in ten years of expert league play, Moyer came in dead last.

As I'm sitting with Moyer, there's a commotion about ten rows behind us. Joe Sheehan, the Tout Wars rookie of the year, slips while climbing over a stadium chair and sprains his ankle. He'll spend the rest of the weekend hobbling around on crutches, holed up nights in his hotel room taking on all comers at Texas hold 'em. As sure-footed as he is in a baseball negotiation, the guy from Baseball Prospectus is pretty lousy at navigating the physical world.

By any reasonable standard Sheehan had a forgettable rookie campaign. His draft plan was wrongheaded, his FAAB pickups mediocre, and his gamble on Randy Johnson a washout. The only reason he finished seventh rather than tenth is that he made up for these shortcomings by working me over like a drunken chiropractor. By Sig's calculations, Sheehan picked up 38 value points in our three trades and gave up only 8. Throw in the Bartolo Colón deal, and his trading record is one of the best in Tout Wars history.

As much as I appreciate Sheehan's brashness, it doesn't make losing to him any more tolerable. When somebody asks him how he managed to salvage a decent season from a disastrous start, he sums it up in three words: "I have *huevos*."

At breakfast the next morning Jeff Erickson passes around a wallet photo. Two weeks before the end of the season, he and his wife, Kim, became parents to Allison Kate, their first baby. Had Erickson had any spare time to attend to the shambles of his RotoWire team, diaper duty absorbed all of it. In the end, Erickson's injury bug was just as bad as mine, if not worse. But in a game that's bound by a single year, where it pays to take risks, the conservative Erickson hadn't made a single blockbuster trade or ballsy free-agent gamble. Fate may have cost him the title, but excessive moderation pushed his Tout Wars team to the bottom of the pack. The guy who looked unbeatable in May finished tenth.

Rick Fogel, the Tout Wars outsider, didn't make the trip to Arizona. The last time I saw him, he was standing in his law office in late September, gazing out at the Chicago River, still haunted by the most unspeakable gaffe: trading me José Guillen. It's pretty clear why he did this. Fogel is still close enough to the amateur game that he expects these leagues to be *fun*. There's nothing he'd rather do than negotiate deals, so the moment he had a chance to make a splashy one, he lowered his guard.

In his law office, Fogel has a collection of mementos from companies he's liquidated: a matchbook from Le Perroquet, a price guide from Spanjer Brothers, an old Dietzgen compass. They are tokens of a life spent searching for crumbs of value, a skill that makes him a formidable Rotisserie player and, this season, provided the fuel for a comeback. Not only did he pick up four of the best free agents of the season, including Baltimore's David Newhan, but he won an astounding 74 percent of his FAAB bids, most of them by $2 or less. His USA Stats team finished fourth. "Two years of playing with the pros," he writes, "and I was in the money both times."

On paper there's no way Dean Peterson finishes third. Not a chance. On the strength of his draft alone, the quietest Tout should have shared the title. While he didn't come to First Pitch Arizona to explain his demise, I'm sure he'd point to his underwhelming pitching staff, which resisted his every attempt to patch it.

But back in September, in the stands at a White Sox game, I caught a glimpse of a deeper problem. Minnesota pitcher Carlos Silva, by then Peterson's property, was cruising toward a win that Peterson desperately needed. But in the seventh inning Silva gave up a home run to White Sox shortstop José Valentin, the Tout Wars property of his chief rival, Trace Wood. It was the kind of moment that would make most Roto players chew on a hot-dog wrapper, but not Peterson. He was clapping.

"You're *cheering*?" I asked.

He gave me a sheepish look.

"It's my favorite team."

On the basis of this, Peterson's narrow defeat makes more sense. On August 7 Peterson had unwittingly torpedoed himself by acquiring Esteban Loaiza, who, in addition to being a total bust for the Yankees, had until recently been a member of the White Sox. Peterson, the perpetual adolescent, the guy who lives in a museum of his own childhood, has a weakness for players on the team he grew up pulling for. This year, in Tout Wars, it proved fatal.

Near the end of Shandler's opening remarks here in Arizona, he pointed to the far corner of the room to make an introduction. "Trace Wood is here," Shandler said, "the 2004 Tout Wars champion." Wood rose stiffly from his chair, forced a smile, and gave the crowd a brusque salute.

Nobody clapped.

If you glanced at his roster, you might conclude that the Prickly One had simply won the lottery when he purchased Johan Santana, who won the Cy Young Award and posted a league-high $46 return on the Black Box. But luck had nothing to do with this. Before the season Wood had argued in print and to anyone who would listen that Santana might be the league's best starting pitcher. He'd come to the draft prepared to spend $25 but landed him for only $19. Nobody at the table feared Wood enough to bid him up.

Trace Wood won Tout Wars by developing a strategy that suits his strengths: an ability to ignore flash and embrace tedium, an affinity for players who've been wrongly dismissed, a lifestyle that allows him to spend 20 percent of his waking hours watching baseball, and, above all, the fortitude to factor out all the social noise and play this game ruthlessly. Not only did he storm back from eleventh place in May to win, he finished with 90.5 points, a new AL record.

Instead of running around interrogating people as I had, Wood spent his time studying players on the field and trolling for clues that the numbers can't tell you: whether a rookie hitter is fouling off a lot of pitches or just missing them entirely; whether a struggling young pitcher is on the verge of harnessing his electric slider. The moment he saw something concrete, he'd act, and with brilliant results. Of all the cheap and surprising pitchers in the American League, Wood had more than half of them on his roster at one time or another.

In the end, just as I'd suspected at the winter meetings, the Tout Wars champion used a blend of numbers *and* scouting to capture the title. Wood believed, as I did, that both schools of thought have power but that they work best when they are used to explain each other. He's just a lot better at the execution than I am. "If I had to pick one of the Touts as a GM, I'd pick Trace," Dean Peterson said. "It's hard to argue with what he's done."

On October 3, the last day of the baseball season, I'd landed at Dulles Airport to attend the coronation of the new Rotisserie king. At fourteen minutes to seven that evening, sitting on the couch in his living room, Wood and I watched the final out of the final game.

It was officially over.

By Wood's own admission, winning Tout Wars is the biggest accomplishment of his working life. It was the fruit of months, if not years, of quiet contemplation and dogged labor and the closest he's come to the standard of greatness set by his idol, Branch Rickey.

"So?" I asked.

Wood turned from the television to look at me. He seemed a little annoyed by the idea that he was supposed to put on a display of spontaneous exuberance. Slowly he raised his arms over his head.

"Woo-hoo."

As a final act, Trace poured three glasses of champagne. It was then, as we clicked glasses with his wife, Lisa, that I finally realized what was so unusual about Trace Wood's evening of triumph.

The phone never rang.

———

The Streetwalkers season ended, for all intents and purposes, on the evening of Friday, October 1, inside a "deluxe" room at the Sheraton Four Points near the entrance to the Bay Bridge.

It was here, about ten minutes after we returned from our ballpark protest, that I saw the story on the wires. José Guillen had settled his dispute with the Angels that morning for a $24,000 payment. Our protest had been a failure. Guillen was on his way home to the Dominican Republic. And there was one more cruel twist: Jacque Jones had been held out of the Minnesota lineup that night for a reason explained only as a "family issue." By midnight back east, Joe Sheehan had an insurmountable lead of seven points.

We would finish eighth.

Sig, Nando, and I were slumped in various poses of exhaustion that evening, our picket signs and leaflets scattered on the floor. The mood was somber but resolute. Our strategy was solid, our mistakes forgivable. We'd done everything in our power to win.

Our choice of pitchers had been inspired. Schilling and Rivera were to finish second and third in balloting for the American League Cy Young Award, and six of our pitching draftees had turned a combined $35 profit on the Black Box, with Brad Radke leading the pack. If we'd kept the gang together, they would have broken the Tout Wars record for wins.

What buried us was our hapless offense. Of the marquee hitters we drafted, only David Ortiz managed to turn a profit. The rest of the lot—Mueller, Mientkiewicz, Phelps, Jones, and Young—put us in a $49 hole. Most alarming was our last-place finish in batting average. In the previous three years, our six best hitters had a combined BA of .285, but this year they lowered that figure by eighteen points. If they'd just performed *normally,* we might have placed in the top five.

Our eleven trades were, at the end of the day, exactly one too many. Our biggest triumph was the Cinquo de Mayo Massacre, which we won by 11 Sig value points, thanks to Guillen and his $23 yield. We came out ahead on Vazquez for Young, blew out Jason Grey in our "pass the trash" deal, and to my boundless surprise reaped a small

profit by reacquiring Ponson. On the other hand, the Schilling transaction was such a bust that Sig can't forgive himself for being out of
the country at the time. "I blame this one on Italy," he said. Overall,
we traded away 97 Sig points and took in 80. If we'd only passed on
acquiring Magglio Ordóñez, we'd have come out even.

In the injury department, the results were so ugly that Sig generated a spreadsheet to decipher them. Sure enough, he discovered, we
were one of four teams to take *five* of the thirty most catastrophic
hits, including Bill Mueller, Luis Matos, and Dmitri Young. Not surprisingly, the name at the top of the list, the costliest injury in the
American League, was Ordóñez.

On the other end of the karmic spectrum, Sig measured each
ballplayer's preseason projection against his actual performance to
produce a list of the top thirty sleepers of the year. This produced another wave of bad news. If it wasn't for Ortiz, who, of course, we
eventually traded, we'd have been the only team with zero.

Since we fared so poorly in both these areas, Sig ran some linear regressions and made a surprising discovery. When you compare the
number of catastrophic injuries each Tout Wars team suffered to its
final place in the standings, there's a 36 percent correlation. And when
you do the same thing with the list of top sleepers, there's a 40 percent
correlation. Mash them together and they explain 51 percent of the
final outcome. In other words, avoiding injuries and picking up sleepers was, at least in this league, more than half the battle.

To Sig, this proves that the Tout Wars championship turned heavily
on one factor: luck. No matter how bright you are, he says, nobody
on earth can routinely predict these extreme statistical deviations.
Not Ron Shandler, not Trace Wood, not even the teams themselves.
In fact, he says, we should be thankful. Given that we were one of the
worst teams in both of these areas, we had a 51 percent chance of
coming in last. "The Streetwalkers are not so pathetic," Sig said.

So why didn't we win?

In the final analysis, there was nothing wrong with my scouting.
Most of the strong hunches I developed about players proved to be
true. Alex Rios, David Ortiz, Sidney Ponson, Gary Sheffield, and Brad

Radke, among others, all took off in precisely the direction I'd expected. All in all, Nando batted about .600 on his suggestions, too. Hunchmaster hadn't set the baseball world on fire, but its 26 percent correlation was, at the very least, a step in the right direction.

Zoladex didn't quite live up to the hype. Sig's creation predicted the performance of all American League players with 55 percent accuracy. That was a bit lower than we'd hoped, but we weren't alone. All the commercial projection systems seemed to be down. "I guess it was just an unusual year," Sig says. (Maybe this had something to do with steroids.)

Even though a couple of her predictions fizzled in September, I should have paid more attention to Andrea Mallis. Her instincts were correct about the Ortiz-for-Soriano trade, which we ended up losing by 3 Sig value points. But what impressed me most was something Mallis had mentioned offhandedly in Oakland: that the New York Mets should trade the streaking Ty Wigginton, because his chart suggested he would "really bottom out" in August. When the month was over, I looked up Wigginton's numbers.

The guy hit *.178*.

Given a second chance, I would have held onto Schilling a month longer, ordered Verizon to block all incoming calls from Joe Sheehan, and kept my big yap shut on the topic of Bartolo Colón. I would have spent less time harassing players, managers, and GMs and more time scouting free agents by myself.

But my biggest regret consists of five words spoken in the Wyndham basement in March: "Sidney Ponson for twelve dollars." After making that enormous blunder, there were two target players left on my draft sheet that I couldn't afford: Matt Lawton and Aaron Rowand. Not only did these two turn a collective $29 profit on the Black Box, they were hitters ten and thirteen on Sig's list of the season's best surprises.

I got a bad deal on both ends of Sidney Ponson.

The sun was setting over San Francisco Bay, and Sig had to drive home to mind the net for his recreational hockey team, the Red Dogs.

I had no idea when I'd see him again. In July—between Tout Wars, European jaunts, NASA research, golf lessons, and ballpark visits— he'd managed to raise the correlation coefficient on his homegrown baseball projection system to .660 for hitters, just a hair below the pros. "Only a matter of time now," he said.

Later, spurred by the Ordóñez disaster, he built a comprehensive database of baseball injuries over the years and a mathematical model for predicting their likelihood. Nothing like it had ever been done, and in a few weeks his findings would be published in the 2005 *Bill James Handbook*, along with an introductory essay written by James himself. Starting tomorrow, with no Tout Wars team to worry over, he plans to take up where he left off, bombarding major-league teams with job queries.

As much as Sig had convinced himself that we were victims of bad statistical sampling, he was plenty disappointed. Though he never admitted it at the time, he said, "there was a one-week period after we made the Magglio trade when I really expected us to win."

Ferdinando "Bonecrusher" Di Fino leaped up to give Sig a bear hug. Over the last few months, they'd bonded—in large part, I'm afraid, by laughing about the dumb ideas and mercurial moods of their employer. The long season had taken a physical toll on Nando. His eyesight had deteriorated. His love life was a shambles. He'd put on fifteen pounds and missed countless hours of sleep watching late games on the West Coast. He had no immediate plans for life after Rotisserie baseball, other than being pretty sure he's never going to do anything like this again.

"My head might explode," he said.

We were all on our feet. This was the end of our little association. "Oh, yeah," Sig said, reaching into his ubiquitous brown backpack. "I need a picture."

After making him promise not to publish our photos in his next brochure over a caption that says "BEFORE," Nando and I scrunched together. Sig pulled his eyes away from the viewfinder to take one last live look at the bedraggled mess in front of him.

He laughed.

"Say José!"

———

In the postseason, unshackled from the pressures of performing on the Tout Wars stage, my players became heroes.

I'm not exaggerating.

In the American League Championship Series between the Yankees and Red Sox, they put on a dazzling show. In Game One, Mariano Rivera overcame his grief at the accidental deaths of two relatives in Panama to shut down Boston. In Game Four, with the Red Sox three outs from elimination, Billy Mueller singled in the ninth inning, tying the game and sparking what would be the greatest comeback in postseason history. Curt Schilling pitched seven dominating innings in Game Six as blood oozed from the fresh sutures holding together his mangled ankle.

Then there's David Ortiz. First, Big Papi won Game Four with a walk-off home run in the twelfth inning at twenty-two minutes past one in the morning. Then in Game Five, he singled with two outs in the fourteenth for his second game-winning hit *in the same day.* In fourteen total postseason games, he batted .400 with five homers, thirteen runs, and nineteen RBI. His three walk-off hits over that span are one baseball record that will never be broken.

In Game Four of the World Series against the Cardinals, the Red Sox were one out away from a sweep when pitcher Keith Foulke scooped up a lazy grounder to the mound. It had been eighty-six years since Boston won a championship, a chasm that stretched beyond the memories of all but a handful of sentient beings. That baseball in Foulke's hand wasn't just a mass of twine and horsehide, it was a historical artifact. And for the rest of time, Red Sox fans will remember the name of the first baseman who caught it.

Doug Mientkiewicz.

The last time I'd seen Jacque Jones before the postseason, he was sulking off to the showers in Chicago, and in the nine games that followed, he appeared to be sleepwalking on the field. On the first of October, two days before the end of the regular season, the Twins charter plane landed in Minnesota, and Jones had a message on his cellphone. His father was dead at fifty-two.

Hardy Jones had been diagnosed in June with liver and pancreatic cancer, and his condition had quickly deteriorated. Jones's teammates and coaches knew, but nobody had said anything about it publicly. Jones wouldn't have wanted that. "Jacque keeps everything inside," Doug Mientkiewicz told me after the news broke. "When he's not smiling, you know something's eating at him. Anyone with a brain knows it was affecting him, but he never makes excuses." Thumbing through my notes from Chicago, I realized Jones had dropped a hint. When I asked him how he was feeling physically, he said, "My body's fine. My *body's* perfect."

Before the last game of the regular season, Jones flew to Sacramento to help make funeral arrangements. The Twins were due in New York for Game One of the divisional series two days later, and it was all but certain Jones wouldn't make it back in time. But on Monday night, he boarded a red-eye in California and arrived in New York at daybreak. When Ron Gardenhire saw him at the team hotel, Jones said he was ready to go.

Gardenhire had every reason to keep him on the bench. Not only was Jones exhausted and emotionally spent, he'd never hit a home run at Yankee Stadium and had a lifetime .161 batting average in the postseason. In the twenty-one times he'd faced that evening's pitcher, Mike Mussina, Jones had fared even worse, batting .142 with *ten* strikeouts. "He just has my number," Jones had told me. Nonetheless, Gardenhire, the big softy that he is, abandoned the numbers and penciled Jones into the lineup for Game One, batting second.

In the first inning, Jones struck out looking. The next time up he managed to make contact, only to ground into a double play. By the sixth, the Twins were clinging to a 1–0 lead, and Jones trudged to the plate to face Mussina for the final time.

He swung at the first pitch, a knuckle curve, and missed badly. The expression on his face was grim. As the capacity crowd looked on, he filled his lungs, regripped his bat, set his spikes, and dug in. Mussina's next pitch was a high fastball well off the outside part of the plate. It should have been ball one, but Jones, being Jones, decided to take a hack. He caught the pitch with the end of the barrel, lashing it the opposite way to left field, the deeper half of a deep ballpark.

The ball took a low arc about even with the bunting on the upper deck. It soared over the close-mown grass where Babe Ruth and Joe DiMaggio once roamed, up toward the white trellises in the outfield, the Dodge billboard, the bullpen, the flagpole, and the granite monuments to Yankee greats. Hideki Matsui, the left fielder, turned to chase, but it was no use. The ball landed in the first row of seats.

Home run.

As Jones rounded first, the Fox microphones picked up his voice—it was hot, primordial. "Woooh!" he shouted, rounding second at the speed of a man possessed. Then "Waauugh!" as he touched third. Once he'd crossed home plate, his back turned to the fences, he made a fist and tapped his chest. Then he kissed his gloved hand, tilted back his head, and pointed straight up at the chilly black sky. It's a gesture that's almost humdrum in sports these days, but this was the first time I'd ever seen Jones do it.

After the game, which the Twins won, my right fielder was so mobbed in the clubhouse that the handlers brought him to a podium in the interview room. I waited for the beat writers to ask a few perfunctory questions, and then I asked him about his dad.

The tears came then. Not the drippy kind you see on Mexican soap operas but the ones that well up slowly and catch the light like little diamonds. I can't remember what he said. I forgot to write it down. Something about wishing his father was here and knowing he's watching over him. As Jones left the podium, I shoved through the cordon of flacks and cameras and boom mikes and stopped to shake his hand. It was hard to know what to say. I wanted to tell him that I lost my dad when I was nineteen or that I sensed something was wrong with him in Chicago, but none of that seemed appropriate.

"I'm sorry," I blurted. "And congratulations."

Jones smiled and lowered his bloodshot eyes to the floor. The circle of people was tightening around us. "Thanks, man," he said, hoarsely. "Thanks a lot."

I watched him walk down the narrow corridor that leads to the clubhouse until he vanished in shadow. It dawned on me that I'd spent the last seven years observing the drama and pathos of sports without actually *feeling* any of it.

Until then.

———

On the last night of First Pitch Arizona, under a bright desert moon, the Touts are milling around on the pool deck. Tomorrow is Halloween. Trace Wood is puffing a Cuban cigar he'd saved for the occasion, and he approaches me, trailing smoke and grinning.

"Okay, butter boy," he says, "time to pay up."

Late in the season, in a burst of graciousness, Wood had offered to let me off the hook. Somebody told him it was physically impossible to eat a stick of butter without throwing up. I'd been tempted to take the reprieve, but a bet's a bet. "Let's go," Matt Berry says, jingling his keys in my face. "Just please don't vomit in my car."

The site of my gastronomic execution is an upstairs dining room at the Gordon Biersch Brewery in Tempe. Ron Shandler has joined us, along with two other conferees who'd apparently caught wind of what was going to happen. I'm about to induce a heart attack, and I'm attracting *rubberneckers.*

It takes a few minutes to explain the situation to the waitress, who is, appropriate to the holiday, dressed like Tinkerbell. After conferring with the chef, she tells me they don't have traditional sticks of butter—it just comes in big industrial clumps. She brings out just such a clump to show us, and it's the size of a basketball shoe. "About half that is fine," I say.

Nobody objects.

Shandler has numerous responsibilities to attend to back at the hotel, but he didn't want to miss *this.* He looks a little worried. If Matt Berry feels the least bit sorry for me, he's doing a fine job of hiding it. "Call the ambulance now," he instructs.

Trace is looking at me with the same smug expression he wore when we made this bet in the first place—when I was in second and he was in tenth. Even then, he *knew* he was going to beat me. In all my travels this year, I have never met anyone who was more supremely confident in his ability to construct a baseball team than Trace Wood. That goes for Theo Epstein, Billy Beane, and, although it's pretty close, Sig Mejdal.

Tinkerbell returns from the kitchen, carrying my butter on a dessert dish. There's a candle in it. The crowd at my table claps and whistles. The other restaurant patrons gawk in horror.

Nobody's exactly sure what to say. Shandler goes first. "Hey, you did what every fantasy guy wants to do," he says.

Trace Wood snorts. "Yeah, you had six guys working for you, you spent who knows how much, you talked to all your players, and now it's come to this."

"Make a wish," Berry says.

Trace reaches across the table and nudges the dish toward me until it's properly spaced between my knife and fork.

"Bon appetit."

———

In the space between the end of the baseball season and this final trip to Arizona, I heard the same question a dozen times.

"So, are you gonna play next year?"

Most of the interrogators were friends I hadn't seen in ten months, who, after having a look at the flamboyant bags under my eyes, meant this as a joke. The question was supposed to make me spit out my pinot noir and lean over the dinner table to say something emphatic like, "No way in hell." You can imagine their reactions when I told them I wasn't sure.

In the beginning, my Rotisserie adventure was supposed to be a noble experiment, an intellectual lark, a salve for professional burnout, and a chance to spend a year getting under the fingernails of baseball—anything but the wakings of a new hobby. The point of joining Tout Wars was to swoop in, use my inside access to dominate the competition, and then vanish forever into the mists of legend. I never considered how it would feel to get my ass kicked.

The trouble with building a Rotisserie strategy around inside information is that it always comes with an expiration date. Minds change, injuries defy prognosis, and performance always trumps opinion. The only way to win Tout Wars by this method alone is to have a live telepathic hookup to every player, manager, and executive in baseball. Someday Sig will figure out a way to do this, but until then a baseball season is an exercise in making adjustments, and that's where my stewardship went horribly wrong.

At times I was too audacious, other times not enough so. I over-thought small moves while acting rashly on larger ones. Sometimes I deferred to Sig's theories, other times to Nando's, never reaping the full benefits of either. By shifting paradigms I wound up standing no-where. Toss in my rookie mistakes, and I was fully cooked.

But even if I could correct these mistakes next season, I've already come to grips with the sad truth: I don't have the deep wiring it takes to play Rotisserie at this level. Winning Tout Wars takes luck, but it also requires mathematical agility, extreme patience, laserlike focus, and an overdeveloped capacity for spatial perception. Lawr Michaels can look at the draft board after ten rounds and, like Garry Kasparov, run through all the combinations of moves in his mind to find the op-timal moment to start buying. Ron Shandler can track twelve devel-oping plotlines at once and calmly run each of them through the filter of his vast experience. Trace Wood, in addition to being a gifted scout, has the talent to make firm calculations and the intestinal forti-tude to never doubt them. It's not surprising to me that all three of these guys were musical prodigies.

To be a perennial contender in this world, you have to be born with some sharp cognitive implement that sets you apart in some phase of the game, whether it's Jason Grey's energy, Joe Sheehan's nerve, Matt Berry's comic timing, or Rick Fogel's nose for value. Other than my two assistants, the most powerful tool I brought to the auction table was a Venti Quad Latte.

As for the gathering feud between the scouts and the Sabermetri-cians, the humanists and the technocrats, I'm honestly sick of the topic. In fact, the whole kerfuffle reminds me of something my dad used to laugh about years ago, when we used to watch college-football games together on Saturdays.

The moment a play is whistled dead on the football field, it's up to the referees to spot the ball at the point where the ballcarrier was tackled. This is anything but an exact science. Sometimes the refs are off by four inches, sometimes four feet. Nevertheless, when it comes time to determine if a team has earned a first down, two grown-ups dressed like crossing guards jog out purposefully from the sidelines dragging a chain that's precisely ten yards long. The sight of it never failed to make my father smirk.

"Here come the chains!" he'd say.

As my dad and I watched delightedly, the crossing guards would use their finely calibrated tool of measurement to determine, to the millimeter, the distance between two completely arbitrary points.

It's a pretty good metaphor for what's happening in baseball. While the scouts, like the referees, preach the value of making a good spot, the quantitative guys, playing the role of the crossing guards, are convinced that all you need is a more accurate chain. What they don't seem to realize is that the only way they'll ever get it right is if they're *both* perfect. In the end, baseball is a game that turns on human tendencies, and human tendencies are fluid. "There is no baseball gestalt," Bill James told me over the summer. "There's simply a lot of strands."

One thing I can say, unequivocally, is that Rotisserie baseball, when played at the highest level, is no trifle. All those people who mock the game for its geekiness or for the prehistoric stats it uses are missing the point. At his rolltop desk in Massachusetts, Dan Okrent didn't sit down to create a game that would revolutionize the way we measure the skills of individual ballplayers. He wanted his game to reward people for building a good *team*. As he imagined it, a strong roster of Rotisserie players, were they to be assembled in a major-league dugout, would win a lot of ballgames, too.

Remembering this, Nando and I decided to run a test. We took the statistical totals for every American League team during the regular season and ranked them by the Tout Wars scoring system.

Here are the results:

Team	Roto Points	Actual AL Finish
1. Boston	117.5	2
2. New York	109.5	1
3. Anaheim	108	3
4. Minnesota	97	3
5. Texas	85	6
6. Chicago	80	7
7. Cleveland	79	8
8. Oakland	77	5
9. Baltimore	74.5	9
10. Detroit	68.5	10
11. Seattle	51	13
12. Tampa Bay	47.5	11
13. Toronto	35.5	12
14. Kansas City	20	14

Only two teams, Seattle and Oakland, finished more than one place beyond their Rotisserie ranking. And it was the Tout Wars scoring system, rather than the actual standings, that identified the Red Sox as the class of the field. If Theo Epstein had built his team by focusing on things like saves, RBI, batting average, and ERA rather than by the turbocharged algorithms he's known to prefer, Boston still might have won the American League.

At the end of the 2004 season, Major League Baseball announced a new record for paid attendance. For all the controversies in the recent past, the game is healthy. And although Rotisserie players may be the last people to earn any credit for the turnaround, I wonder where the game might be if those legions hadn't been there to bail it out in the lean years after the 1994 strike. Without them, Trace Wood likes to say, "Baseball would be hockey."

As it stands today, for every person on earth who is paid to run a big-league ballclub, there are a hundred and fifty thousand more doing roughly the same thing in their own spare time. Ten months ago, I assumed that the game was *the game* and Rotisserie was just a preposterous satellite orbiting in its gravity. Now I know that I was wrong.

It's the other way around.

———

First Pitch Arizona ends on Halloween, and that afternoon I'm rolling my dented wheelie bag down the aisle of one last airplane cabin. After three days in the company of my Tout Wars opponents—and despite a formal invitation from Jason Grey—I still haven't decided whether to play next year.

There are so many reasons to say no that I'm hesitant to list them. If all my labors this season yielded an eighth-place finish, I shudder to think what will happen if I try to manage my team in stolen moments between columns and diapers. And while it was fine to try Tout Wars once, joining the league a second time borders on the fraudulent. There are more deserving candidates.

But the trouble with this insidious game is that once you've played it, every other form of fandom is a pale substitute. In the last six months, baseball had taken on an entirely new profundity for me. Suddenly there was no such thing as a meaningless tilt between two sorry teams I didn't care about. When I clicked on a ballgame, there was always some plotline in progress. Maybe the guy at the plate was a minor-league call-up I decided not to FAAB because the scouts warned me about a hole in his swing. The next pitch, then, would be a short morality play. If the guy hit a home run, I was a dope. If he struck out on an inside fastball, I was a Nobel laureate. Baseball had become an extension of my ego.

For all that my wife has endured this year, there were times when I could tell that she'd enjoyed watching this process. Not because I've been easy to live with but because playing this game has drawn out emotions in me that might otherwise lie dormant. "Hey," she said one Saturday in June after finding me on the floor in my office, my back in spasms, moaning about my slumping team, "you always said you needed a hobby."

If nothing else, joining Tout Wars accomplished one of my aims. I have a renewed faith in baseball and a trunkload of memories of a year spent in its intimate company. Meeting Mariano Rivera at the airport and Calvin Reese on the subway. Jumping for joy with José Guillen and sharing a beer with my third baseman. For the rest of my life I'll be an ardent fan of Jacque Jones, and if you say the words "Big Papi" or "Dougie Baseball" or "Miguel Batista's novel," I have to smile despite myself. It's true what Ron Shandler says. I did what every fantasy guy wants to do.

But am I really one of them?

Out my window, there's a gorgeous view of the Rockies in twilight. The movie on this evening's flight is *Old School*, a panoply of fart jokes and streaking that offers exactly the level of intellectual engagement I'm looking for. While I did manage to hold down that butter, my gallbladder is twitching like a Chihuahua.

Nevertheless, after ten months of baseball immersion, I'm starting to feel a now-familiar reflex. Inside my bag, there's a copy of the 2005 *Bill James Handbook*, hot off the presses, with the stats for every player in the majors last season. As study guides go, it's second only to the *Baseball Forecaster*, which won't be out for a few more weeks.

Just to be perfectly fair, I pull out the *Handbook* and place it on my tray table. Between its covers, there are 311 pages of statistics in a typeface small enough to induce glaucoma. There's a list of the pitchers who led the majors in the percentage of sliders thrown and a ranking of the league leaders in stolen-base success percentage. There are a handful of essays with subheads like, "A Few Words on High Pitch Outings."

If I open this book, it's all over.

It occurs to me, then, that it was a moment just like this, a quarter of a century ago, that gave rise to this silly game in the first place. On that long flight to Texas in 1979 when he first sketched out the rules, Dan Okrent was almost precisely my age. He'd gone to the same college as I had, moved to New York, burned out, and decided to write a book about baseball. Just as it was then, the season is over. There are no box scores to check, no game stories to examine. When Okrent told me he'd felt "bereft of baseball" on that Pan Am jet, I thought he was a drooling idiot.

Now I get it.

"Headset?" the flight attendant asks.

"No, I think I'm good."

Final 2004 Tout Wars American League Standings

1. Trace Wood, The Long Gandhi, 90.5
2. Ron Shandler, Baseball HQ, 81.0
3. Dean Peterson, STATS, Inc., 76.5
4. Rick Fogel, USA Stats, 73.0
5. Matt Berry, Talented Mr. Roto, 70.0
6. Lawr Michaels, CREATiVESPORTS, 69.0
7. Joe Sheehan, Baseball Prospectus, 65.0
8. Streetwalkers, 58.0
9. Gene McCaffrey, Wise Guy Baseball, 57.0
10. Jeff Erickson, RotoWire, 51.5
11. Jason Grey, Mastersball, 48.5
12. Steve Moyer, Baseball Info Solutions, 40.0

Epilogue

October 2005

The Streetwalkers

Miguel Batista had 31 saves in 39 opportunities as the closer for the Toronto Blue Jays. He recently made his musical debut playing Native American flute on Navajo artist Radmilla Cody's album "Spirit of a Woman." He continues to work on his detective novel.

Bubba Crosby bounced between the Yankees and the minor leagues in 2005, but by September was making regular starts in the Bronx. While chasing down a ball in Game 5 of the American League Divisional Series, he collided with fellow outfielder Gary Sheffield, allowing the Angels to score two runs. The Yankees lost and were eliminated from the postseason.

José Guillen met with an anger-management counselor during the off-season and later signed with the Washington Nationals. During an interleague series with the Angels in June, he had to be restrained from charging his former teammates and later called Angels manager Mike Scioscia "a piece of garbage." In September, he was suspended for throwing bats, a helmet, and a shin guard on the field after being ejected. He hit 24 home runs.

After an injury to the minor leaguer who was slated to replace him, the Minnesota Twins signed **Jacque Jones** to a one-year contract for $5 million. Though he was disappointed by his season totals, which were nearly identical to his 2004 numbers, he led the team with 23 home runs and 6 game-winning hits. Before what was likely his last game as a Twin, Jones removed himself from the lineup to spend the final hours in the dugout with his teammates.

Doug Mientkiewicz decided to keep the ball he caught to end the 2004 World Series, rather than give it to the Red Sox for posterity. This resulted in a public feud that was chronicled on page one of *The New York Times*. Not long afterwards, he was traded to the Mets, where his struggles continued. In June, hitting only .219, he pulled a hamstring while warming up in the batter's box. "Would I like to be in there every day?" he said to a reporter after losing his starting job. "Yeah, of course. Everybody would. But that's why it's called a team and not the New York Mientkiewiczs."

Bill Mueller returned to the Red Sox in 2005 after the team exercised a $2.5 million contract option. He played in 150 games, raised his batting average to .295, and finished second among American League third basemen in both fielding percentage and on-base percentage. "There are bigger, faster, stronger, more overall gifted athletes on the team," wrote *Boston Globe* columnist Bob Ryan. "But there are no purer professionals."

Magglio Ordóñez flew to Austria for specialized shock-wave treatments on his knee by the same doctor who worked on downhill skier Hermann Maier. Later he signed with the Detroit Tigers for $75 million over five years. He played three games in April before missing the next ten weeks with a hernia.

David Ortiz earned more All-Star votes than any other major-league player. He hit 47 home runs, led the majors with 148 RBI, and made a case for becoming the first designated hitter to be named league

MVP. In a September ceremony at Boston's Logan Airport, Song Airlines named its newest Boeing 757 in his honor. It's called *Big Papi*. "Dude, you should see it," Ortiz said after taking a tour. "They put TVs in every seat!"

Let go by Cleveland, **Josh Phelps** signed with the Tampa Bay Devil Rays and hit 4 home runs in May. He was sent down to the minors in June and did not return. When asked in an interview during the season to reveal his biggest guilty pleasure, he responded, "Bookstores."

On Christmas Day 2004, **Sidney Ponson** was approached on a beach in Aruba by a group of citizens who accused him of menacing people with his personal watercraft. Ponson allegedly punched one of the men, who turned out to be a judge. After spending eleven days in jail, he decamped to Florida, where he was arrested for DUI. In August, while struggling with a 6.21 ERA, he was arrested again near Baltimore after failing a sobriety test. The Orioles terminated his contract.

Mariano Rivera blew 2 saves in early April, both against the Red Sox, then went on to close 31 straight. He continues to sign autographs for anyone who asks nicely.

Dmitri Young opened the season by hitting 3 home runs on Opening Day, but only managed to hit 18 more all season. He got into a feud with Tigers manager Alan Trammell, who was fired at the end of the year. The Tigers have not played in the postseason in eighteen years.

The Founders

Lee Eisenberg, now a full-time author, recently published *The Number: A Completely Different Way to Think About the Rest of Your Life*. A Midwestern transplant, he now divides his time between Chicago and Madison, Wisconsin.

Rob Fleder showed up at the wrong location for the 2005 AARP Rotisserie draft and spent the first five rounds issuing bids by phone while riding in a series of conveyances: a taxi, a crosstown bus, and a pair of elevators. He spent three months in a battle for first place.

Bill Gamson participated in the National Baseball Seminar for the forty-fifth time in 2005 and won the American League title by just under 7 points. He didn't make a big deal out of it, of course. The season before he won by 20.

Peter Gethers published *Midas*, the latest in a series of best-selling thrillers written under a pseudonym, Russell Andrews. His three best-selling books about traveling the world with his cat, Norton, have been packaged in a single volume. Lately he's been finishing a screenplay, editing two books, and spending time at his house in Sicily, where he still can't figure out how to get ballgames on Italian satellite TV. His AARP team finished last.

Dan Okrent concluded his tumultuous stint as the first public editor of *The New York Times*, which he has taken to calling "my last job." He's working on a book about Prohibition to be published in 2008. He finished fourth in his league this year and still hasn't won the game he created.

Corlies "Cork" Smith, the esteemed book editor who hosted the first Rotisserie auction in 1980, passed away in November 2004. During his literary career, he published Jimmy Breslin and Calvin Trillin and discovered Thomas Pynchon. His Rotisserie track record was only slightly less distinguished.

Glen Waggoner is working on a forthcoming book, *A Whole New Ballgame*, with former Philadelphia slugger Mike Schmidt. He hosted the 2005 AARP Rotisserie League draft, which was, for a few people at the table, the twenty-fifth anniversary of the first time they ever did this. Waggoner passed the time by pouring gin martinis and spending $33 on Jim Thome, who hit 7 home runs all year.

The Touts

Matt Berry is suddenly everywhere. If he's not providing fantasy content for five or six Web sites, he's appearing as a fantasy expert on ESPN's morning show "Cold Pizza," writing a fantasy basketball magazine for the NBA, hosting his own Friday night fantasy radio show in Los Angeles, or working on a screenplay for a film adaptation of the cartoon *Johnny Bravo*. After oversleeping, he arrived at the 2005 Tout Wars auction an hour late. He finished eleventh.

Jeff Erickson is the new co-host of "Fantasy Focus," a talk show on XM Satellite Radio that airs weekdays at noon EST. Aided by a late surge of offense, his Tout Wars team finished eighth.

Rick Fogel turned fifty this year. He's spent most of his time trying to figure out how the new bankruptcy laws passed by Congress will affect his clients and watching another fruitless season for the Cubs. As usual, he showed up at the Tout Wars draft with a few notes on a legal pad. He finished third, which is nothing new.

Jason Grey has seen a 60 percent increase in subscribers to his Web site and has cut down to four Rotisserie leagues to spend more time writing. For clubhouse news gathering, he's ditched his Pocket PC in favor of an iPod voice recorder. As usual, Grey spent less than a quarter of his money on pitching. He had the lead as late as August 12, but stumbled and wound up fifth.

On the morning of July 29, 2005, Cathy Hedgecock died of cancer. She'd been asleep in bed next to her husband, **Lawr Michaels**, and her dog, Macaroni, who was curled up beside her. She was wearing a cashmere sweater, red pants with black moose, and a pair of pink pig slippers, a gift from Lawr. To fill his days in her absence, Michaels is working with his band Strictly Olga on a forthcoming album whose tentative title is "downward facing dog." He worked all season to keep his Tout Wars team ensconced in a field of positive energy. It came in fourth.

Steve Moyer has expanded the Baseball Info Solutions empire to the minor leagues, where he has started sending scorers to collect data. Bill James became a formal investor in the company. In Tout Wars, he changed his strategy a bit, spending 40 percent of his budget on pitching and collecting a fair number of superstars who were under thirty. He finished seventh. "I'm really thinking about quitting," he says.

Mat Olkin retired from Tout Wars and moved to Connecticut with his wife, Laura, and their four horses. He continues to work for the Mariners as a player-management consultant, but has made only one concession to status. "I bought a cellphone," he says.

Dean Peterson signed up to participate in four additional fantasy leagues this season, bringing the total to seventeen. While he drafted four White Sox players on his Tout Wars team, they were, apparently, the wrong four. The White Sox won the 2005 World Series while his team finished dead last in Tout Wars.

Ron Shandler gave notice in January that he would not return as an adviser to the St. Louis Cardinals. He says he was uncomfortable with the competing motives of being a team contributor and a Rotisserie pundit. "I may be the only person in history who will choose fantasy baseball over real baseball," he wrote on his site. Meanwhile, sales of the 2005 *Baseball Forecaster* rose 15 percent. His Tout Wars team held down first place for several weeks early in the season but floundered later thanks, in large part, to a horrible trade with Lawr Michaels.

Joe Sheehan continues to write columns for Baseball Prospectus and is now appearing once a week on ESPNEWS. Despite failing to make a single trade with the Streetwalkers, he finished second.

Defending Tout Wars champion **Trace Wood** was honored as the Fantasy Baseball Writer of the Year by the Fantasy Sports Writers Association. Assuming others would copy his strategy of studied dullness at the Tout Wars draft (they did), he spent more on superstars, leaned on some untested rookies, and made a few hasty trades. He came in ninth. "My team was like Apollo 1," he says. "Lots of system failures."

The Front Office

While searching for meaningful employment, **Ferdinando Di Fino** passed the time with temporary jobs at a handful of places ranging from Court TV to a booth at the New York State Fair that sells fried dough. In the meantime, he accepted an invitation to draft a team in the inaugural Tout Wars "Mixed League" competition. This was a direct violation of his vow to never again play fantasy baseball. He came in second.

Andrea Mallis attended baseball's winter meetings in Anaheim in December 2004 and had audiences with a dozen general managers. While she remains in regular contact with one team, she's still a free agent.

Sig Mejdal left NASA in April 2005 to take a position as senior quantitative analyst for the St. Louis Cardinals. The next draft he attended after Tout Wars was Major League Baseball's amateur draft, which he monitored for the team using the same laptop that contains Zoladex. He still takes phone calls from his old Rotisserie mates, though he insists that everything he says is "off the record." The Cardinals finished the 2005 season with the best record in baseball, but lost the National League pennant to the Houston Astros in six games.

August Walker, better known as Gus, was born in New York City on May 3, 2005, at 1:45 P.M. He weighed 7 pounds, 1 ounce, was 19.5 inches long, and posted an APGAR score of 9.9. It's early yet, but he appears to be left-handed.

Sam Walker returned to Tout Wars in 2005 to draft a second incarnation of the Streetwalkers Baseball Club. With only two nights to spare on the evaluation of American League ballplayers, he arrived at the draft in New York fully expecting to be thumped like a traffic cone. Six months later, he won. Maybe it was the butter.

Index